Palaeography
for Family and Local Historians

LEGERE, INTELLEGERE

Palaeography
for Family and Local Historians

HILARY MARSHALL

Phillimore

2004, Reprinted 2010, 2021

Published by
PHILLIMORE & CO. LTD

© Hilary Marshall, 2004, 2010

ISBN 978 1 86077 651 9

Contents

Preface

This book aims to help genealogists and local historians unravel the palaeographical difficulties posed by some of the classes of records which could most enable them to make further progress with their research. Many of the older documents which contain valuable material are written in scripts which are unfamiliar to modern readers, often use abbreviations and may use extra characters and symbols. In addition, many records produced before Lady Day in 1733 were written in medieval Latin which, often an obstacle in itself, is more heavily abbreviated and uses yet more symbols.

Such records sometimes followed a general pattern, so a familiarity with set forms of words, in addition to divers types of handwriting, will enable searches, transcriptions and translations to be made with greater speed and assurance.

Considerable problems may well have been overcome to discover documents relevant to one's research, and the question of reading them then becomes paramount. This can be a frustrating and tantalising situation.

Diligence and intelligent guess-work may enable a good start to be made, especially if the document is in English, but may also lead to pitfalls, and confidence is hampered by having no fair copy against which to make a check.

Two methods in particular, jointly or severally (to use an expression found in records), can be used for acquiring a working knowledge of the reading of old documents. Problems of handwriting, strange spelling, and stranger abbreviations can be resolved, and experience gained of recognising differing kinds of letters and scribal idiosyncrasies, either by attending classes of practical instruction, or by working carefully through parallel texts with commentary. For the latter method it is hoped that this book, giving such texts in a wide variety of hands from the 1400s to the 1700s, and in graduated order of difficulty, together with an exposition of the forms of letters and abbreviations in them, and suggestions for overcoming problems of deciphering, will fill a gap and spur the reader on to success.

Those who use this book will not need to be persuaded of the great enjoyment, indeed excitement, to be derived from pursuing research into family or local history and the pleasures of discovery, of working from the known to the unknown and of piecing together the evidence gathered to throw new light on old times. It may well be that they will also find great enjoyment and reward in the deciphering of documents, the means to that end.

Acknowledgements

My thanks go foremost to John Moore who has given unstintingly of his interest, experience and ability in helping to produce this book. He has contributed the sections on abbreviations in documents and on the characteristics of individual letters (chapters 4 and 5). In addition he has collaborated over the transcripts, making many valuable recommendations. For his help I am most grateful.

I am also grateful to Dr Paul Brand for his advice on the document in Anglo-Norman French; and to Dr Lesley Boatwright for reading and for useful suggestions.

Without permission to publish the reproductions there could have been no book, so I should like to express my great gratitude to The National Archives for authorisation with regard to the majority of the documents used; also to the College of Arms for their kindness in allowing the use of a pedigree from one of the visitations; and to the record offices of Berkshire, Hampshire and Herefordshire, the Surrey History Centre, the London Borough of Richmond upon Thames Local Studies Collection, and the Revd G.T.G. Sykes, vicar of the parish of Bromyard in Herefordshire.

In addition I thank John Price, Miriam Scott and Dr Stephen Taylor for each drawing my attention to a document for the book; and those of my family and friends, particularly my daughter Elizabeth, John Moore and Cedric Jeffery, who have extricated me from computer problems.

Abbreviations

For abbreviations of classes of record at The National Archives, see separate list. Irregularity of abbreviations is due to required method of citing references.

bdl.	bundle
cf.	confer
d	dorso
D.N.B.	Dictionary of National Biography
East	Easter
ed(s).	editor(s)
edn	edition
f.	feminine
f(f)	folio(s)
l(l).	line(s)
lit.	literally
m.	masculine
m(m)	membrane(s)
MSS.	manuscripts
n.	noun
no(s).	number(s)
O.E.D.	Oxford English Dictionary
P.C.C.	Prerogative Court of Canterbury
p(p).	page(s)
PRO	Public Record Office
q.v.	quod vide
r	recto
ref:	reference
rot	rotulus
TNA	The National Archives
v.	vide
v	verso

Descriptions of Classes of Records Used in this Book and Preserved in The National Archives

ADM 106	Navy Board Records
C 1	Court of Chancery: Six Clerks' Office: Early Proceedings, Richard II – Philip and Mary
C 139	Inquisitions Post Mortem, series I, Henry VI
C 54	Chancery; Chancery Division of the High Court; and Central Office of the Supreme Court of Judicature, Enrolment Office: Close Rolls
C 65	Chancery: Parliament Rolls
C 66	Chancery; Chancery Division of the High Court; and Central Office of the Supreme Court of Judicature, Enrolment Office: Patent Rolls
C 139	Inquisitions Post Mortem, Series I, Henry VI
CP 25/2	Court of Common Pleas: Feet of Fines Files, Henry VIII – Victoria
DL 30	Duchy of Lancaster: Court Rolls
E 115	Exchequer: King's Remembrancer: Certificates of Residence
E 133	Exchequer: King's Remembrancer: Depositions Taken before the Barons of the Exchequer
E 134	Exchequer: King's Remembrancer: Depositions Taken by Commission
E 179	Exchequer: King's Remembrancer: Particulars of Account and other Records Relating to Lay and Clerical Taxation
PC 2	Privy Council: Registers
PROB 6	Prerogative Court of Canterbury and Related Probate Jurisdictions: Administration Act Books
PROB 11	Prerogative Court of Canterbury and Related Probate Jurisdictions: Will Registers
REQ 2	Court of Requests: Pleadings
RG 4	General Register Office: Registers of Births, Marriages and Deaths surrendered to the non-parochial registers commissions of 1837 and 1857
RG 6	General Register Office: Society of Friends' Registers, Notes and Certificates of Births, Marriages and Burials
SC 2	Special Collections: Court Rolls
SC 12	Special Collections: Rentals and Surveys, Portfolios
SP 9	State Paper Office: Williamson Collection; Pamphlets, Miscellaneous
SP 12	Secretaries of State: State Papers Domestic; Elizabeth I
STAC 1	Court of Star Chamber: Proceedings, Henry VII
STAC 5	Court of Star Chamber: Proceedings, Elizabeth I
WARD 9	Court of Wards and Liveries: Miscellaneous Books

1

Scope and Use of the Book

Palaeography, the study of early handwriting, can have many facets, including that of dating manuscripts, and can cover a vast period, but in this book the study is confined to the reading of documents of interest to family or local historians during the timespan most likely to be useful to them.

The book outlines the many types of letter to be found in the documents so that, when a letter seems unidentifiable, a check may initially be made to find that which seems most likely, and then further search made if need be. This will gradually accustom the eye to the diverse shapes of letters.

The sections on abbreviations, making a transcript, and the characteristics of individual letters should be read and examined before the transcriptions are undertaken; similarly the chapter on medieval Latin should be read before embarking on the Latin section.

In many past publications a transcript, in addition to adhering to the spelling and eccentricities of a document, would include abbreviations closely replicating what appeared in the document. This was known as record type and may be seen for instance in *Extracts from the Court Rolls of the Manor of Wimbledon* (published in 1866). This is not now done and various methods of representing documents on paper are used. Since part of the object of this book is to acclimatise the reader to the scribe's intention in the use of abbreviations and of additional characters, the letters indicated by them have been printed in square brackets. The word 'transcript' in the book therefore denotes a copy in which the abbreviations etc. have been extended to show the letters indicated by them and to elucidate the meaning of the wording. Similarly, for the sake of brevity, 'document' refers to the reproduction of a document, and 'Latin' should be taken to mean medieval Latin (which of course includes most classical Latin) unless otherwise described.

No two transcribers are likely to have exactly the same outlook on how to treat abbreviations, certain letters, punctuation etc. In *Editing Records for Publication* (1977) R.F. Hunnisett outlined his ideal method of making transcripts, in the hope that this would become the standard. However, those proposals were made for transcribers producing work for others to explore rather than for those learning to read documents. For the latter, it is hoped that the transcripts, which aim to include all curious spelling, capital letters and an exact indication of letters represented by abbreviations, will help to unravel the more obscure minutiae of the documents in the book and hence documents in general.

The English and Latin documents are grouped separately on the grounds that practice and improved ability with the English examples will provide a good basis for the Latin ones (for a few of which, where entries are short, the translations are interlined). Each group is in approximate order of difficulty. Those who have some experience of reading records may like to omit detailed examination of the earlier English samples.

Readers will decide for themselves how to use the book. The planned intention is to print parallel texts wherever possible for easy checking. It is suggested that the first part of the document, unless found to be fairly well within a reader's scope, should be examined together with the first part of the transcript. Then, as the eye becomes accustomed to the types of letters, scribal peculiarities and general style of writing, an exact transcript should be made, with recourse to the alphabet of letters given in chapter 5 and, as required, the Latin vocabulary. From time to time the printed transcript should then be consulted to check accuracy. In this way, problems will be highlighted and perhaps the puzzle of disentangling the writing, abbreviations, grammar etc. will be more enjoyable. It is important to make a meticulous check against the transcript in the book to establish a basis from which to make progress.

The following conventions should be noted:

Abbreviations

Omitted letters indicated by abbreviation signs or symbols and superscript letters have been enclosed in square brackets, and the superscript letters placed on the line. The sign '&' has been retained and denominations of money (li, s and d), as also '&c.', have not generally been extended. A short list of abbreviations, other than those in the documents, will be found on page ix. Marks identical with abbreviation signs, but of no actual significance, have been ignored.

Capital and small letters

Capital letters are erratic in old documents at the best of times, but have been reproduced as they occur. In some scripts the capital and small letter can be alike and in such instances transcripts include the form which appears to be the more likely. In translations where very long sentences occur, capital letters have in some cases been retained to introduce a new phase of the passage.

Individual letters

A great variety of letters, covering the scripts in the book, with some additions, appears in chapter 5.

Opinion varies on the letters *i* and *j*, particularly with regard to their use in Latin. They are often used interchangeably. The intention here, in the case of documents in English and Anglo-Norman French, has been to transcribe according to likely spelling; and in the case of Latin documents to transcribe them both as *i* (with occasional exceptions such as initial letters of English names rendered into Latin and the final digit of small Roman numbers).

The letters *u* and *v*, although also used interchangeably, fall into a slightly different category and have been transcribed according to what is clearly intended.

In some contexts little distinction is made in the use of *c* and *t* which are in any case often written in very similar form. These have been reproduced as appears to be intended. If an interchangeable *c* or *t* is hidden within a Latin abbreviation, *t* has generally been preferred unless the document clearly contains the letter *c* in a comparable context. Similarly, in transcripts of English documents, extended words have been spelt to conform with the spelling used in the documents.

Thorn and yogh

For a note on these characters, see pp.38 and 39. Thorn is represented by the letters *th* in brackets; yogh by the letter *g* in brackets.

Punctuation

This is very inconsistent in old documents and marks occur which are unlike those in current use. Due to its capricious nature, the fact that forms resembling punctuation sometimes appear when only intended to signify abbreviation, and the constraints of printing, punctuation (other than hyphens and brackets) has been omitted unless helpful to the sense.

Italics

These have been used in transcripts on occasion to indicate postulated letters where there are uncertainties arising from slight disrepair, doubtful writing, or omitted abbreviation. Italics are also used for translations where they are interlined; and, in the notes, for Latin words and specific letters so that they are easy to locate.

Brackets

Square brackets, in addition to being used in transcripts for the extension of abbreviated words, are used occasionally in translations to enclose words added to make good sense. Words which are interpolated in the manuscript text are enclosed in angle brackets in the transcript.

Names

Christian names. In translation Christian names have been regularised.

Surnames. In translation these have been left in the form found in the document.

Place-names. In documents the endings of place-names, particularly those in Latin, are frequently abbreviated. As the Latin for counties, cities etc. can have varied forms, and smaller places perhaps had in any case no known Latin name, the tradition has been followed in the transcripts of indicating such endings with an apostrophe. Most place-names other than those of counties have been left as they are spelt in the document, although in many cases it is entirely clear what place is intended and what the spelling would then be.

Line fillers

These marks, which occur in many variant forms at the ends of lines in some documents, have been omitted.

Commentary on documents

These are intentionally brief, and to some extent random, since the aim of the book is to improve ability in palaeography rather than to teach genealogy or local history (though the hope is that horizons for research may be broadened). In general the genealogical examples have been chosen for interest (in addition to considerations of script, type, size, contrast, condition, legibility etc.), and therefore include rather more details of relationships than is average. They demonstrate, nonetheless, the type of material which may be found in similar documents. Further reading is suggested in some of the commentaries and in the bibliography.

Latin

The book should be self-sufficient as far as Latin vocabulary is concerned, but help with Latin grammar and syntax may be needed from a text book, preferably one relating to medieval Latin (for which see p.17). Books on Latin generally are noted in the select bibliography, together with others which have some relevance to the transcribing or understanding of Latin documents.

Documents

Most of the reproductions in the book are of MSS. at The National Archives (formerly Public Record Office) at Kew in Surrey, but the geographical spread of their content covers most counties in England. Some relate purely to local history but the majority relate chiefly to family history and have been chosen in most of these cases to illustrate at least two generations. The latter records, nevertheless, have a local setting and therefore impart colour and add personalities to the places of their subjects' habitation. Whatever the content, however, the object of the book is to try to demystify the problems of palaeography and turn bewilderment to pleasure and understanding.

2

Transcripts and Transcription

Having, perhaps with time and difficulty, identified what may prove to be a fruitful document, it is then necessary to resolve the eccentricities of the writing.

Opinion varies on the extent of experience necessary for the reading of documents, but it is undoubtedly very demoralising to flail about hopelessly in the deep end when gentle progress from experience in the shallow end can gradually bring confidence. Even to open a basic book on a foreign language somewhere in the middle induces a feeling of despair at any possibility of mastering that language. It is therefore most important for the inexperienced student to work gradually from the least complex examples of records onwards.

Documents differ greatly in difficulty, not only depending upon whether the original is in English, medieval Latin or even, in the case of some early documents, in Anglo-Norman French or Anglo-Saxon, but also because the writing itself can vary from the beautifully penned and regular writing of, for instance, some clergy in their parish registers, to the appalling scrawl seen in some depositions of the same period.

It is thus a fallacy that writing becomes more difficult to decipher in proportion to its antiquity. The writing of documents of the tenth century can be far more regular in form than that of documents written many centuries later. In general, however, it is true to say that, whereas many modern hands are very inconsistent, most old hands are more capable of being decoded in a logical way, given time and patience.

After a little practice the whole process can be much like working on a crossword in that a first attempt may yield only an incomplete resolution of the wording but, by shrewd use of what is, in the context, clear, and by building progressively on what appears certain, it may be possible to resolve most, if not all, of the outstanding problems. In the case of palaeographical difficulties, most of this resolution, at least with regard to English documents, will be achieved by careful scrutiny and comparison of letter-forms.

Making a Transcript

Importance of accuracy

Anyone learning to read MSS. should make a transcript reproducing exactly the idiosyncrasies of the spelling in the original. Abbreviations in English documents are not very numerous and their meaning is generally self-evident. On the other hand, documents in Latin are often heavily abbreviated, both in the middle of words and at the end. It is fortunate, however, that the abbreviations are generally of a regular character and can usually be unravelled by acquiring a knowledge of the signs, and by the use of suitable reference works (see chapter 4 on abbreviation, chapter 3 on Latin, and the bibliography).

The use of capital letters, other than for the initials of names etc., seems very arbitrary in documents (though there does appear to be a tendency for initial capitals to be applied to nouns, as in German, and sometimes to legal terms or for the introduction of a new clause). However, a true transcript should reproduce them as written.

Seldom is every letter of a document clear at the first reading, even for the initiated. For the novice, a very considerable number of queries may arise. Precision is of the greatest importance and it does need to be emphasised that any guesswork should be very carefully marked as such when a written version of a document is made. Otherwise misreadings may go unremarked during checking and even cause others elsewhere. A simple mark such as a dot or underlining under the suspect letter or letters of a word will suffice, and is much more useful than a question mark against the whole word. It is better not to spend too long wrestling with words which seem difficult, as subsequent revision may well resolve many problems.

A method should be adopted to distinguish between letters which are directly transcribed and those which are indicated by signs of abbreviation. This may be to enclose such letters in square brackets, as in the transcripts in this book, to render them in italics, or to mark them clearly in some other way according to individual choice, provided such marks are not ambiguous or identical with anything in the text. Deletion or interpolation should also be reflected in a transcript.

Use of a list, such as that in Martin's *Record Interpreter*, should make it possible to deduce correct endings for Latin counties and fairly important place-names when indicated by a suspension mark, but perhaps only from several variants. In the case of the abbreviation at the end of many smaller place-names, it is often quite uncertain what any extended version might be (and very possibly was so for the scribe in question). In the transcription of Latin documents therefore it is customary to use an apostrophe to indicate unknown or uncertain endings.

It is worth consigning work on transcripts etc. to a word processor or computer, as amendments and additions are then easily made. It can, however, be valuable to print out a first attempt, and even several subsequently improved 0s, since for most people errors are more easily detected on paper than on screen.

Deciphering the Text

Familiarity with the letters

If a hand is unfamiliar, and also the wording, perhaps little in the first lines will be immediately readable; but some words, even if only the simplest and most usual, will probably stand out as indisputable, and the letters comprising them will then be useful for comparison. Sometimes, however, a document starts with standard wording in which case, even for the experienced reader, it is worth reading it to become acquainted with the forms of the letters of known words or phrases. The preamble to a will, for instance, can be quite long and helpful in acclimatising the eye to the individual scribe's writing, so it is useful to work carefully through the first lines of such a document, even though their meaning may be clear and their import irrelevant to the requirements of the search.

On a first revision of a transcript, it will be remarkable to what extent it has proved possible to acquire some familiarity with the writing, and how, from experience and by basing deductions on comparison of letters, many more words will fall into place. Sometimes, indeed, a puzzling word considerately appears again, written more clearly, in a later part of a document. Gradually, with each additional revision, some difficulties will almost certainly be resolved and, although one should be on one's guard against hasty conjectures, nonetheless the meaning of the passage as it emerges will undoubtedly give some further leads.

Comparison of letters is thus cardinal to the deciphering of documents. Also valuable is comparison of the joining of two or more juxtaposed letters. Although forms of writing may be grouped into categories such as court hand or secretary hand, yet within those categories the idiosyncrasies of scribes vary greatly. The examples of letters in chapter 5 should greatly diminish these problems.

Sometimes, particularly with capital letters which are notoriously confusing and are likely to be a problem for the transcription of names, it can be worth writing out an alphabet, as far as possible, of the forms of the letters found in a document. This can help to reduce the chances of error, though some scribes are not wholly consistent and may unhelpfully use more than one form of the same capital letter. Small letters also may have several forms in the same hand, depending on their position in the word or on the whim of the writer.

In the case of lists of names, such as occur in lay subsidies and rentals, uncertainty over the initial letter of a surname can often be resolved by running the eye down a number of the Christian names to find a similar letter which in the context is certain.

Different letters (particularly vowels) do sometimes, in the same hand, resemble one another. An open letter *a*, for instance, may strongly resemble a *u*. Close scrutiny of those which are beyond doubt will generally resolve this problem, but occasionally there will be slight uncertainties of interpretation, particularly with names, and these should be marked as possible ambiguities. Some difficulties can be overcome by trying visually to follow the route of the writer's pen; this tactic is more valuable for work on an original manuscript rather than on a reproduction.

Other problems arise from inexplicable abbreviation or cursive handwriting in original documents. It is worth examining another part of the document or book, perhaps at or near the beginning of the work, where a clerk may write in their entirety, and more legibly, words which the ennui of repetition causes him to write less fully or regularly at a later stage.

One of the great problems for transcribers is the deciphering of names of people and places. Severe damage can be done to one's efforts by a quick guess bolstered by optimism. To query a likely possibility is much better than to leave as apparently definite an over-enthusiastic conjecture. Subsequent internal evidence will often resolve queries.

In the case of parishes, it is useful to consult printed books, such as Lewis's *Topographical Dictionary*, Smith's *Genealogical Gazetteer of England* or Bartholomew's *Gazetteer of The British Isles*, to test whether a place-name is likely. To identify a parish, the alphabetical list of parishes in Crockford's *Clerical Directory* can be helpful, but a shorter cut when the county is known is to consult *The Phillimore Atlas and Index of Parish Registers* where the parish listings are alphabetical under each county heading. Having done so, it is necessary to justify one's deductions, and maps may sometimes prove helpful.

Names, in the absence of any set spelling, often occur in different forms in the same document and, in the recording of entries in parish registers etc., much depended on pronunciation (possibly heavily influenced by local accent) as heard by the writer.

Minims

One of the principal problems of transcription is in determining the letters represented by minims (the short vertical strokes which, occurring in varying numbers, may produce the letters *i*, *m*, *n*, *u* and *v*). Not only may the letters *u* and *v* be written identically, but they can also be indistinguishable from the letter *n* if no rounding occurs at the top of that letter. The very word minim may appear as a row of ten minims, minimum (and several other Latin words) as a row of fifteen. These examples are, of course, extreme; more likely, and treacherous, are problems caused by the writing of different words in an identical style: such as *sine* (without) and *sive* (or), or *iudicium* (judgement) and *indicium* (proof). This ambivalence is especially problematic in the rendering of unknown surnames and place-names; an open mind is particularly needed for alternative possibilities (e.g. the surname Daines may appear, give or take the position of the dot, the same as Davies).

Minims generally present a special challenge in the deciphering of Latin documents in which runs of minims frequently occur, e.g. in *dimidium* (a half), *munimentum* (document etc.), *vinum* (wine), *communis* (common), *nominum* (of names), *omnium* (of all), *lumini* (for the light, which sometimes occurs in wills).

The keenly observant eye may accurately assess the number of minims, but it is surprisingly easy to gain a wrong impression of that number. This can be avoided by placing paper or thumbnail (in the case of a photocopy) across them all and gradually withdrawing it while counting.

In disentangling the puzzles presented by minims it may also be helpful to list all the possible permutations of the number of minims causing trouble, and so to find what may fittingly apply. The dotted *i* should of course be helpful in interpreting words which might otherwise be ambiguous. However, in some documents there is a marked absence of the obliging dot. Even when it is supplied by a kindly scribe, it may well not have landed immediately above its partner, but have strayed (generally forward). An analysis of the position of the dot over other words in the text, where that position seems regular, can enable fair speculation to be made about the minim to which it relates in a difficult word.

Further hazards

One of the pitfalls of reading documents lies in the entanglement of letters that can occur between the lines, either because the lines are very close together or because the letters have particularly long ascenders and descenders. In such cases it is useful to scrutinise the way in which the scribe's pen has travelled in both lines of writing. A magnifying glass can be a great asset here. However, despite the possible overlap above and below lines (but keeping it well in mind) it is very helpful to place a ruler, preferably transparent, under the line in question, if working from a photocopy, or a long slip of paper (acid-free paper being provided in some record repositories) if working on original documents.

This will also help to keep a clear view when working on very large documents such as the prodigiously wide chancery proceedings; it can be particularly effective for avoiding the easy mistake of returning to a subsequently repeated word or phrase, such as 'Item', 'Furthermore' or 'the aforesaid lands and tenements' and thereby missing an intervening section. The phenomenon of writing once rather than twice is known rather attractively as haplography; the opposite as dittography. These risks can also be avoided by numbering lines on photocopies or at least on transcripts (which will assist quick reference from one to the other).

Too much rather than too little can also be a problem. The eye can be greatly confused by the ink-marks showing through from the reverse side of the page. It may help to examine the slope of the writing in question as distinct from the slope of that showing through from the other side.

In some documents the scribe gives many words a gratuitous abbreviation mark which is purely a formality and can be ignored. The habit of attaching such marks to words seems to be a legacy from the writing of Latin documents. Particularly disconcerting is the line often placed through the letters *ll*, which on first impact suggests *tt* (though comparison is likely to show *l* quite unlike *t*).

Mistakes do occasionally occur in manuscripts. To err is human. However, before concluding that the error is on the part of the writer, it is worth checking several times for the possibility of its being on the part of the reader.

The deciphering of original documents faint with age can often be achieved by the use of an ultra-violet lamp (generally available in record repositories) which sometimes can make magically legible a passage almost invisible to the naked eye. Of the many types of magnifying glass, perhaps the most useful is that which has a small inset area for greater magnification and a battery-operated light.

Strange spelling and other peculiarities

The spelling in documents written in English can be very inconsistent. Not only will it appear different from modern usage, but words may occur in the same document in a number of variant forms. This should not be put down to a lack of vigilance or education on the writer's part but rather to the fact that spelling took a long time to crystallise into a regular form. However, *Johnson's Dictionary*, published in 1755 (and some lesser, previous attempts at dictionaries) no doubt did much to produce an increasing regularity. Most English spellings of the 15th century onwards are perfectly intelligible when seen in print. However, they are less so when taken in conjunction with other problems of contemporary writing.

The forms of *u* and *v*, being often used interchangeably, as also *j* and *i*, cause trouble. For example (given a changed initial vowel, four minims at the beginning and perhaps other problems of deciphering) 'inioye' may not immediately suggest the word 'enjoy'. See more about these letters in chapter 5.

The small letter *c*, being often used instead of *t* (and the two letters being also frequently very similar in form) can cause problems; *y* often supplants *i*; consonants are often doubled and *e* makes a frequent appearance at the end of words.

Other forms of spelling, which may seem peculiar to the modern eye, frequently occur. Words are unexpectedly joined so that the word 'shalbe', encountered in a document, can perplex until it is divided into 'shall' and 'be'. Elision of the definite article, 'the', and a merger with a following word beginning with a vowel, is very common, giving rise to such forms as 'thother', 'thelder', 'thone', 'thaforesaid'. Thus for any curious word beginning with the letters *th*, it is worth suspecting this possibility. Sometimes the letters *au* are written rather than an expected letter *a* producing, for instance, 'graunt' and 'Frauncis'. For greater confusion, more than one of these peculiarities may occur in one word as, for example, in 'thauncient', 'tharchaungell', 'tholly' (the holy).

Other small idiosyncrasies abound. For instance, field is commonly 'feild'; month is often 'moneth'; September, October etc. may appear as '7ber', '8ber' etc.; the Greek 'chi rho', as seen in churches, representing Christ, looks much like 'Xp', and is frequently used for the first part of the Christian name Christopher; small bewildering marks of varying aspect often appear at the end of lines and are no more than devices to justify the end of the line or, in some cases, act as a guard against fraudulent interpolation (though not, of course, in the case of, say, a registered will). Pairs of some letters, e.g. *st* and *sc* may be joined by ligatures which alter their appearance.

It is easy to be caught unawares by an unexpected encounter with the old symbol called 'thorn' which resembles the letter *y* but equates with the letters *th*; or that called 'yogh', resembling a long *z* but representing a value of the letter *g* or sometimes *y*.

Archaisms naturally occur, e.g. 'sithence' (since), 'fader' (father), 'eftsones' (soon). In particular, inventories are full of words which are now unintelligible to most people but which can generally be found in Halliwell's *Dictionary of Archaisms and Provincialisms* and other books listed in the bibliography. The *Oxford English Dictionary* is a remarkably rich source for interpreting obsolete terms.

Latin

Documents in Latin are naturally more difficult to understand (and indeed it appears that it was for this reason that legislation was passed in the 1730s that legal documents should no longer be written in that language) but much help may be derived from a study of similar documents in English. Thus the perusal of a manor roll of *c.*1735 will suggest the type of material, standard phraseology etc. which may similarly be found in Latin before 1733. If the style of handwriting persists over the period, the eye will meanwhile become attuned to the vagaries of the scribe's writing. Equally, in the previous century, whatever the many distresses of the Commonwealth, a benefit to the transcriber is that during most of that period documents were written in English.

Much of the above relates to the process of learning but with an armoury of knowledge and experience (and with the constraints of time spent in repositories), abstracting the vital matter from documents at a later stage will be achievable at greater speed (and with the prudent omission of much of the wording). A groundwork of transcribing in detail and at a leisured pace should provide the ability and confidence to make this possible.

Understanding the Documents

History

It is useful, and interesting, to have some idea of the type of information which can be gleaned from particular documents, and of their provenance. For types of document housed at The National Archives help is to be found in the introductions to the class lists, in the files of the *Guide* and in the leaflets there on specific subjects and types of record (as also from excellent past works on the records by Thomas, Scargill-Bird and Giuseppi, and the *Guide to the Contents of the Public Record Office*, published in three volumes during the 1960s). Other very useful books written specifically to describe genealogical material there are the *Dictionary of Genealogical Sources* by Stella Colwell, and *Tracing Your Ancestors in The National Archives* by Amanda Bevan. Local repositories have varying degrees of information; books on genealogy and local history are helpful; and useful introductions to indexes, transcripts and abstracts of records appear in the publications of local archaeological and record societies and of the Selden Society.

Dates

Until 1752 the year in England began on Lady Day (25 March) so that before that year dates shown in documents for the period 1 January to 24 March of a given year fell historically in the following year. Thus 7 February 1673 is historically 7 February 1674. For some years preceding the change some records helpfully gave both years in the form of, for instance, 1741/2. Unless the earlier system is borne in mind, many interpretations of dates will be wrong, sometimes with puzzling effect such as the date of probate appearing to occur before the testator's death. Also in 1752 the calendar was reformed by the omission of a period of 11 days, from 3 to the 13 (inclusive) of September.

Documents were often dated by saints' days and the regnal year. The exact date can be worked out from *A Handbook of Dates for Students of English History* by C.R. Cheney, which, amongst much other useful information, includes a list of saints' days, tables of of regnal years, and tables from which to work out the date of, for example, Tuesday before the feast of St Barnabas in a particular year. See pp.14-15 for a note on the Latin wording of dates.

It is worth noting that Charles II, despite the Commonwealth and his own absence, dated his documents on his restoration in 1660 as though he had reigned from the time of his father's death in 1649, so that what was apparently the first year of his reign was deemed his twelfth.

Kinship

A word should be said here for family historians. The relationships mentioned in documents are not always what they seem. For instance, reference to a brother or sister frequently indicates a brother-in-law or sister-in-law. On the other hand, a person referred to as 'mother-in-law' or 'father-in-law' is likely to be a step-mother or step-father. The word 'cousin' can cause much confusion. This may, as one might expect, indicate in the strict modern sense an uncle's or aunt's child, but there is a strong likelihood that it will denote some other relationship. This is not a question of error or vagueness but in earlier times was normal usage. The term often refers to a nephew or niece, but may mean a more unlikely affinity. In the chancery case of Sacheverell versus Stanhope in 1602 the opening sentence of the bill of complaint refers to the plaintiff's cousin. As the bill progresses it becomes apparent that this cousin was the plaintiff's great-grandfather.

3

Differences between Medieval and Classical Latin

The medieval Latin considered here is that used in records of interest to genealogists and local historians up to Lady Day in the historical year of 1733, the beginning of that year as then computed. This change followed an Act of Parliament of 4 Geo. II, c.26 (1731). Many documents, including chancery proceedings (except some very early ones which were written in Anglo-Norman French) and most wills and parish registers before this time were written in English, but such legal documents as feet of fines, inquisitions post mortem and, almost invariably, manor rolls were written in Latin. Although these documents in Latin, with their accompanying problems of writing and heavy abbreviation, may look very daunting and enigmatic, the medieval Latin required to translate them is for several reasons easier than the classical Latin learned at school. Those who wrote were after all not Romans and were having to translate English into Latin. The order of words is much more akin to that of English, and the grammar presents fewer complications. In addition, much of the wording consists of stock phraseology e.g. *secundum consuetudinem manerii* (according to the custom of the manor); or *in cuius rei testimonium* (in witness whereof). The meaning of such standard phrases may become familiar by initial study of similar documents in English (see p.10).

In general terms, there is very little difference between classical Latin and medieval Latin as encountered in the records in question and it is not difficult to make the transition, nor is it necessary to have a solid classical background. Indeed, past a certain point of knowing necessary Latin grammar, the fewer classical authors one has read the easier that transition is likely to be. Some of the differences and anomalies will not appeal to the classical mind and will be more easily assimilated by those with, as reputedly Shakespeare, small Latin.

A basic difference to be remembered, nonetheless, is that the letters *ae* of classical Latin words are normally reduced in medieval Latin documents to the single letter *e* (although sometimes they are represented by a diphthong). This is noticeable especially in the endings of nouns and adjectives, and can be misleading on first impact in such words as *ille* for *illae*, *Johanne* for *Johannae*; and causes other parts of words to look unfamiliar, e.g. *eger* for *aeger*, *hec* for *haec* or the prefix *pre-* for *prae-*.

Order of words

Although the order of words will not be quite as in English and verbs will often occur at the end of sentences or clauses as in classical Latin, there is, however, a tendency for it to be more like that of English than of classical Latin. An exception to this greater simplicity occurs in the method of expressing regnal years (q.v. under dates).

Grammar

Here also in most documents a greater simplicity will be found, even to the extent that the accusative and infinitive tends to be replaced by *quod* (that) with the indicative. The ablative absolute is only used occasionally e.g. in a will: *debitis meis solutis* (my debts having been paid) but appears to occur (though opinion varies) in the wording *teste* (he or she e.g. the queen) being witness and *his* (or *hiis*) *testibus* (these being witnesses).

Verbs

In the nature of the information to be found in documents, there is no great variety of tenses. Most verbs are in the present or perfect tenses. The future perfect sometimes occurs, but the future, imperfect and pluperfect are rare. Other than in the case of, for example, wills and grants, verbs are mainly in the third person. The subjunctive mood occurs from time to time.

Nouns

There is little call for the vocative case. The change from *ae* to *e*, already noted, gives rise to instances such as: *Egidius dat unam acram terre Elizabethe filie sue* (Giles gives an acre of land to his daughter Elizabeth).

Prepositions

These are far more widely used than in classical Latin, and sometimes with different and additional meanings. For instance *de* means not only 'concerning' and 'down from', but also can frequently be translated as 'of' (before place-names, not as a substitute for the genitive case); *ad* frequently has the meaning of 'at'; *per* often means 'by' where *ab* would be used in classical Latin; *cum* has extended uses e.g. *cum baculo* (with a stick), *cum pertinentiis* (with appurtenances); *super* occurs in an abstract sense e.g. *super sacramentum suum* (on his/her oath).

Articles

Unus etc. is often used for 'a' or 'an' in descriptions of property. It is worth mentioning here that the French *le* is sometimes used to indicate the word 'the' in names of lands.

Vocabulary

Since medieval Latin relates to a period more recent than when classical Latin was spoken, much new vocabulary was required. For this, however, recourse to Latham's *Revised Medieval Latin Word-List* will almost always overcome problems of definition. Another source is the excellent *Dictionary of Medieval Latin from British Sources* which, published in a series of fascicules from 1975, has now reached a point a little over half-way through the alphabet. This is immensely detailed and includes numerous quotations, as examples, from original manuscript sources.

There are a few treacherous words, however, which have different meanings in classical and medieval Latin so that even, or perhaps especially, for those with a good knowledge of Latin, a certain wariness is advisable. The following are examples:

	classical Latin	medieval Latin
dominus	master, lord	Sir, Lord (also used for some clerics)
exitus	way out, death	also issue, heirs
miles	soldier	knight
nepos	grandson	nephew
neptis	granddaughter	niece
filiolus	little son	also godson
filiola	little daughter	also goddaughter
villa	house	town or smaller place
continuo	continue (etc.)	adjourn

Occasionally a writer, apparently uncertain whether his Latin would be correctly understood, will confirm its meaning in English, e.g. *cum muro lateritio Anglice* a brick wall. Many medieval Latin words appear in various forms and sometimes with different genders, for instance, *herietum, herieta, harietum, harrietum, harieta, heriotum, heriota, hariotum,* and others similar (heriot i.e. feudal death-duty, frequently mentioned in manor rolls); *duodena, duodenum, duodenarius* (a dozen). The above dictionaries indicate dates at which the variants have been noted.

Dates

Days of the week. These can perhaps be most easily remembered by their similarity to the French or Italian i.e.:

Dies

Lune	Lundi	Lunedi
Martis	Mardi	Martedi
Mercurii	Mercredi	Mercoledi
Jovis	Jeudi	Giovedi
Veneris	Vendredi	Venerdi
Sabbati, Sabbatinus	Samedi	Sabato
Dominica, Dominicus	Dimanche	Domenica

The names of months are self-evident.

Much dating is in relation to Easter, saints' days etc., e.g. *in festo natalis sancti Johannis Baptiste*: on the feast of the birth of St John the Baptist (29 August); *in crastino festi Sancti Andree*: on the morrow of the feast of St Andrew (1 December).

The year is frequently given by the regnal year and can involve a somewhat prolix expression introduced by the word *anno* which agrees, after considerable intervening verbiage, with the ordinal number at the end of the phrase, e.g. *anno regni regis* (often shortened to RR with abbreviation signs) *Henrici quarti post conquestum Anglie decimo* (in the tenth year of the reign of King Henry the fourth after the conquest of England); or *anno regni domini nostri Caroli secundi dei gratia Anglie Scotie Francie et Hibernie regis fidei defensor &c. vicesimo septimo* (in the twenty-seventh year of the reign of our Lord Charles the second by the grace of God king of England, Scotland, France and Ireland defender of the faith &c.). Not infrequently, after this extensive method of defining the year, the scribe then generously supplements it by adding the year in arabic numerals. If not, however, it is necessary, in order to identify the year, to know on which day of the year a monarch's reign began (for which, as for saints' days etc., see *A Handbook of Dates for Students of English History* by C.R. Cheney). Other details on dates are given on p.11.

Roman numbers which appear in dates and in sums of money are not universally understood. The letters representing them are the same whether large or small, but there is a tradition in the case of the latter for a final digit *i* to be written with a long stroke (shown in the texts as *j*). The small numbers can be more treacherous to transcribe since the *v* (5) often has a long tail and greatly resembles the *x* (10), and they both can look remarkably like the letter *p*. Briefly, up to the number 100 (Roman *c*) the components of the numbers will be *i*, *v*, *x* and *l* (for 1, 5, 10 and 50). For the purposes of this book, additions of these numbers will in most cases suffice, e.g. *iij*=3, *viij*=8, *xvj*=16, *liij*=53. However, *i* before *v*, *x* or other larger number means that it is subtracted from the following number, thus *iv* (as also *iiii*)=4, *ix*=9, *xix*=19 (10+9), *xxiv*=24; *x* before a larger number also signifies subtraction so that *xl*=40, *xc*=90. The system continues with the larger numbers *D* (500), *M* (1000), both usually capital letters. Thus it is a question of adding the numbers up, except that a smaller number before a larger number indicates subtraction from that number. Useful lists of cardinal and ordinal numbers in words can be found in Stuart's *Latin for Local and Family Historians*, but such written numbers in this book will be found in the vocabulary. It is worth checking one's rendering of the figures in a list as in, for instance, a lay subsidy or rental, with any total given at its foot.

Proper names

Christian names

In medieval Latin these are usually straightforward (e.g. *Henricus, Ricardus, Margareta*) although some may seem obscure, such as *Egidius* (Giles), *Audoenus* (Owen), *Galfridus* (Geoffrey), *Ludovicus* (Lewis). It is worth remembering that the letter G sometimes occurs as the initial of alternative variations normally starting with W, e.g. *Gulielmus* rather than *Willelmus*, *Gualterus* rather than *Walterus*. Latin names which are identical with English names such as *Maria* and *Anna*, should ordinarily be translated as Mary and Ann(e). Some names have more than one possible translation. For instance *Isabella* and *Elizabetha* can be interchangeable, and *Matilda* is sometimes to be translated as *Maud*.

Some masculine Latin names have a curiously feminine appearance. For example *Lucas* (Luke), *Andreas* (Andrew) and *Thomas* and *Adam* all have 1st declension feminine endings for the accusative, genitive, dative and ablative cases. This is confusing and leads to curious genitive cases such as *Andree* and *Ade* and deceptive ablatives such as *Andrea* and *Ada*.

Much care needs to be taken in discriminating between the endings of cases of *Lucas* and *Lucia* (Lucy), *Matheus* (Matthew) and *Mathias* (Matthias) and *Johannes* (John) and *Johanna*

(Joan). In the latter case the ablative of *Johannes* is identical with the genitive and dative of *Johanna* (i.e. *Johanne*).

A useful list of Latin Christian names appears at the end of Martin's *Record Interpreter*; and a page of declensions of Christian names is to be found in Gooder's *Latin for Local History*.

Surnames

Again Martin's *Record Interpreter* has a Latin list, as does Wright's *Court-Hand Restored*. However, although Latin versions of surnames certainly appear in quite early records, the great majority of Latin documents likely to be used by genealogists and local historians do not translate surnames. There is, however, sometimes a token mark of abbreviation.

In these early documents surnames may simply be rendered as a translation of an occupational surname, thus: *Piscator* (Fisher), *Caretarius* (Carter), *Senescallus* (Stewart i.e. from steward), *Marescallus* (Marshall, Marshal); or can be of local significance, as *de Monte* (Mount), *de Lacu* (Lake), *de Morisco* (Moore), *Collinus* (Knollys), *de Stagno* (Poole); and amongst other Latin equivalents such as *de Sancto Johanne* (St. John), *de Nova Terra* (Newland) are the enjoyable *de Blanco Pane* (Whitbread), *de Botellis* (Butler), *Nigeroculus* (Blackey), *Hastifragus* (Brakespere), *Ala Campi* (Wingfield), *de Mortuo Mari* (Mortimer), and *cum Barba* (Beard, Witheberd).

Place-names

Lists of Latin place-names in Great Britain and Ireland can be found in Wright's *Court-Hand Restored* and, with separate lists of names of bishoprics in England, Scotland and Ireland, in Martin's *Record Interpreter*. Abbreviated place-names in documents can therefore often be extended (but see a note about this on p.3) and translated.

Miscellanea

Other small variations may occur e.g.

michi	for	*mihi*	to me
nichil	for	*nihil*	nothing
animabus	for	*animis*	to or for (etc.) souls
hiis	for	*his*	by (etc.) these
dampnum	for	*damnum*	damage

Words beginning *ob-* may often in medieval Latin begin *op-*. The letter *c*, as noted in an earlier section, sometimes replaces an expected *t*. *Premissa* is used with the meaning of 'the aforesaid' as well as 'premises'.

Alarmingly for genealogists the *Dictionary of Medieval Latin from British Sources* quotes two instances from the late 14th century where *filia* means granddaughter rather than daughter; and quotes also the use of *filius* as son-in-law, though usually with *in lege* (see comment on kinship on p.11).

Sometimes curiosities occur over the initial *h* which is occasionally added, as in *hostium* for *ostium* (door), or subtracted, as in *yemalis* for *hiemalis* (wintry).

The suffix *-que* (translated as 'and' before the word to which it is usually attached) sometimes appears detached from the previous word, e.g. (in a will): *corpus que meum sepeliendum* (and my body to be buried).

Abbreviations

Where abbreviations occur, as they do extensively in Latin documents, see chapter 4; also the list in Martin's *Record Interpreter*, or in Cappelli's *Dizionario di Abbreviature latine ed italiane* (for further notes on both of which see p.22). Chassant's *Dictionnaire des Abréviations Latines et Françaises* may also be useful. In the latter two books the examples shown are in writing as from records.

Books

For further detail on the grammar and use of medieval Latin, see Stuart's *Latin for Local and Family Historians* and Gooder's *Latin for Local History* (the latter in conjunction with Kennedy's *Shorter Latin Primer* of 1931). Both include practice exercises.

For translations of documents found in the course of research it is necessary to have, or have access to, Martin's *Record Interpreter* and Latham's *Revised Medieval Latin Word-List*, in addition to a classical Latin dictionary, such as Lewis and Short.

Other books are listed in the bibliography, including some parallel texts. These, even though they seldom include reproductions of original material, are of particular use for acquiring a knowledge of the forms of wording and translation of documents.

4

Symbols used for Abbreviation in Manuscripts

The conventions for the spelling and grammatical construction of Latin words have been more or less established for several thousand years and the spelling used in documents of interest to family and local historians is essentially the same as that found in a modern Latin dictionary. There are a number of differences between medieval and classical Latin usage, but these are dealt with in the chapter on the Differences between Medieval and Classical Latin.

Medieval and later Latin documents, however, make extensive use of various forms of abbreviation and this is the feature that readers new to Latin historical documents can sometimes find confusing. Fortunately, the principles underlying the methods used for abbreviation remained much the same during the whole of the medieval and post-medieval periods, not only in England but throughout Europe.

No standard system for English spelling was adopted until dictionaries became generally available in the 18th century. As a consequence, the spelling of English words in earlier documents, although usually readily understandable, tended to be phonetic and variable. Inconsistencies in the spelling of quite common words can frequently be found in a single document, even though it has clearly all been written at the same time by the same individual.

The use of abbreviation in records written in English is much less common than with those written in Latin, but some examples will still be found in the majority of early documents, whatever the language.

The scribes of this period followed fairly strict rules and the various signs, symbols and conventions employed by them are discussed and illustrated below. The abbreviations that they used, however, can be divided into two categories: specific abbreviation symbols that indicate precisely what letters have been omitted; general abbreviation symbols, where the scribe considered that the nature of the missing material could readily be deduced from the grammar and the context. Both types of abbreviation saved space (and hence expensive writing materials) as well as time by resorting to what can be regarded as a kind of shorthand.

1. Contraction (the omission of one or more letters in the middle of a word) or suspension (the omission of one or more letters at the end of a word) are commonly indicated by a horizontal line above the word, sometimes passing through the ascenders of the taller letters. The line may be looped or ornamented with vertical dashes. In all such cases, the line represents a general abbreviation symbol where the identity of the missing letters has to be deduced from the letters supplied and from the context.

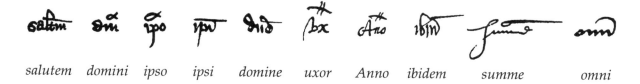

salutem	domini	ipso	ipsi	domine	uxor	Anno	ibidem	summe	omni

This sort of contraction was also widely used with the more common Christian names.

Nycholas	Johannis	Willelmo	Ricardo	Johanna

A line above a vowel often indicates the omission of the letters *n* or *m*.

nomine	matrimonium	indentatum

But beware. There are some hands where a horizontal flourish over a final *n* or *m* is purely ornamental and does not imply any form of contraction.

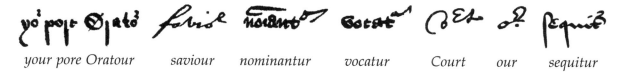

commen	man

2. A hook-shaped mark above the word can sometimes be a general omission symbol, but it usually indicates the omission of the letters *er*.

Manerii	verba	termino	Reverend	every	forever	interest	terme

3. A superscript symbol, possibly based on the 2-shaped *r* used in medieval court hands but somewhat variable in form (as shown in the examples given here), commonly represents the letters *ur*. It normally appears at the end of a word, but not always.

your pore Oratour	saviour	nominantur	vocatur	Court	our	sequitur

4. A superior symbol, shaped like the Arabic numeral 9 and inserted at the end of a word, represents the ending –us.

huius   baptizatus   Ricardus Hunt sepultus erat   unius

5. A symbol, similar to symbol number 4 but placed on the line at the beginning of a word, represents the prefix con- or com-.

confirmata   confidencia   commendo

6. A symbol at the end of the word shaped like the letter z can sometimes be a general suspension symbol, but there are a number of applications where it is much more specific.

Where the symbol follows the letter –b, the Latin ablative plural ending –bus is indicated.

duabus   omnibus   nobilibus

Where the symbol follows the letter q it always represents –ue

Annoque   uterque   absque   quinque

The same symbol may also be used at the end of a word to indicate the letters –et, for example, in the abbreviation of Latin words such as licet, debet, etc.

7. Where words ending in –ar or –or finish with a 2-shaped r which has a downward curving mark through its horizontal baseline stroke, it indicates that letters have been suspended and in this case the genitive plural ending –arum or –orum is indicated.

Rotulorum   quorum   librarum   Annorum   regnorum

8. A looped stroke curving downwards appended to the last letter of a word generally indicates the suspension of one or more letters, although some scribes just used it as an embellishment, particularly with the letter *d*. In English texts, such a symbol commonly represents –*es* (but sometimes –*is*, –*ys* or simply –*s*).

subjectes   landes and tenementes   poundes   thereaboutes   profittes

9. Any superscript letter generally (although by no means always) implies the omission of at least one letter. Superscript vowels frequently imply the omission of the letter *r*.

principis   contra   praye   quam

After the letter *q*, however, the missing letter is always a *u*.

10. Where a word ends with the letter *t* and the cross stroke of the *t* finishes in an upward hook, this is a general abbreviation indicating that a letter or letters have been suspended.

tentam   Ducatus   viginti

11. There is a group of special contraction symbols associated specifically with the letter *p*.

Where the *p* has a horizontal line through the stem, this usually represents *per*, but it can also represent *par* or occasionally *por*.

per   super   corpore   parte   parish   personally   perfect

Where a pen stroke from the head of the *p* comes down to the left and loops back towards or across the stem, this represents an abbreviation for *pro*.

pro   *proprias*   *profyttes*   *provyde*   *proximus*

With a *p*, the presence of a hook-shaped mark above the letter similar to symbol number 2 represents *re*, rather than the *er* implied with other letters

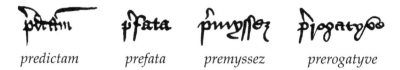

predictam   *prefata*   *premyssez*   *prerogatyve*

Another abbreviation mark is also used with *p* to represent *re*, but its use is far less common and it tends to be found only in some later documents.

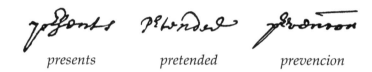

presents   *pretended*   *prevencion*

12. Scribes often found it convenient to represent the word *et* or its English equivalent *and* by a single symbol. The exact form chosen varied widely with different hands, but the reader will generally find no difficulty in identifying it from the context.

Et cetera was generally abbreviated to an *et* symbol followed by the letter *c*.

In Latin documents, there are many other conventional forms of abbreviation that were in common use but cannot be deduced directly from the above rules. Anyone who regularly transcribes such documents will find it essential to have access to one of the published lists of Latin abbreviations. *The Record Interpreter*, compiled by C. Trice Martin, contains a list of abbreviations based on English historical manuscripts as well a useful list of some of the abbreviations found in documents written in Anglo-Norman French.

A more comprehensive list of Latin abbreviations, based on documents in the Vatican archives but still highly relevant to British manuscripts, is the *Dizionario di Abbreviature latine ed italiane* (otherwise titled *Lexicon Abbreviaturarum*) by A. Cappelli. Although this is an Italian publication, copies can be obtained from many of the better bookshops in the UK.

5

The Characteristics of Individual Letters

The letters illustrated here have been taken from documents written between about 1400 and 1750. The characteristics of the letters used over this period varied considerably, depending both on the date when the document was written and on the purpose for which it was produced. Earlier records tend to be in some sort of court hand.

Although court hands were all based on the early Caroline minuscule script, a number of distinctly different styles began to develop after about 1200. This divergence was due to the way in which the scriptoria or groups of professional scribes serving the different royal courts and departments of state began to develop their own house styles to suit their own particular requirements. As a result, the documents produced by various government offices, which included the kings' courts, were written in specialised departmental hands, each with its own conventions and idiosyncrasies. These different hands are usually referred to generically as court hands.

Some forms of court hand continued to be used until at least the early 1700s but, from 1500 onwards, more and more documents came to be written in secretary hand. The latter form of handwriting remained in widespread use, both for official records and private correspondence, until well into the 18th century, when it was gradually replaced by a new style of lettering much closer to that of modern hand-writing. This was known as Italic hand (because the new style originated in Italy) but the term must not be confused with the sloping letters that we now associate with the word 'italics'.

Many of the letter forms used in these early documents were very different from those of modern handwriting. The examples given here have been selected and copied from original documents, many from documents transcribed in the present book. The intention has been to provide a representative sample of the forms and characteristics of the different letters that a reader is likely to come across when extending research in local and family history to the use of original early manuscripts.

It can sometimes be particularly difficult to recognise some of the more exotic forms used by early scribes to represent capital letters. By their nature, these occurred less frequently than did the small letters and, as a result, gave the scribe more opportunity for elaboration and even a degree of ostentation. The latter was especially the case with the initial letters used at the beginning of a manuscript, which often received special attention.

As has already been stated, it is a good general principle of palaeography that the reader should compare different instances of the same letter in the same document. This can help because, in many cases, the use of a particular form of letter in a familiar word makes it fairly easy to deduce what that letter is likely to be, but it is much more difficult to do this with capital letters because of their less frequent appearance in the text. This can often be a particular problem in the interpretation of surnames and place-names. It is hoped that the examples given here will help the reader by providing a quick reference for a check on the more unfamiliar letter forms and also show the way in which the structure of individual letters developed during a period when rapid changes were taking place in the basic shapes of the letters used to record the written word.

The examples given here are taken from many different styles of handwriting, some of them much easier to read than others. With certain hands, it is well known that confusions can arise between pairs of different letters that have a broadly similar shape. In cases where such confusions have been known to create problems, this is pointed out in the comments on the individual letters.

In making use of the letters illustrated, it is important to realise that they can only represent a selection of the many different letter forms that a researcher reading original historical documents can expect to come across. Those seeking to learn the technique of document reading must train themselves to study each new style of handwriting that they encounter and try to become familiar with the idiosyncrasies and conventions of the individual scribe. Any specific document will, of course, only feature a limited number of the different letter forms illustrated here.

a

Two basic forms of small *a* are found, those with a head and those without. It is sometimes possible for the more open-topped forms of the letter *a* to be confused with the letter *u*.

A special type of small *a* was used when the letter was written above the line. This often took an open-topped form, especially in earlier documents.

A

There are normally few problems in identifying the letter *A* and little likelihood that it will be confused with any other capital letter. There are some scripts, however, where the form of the small and the capital letters were more or less identical and in this situation it can sometimes be difficult to be sure whether a small or a capital letter was intended. As indicated elsewhere, this is true of a number of other letters.

b

Most examples of *b* can easily be recognised. Where the lower loop is open-topped there is some possibility of confusion with the letter *l* or between a badly written *lb* and *bb*. Less commonly, this form of *b* can also sometimes be confused with certain forms of the letters *u* and *v* (see the notes relating to those letters).

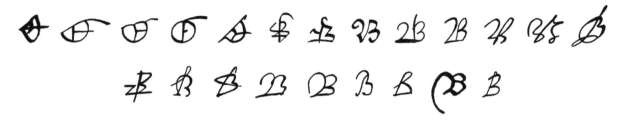

B

Some of the earlier examples of the capital letter *B* may be unfamiliar. In manuscripts where these early forms were used there is sometimes the possibility of confusion with contemporary forms of the letters *D, C, E* and *G*.

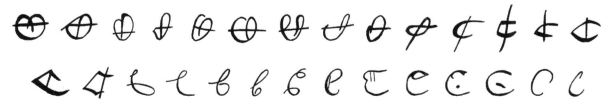

c

In secretary and court hands, there is often confusion between the letters *c* and *t*. Indeed, in some of the early court hands it can be almost impossible to know which of the two was intended. In most cases, however, the scribe was careful to make a clear distinction between the two letters. This usually consisted of the vertical stroke of the letter *t* being extended further upwards or the horizontal stroke further back. Individual scribes had different customs and unambiguous examples of the two letters should always be compared in each new script encountered.

C

The 'hot cross bun' forms of the letter *C* were frequently used in documents written before 1700. In later documents the letter took on a more modern form but there is the possibility, in some cases, of confusion with some forms of the letter *E*.

d

Although the uncial form of the small letter *d* (the form to the left side of the first row of letters) was widely used up to the 18th century, there is rarely any problem in recognising it. It gradually gave place to the more modern form.

D

Some forms of the capital letter *D* may be unfamiliar at first sight. There is some chance of confusion with early forms of the letter *B*, but there are distinct differences between the two and a comparison of the examples shown here should make it possible to identify them. In later hands, there was a reversion to the Roman form of the letter which is also the modern form.

e

The small letter *e* occurred in many different forms in different hands. In most cases it can be readily distinguished from other letters but, depending on the particular form that it takes, it can sometimes be mistaken for a *c*, an *o* or an *r* and, occasionally, when it occurs at the end of a word, for an *s*. It is not uncommon for a scribe to have used several forms of the letter *e* in the same document.

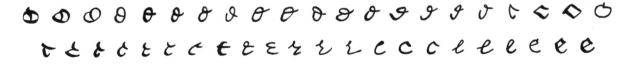

E

There are possible confusions between some forms of capital *E* and contemporary forms of the capital letters *C* and *G*.

f

There has often been confusion between the small letter *f* and the long forms of the small letter *s* (see the examples given under that letter). The only difference is the short horizontal dash across the centre of the *f* and this is not always very clear. The confusion is sometimes confounded if the long *s* also has a short horizontal dash (although it is very rare for this to extend across to the right side of the vertical stroke) or if the following letter is close enough to the *s* to run into it. See also the comments on the *st* ligature.

F

Before about 1700, the capital letter *F* was almost always represented by a double small *f*. The modern form of *F* only came into use with the introduction of the Italic form of handwriting. The double letter form still occasionally persists with some families who prefer to retain *ff* as the initial letters of their surname.

g

There were a number of different versions of small *g*, some with the lower loop open and some with it closed. It is not normally too difficult a letter to identify, although it can sometimes be mistaken for the letter *q*. Where the stroke across the top is faint or has faded, it can also be misread as the letter *y*.

G

The capital letter *G* can sometimes be one of the more difficult letters to recognise. Some early examples took rather curious forms. The main feature to look out for in all the circular forms of the letter is the strong hook or curved stroke at the top right. This often helps to distinguish it from contemporary forms of capital *C*. One or two forms might also be misread as capital *B*.

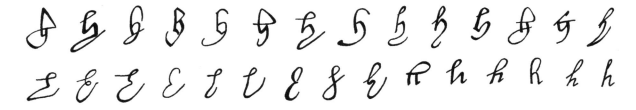

h

A letter that can be unfamiliar at first acquaintance is the very common secretary form of the small *h*. The first nine characters in the second row show various examples of that particular letter. In cursive examples of secretary hand, there was a tendency to run the letters *th* together as a ligature. See plates 29 and 32.

H

In Tudor and Stuart documents in particular, there were a number of hands in which the capital *H* and small *h* were written in more or less the same way and the decision as to which was actually intended can only be made on the grounds of context or (and this can be rather unreliable) size. It is not normally difficult to distinguish them from other letters, although there have been occasions when a capital *H* has been misread as a capital *N*.

i j

The Roman alphabet had only one symbol to represent these letters, the straight *I*. At the time when the documents transcribed here were written, there was no distinction between the symbols used to indicate the vowel *i* and the consonant *j*. The letter appeared in two patterns, the long and the short. There was a convention that where *ii* was written, especially when this occurred at the end of a word, the second letter of the two was elongated (see the examples illustrated). The short *i* is the more usual form and, of course, *i* is by far the more common letter, but in many cases the short *i* symbol was used to represent the consonant *j*.

It was often the custom in early documents not to put a dot over the letter *i*. The simple vertical stroke which forms the short *i* is known as a minim. Quite serious problems can arise with words in which the letter *i* is associated with other letters such as *m* and *n* also essentially made up from minims. For a comment on this, see the notes on the letters *m* and *n*. A single *i* without a dot can appear very similar to the letter *r* (note the final example given here).

Note: when the letter *i* was used in Roman numerals, the final letter of a sequence invariably took the long form, e.g. *viij* or *xj*.

I J

As with the small forms of these letters, there was no distinction between the symbols used to represent the vowel *I* and the consonant *J*. The scribes used a variety of different forms, some more similar to a modern capital *I* and some to a modern capital *J*, but these were often used randomly in words like *Indenture* or *James* to represent either the vowel or the consonant. Generally, it is only the context that indicates which letter was actually intended.

k

There are many variations in detail, but all forms of small *k* tend to feature a loop above a cross-stroke or leg to the right of a strong vertical stroke rising above the line. This makes it distinct from any other letter.

K

Apart, perhaps, from an increase in elaboration or size, the earlier forms of capital *K* generally follow the form of the small letter, from which it is often barely distinguishable. Some versions resemble the letter *R*, with which it has occasionally been confused. In later scripts there was a reversion to the Roman form of the letter resembling the modern *K*.

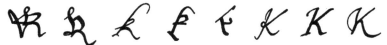

---

l

Small *l* is a letter with a very simple shape and it is, therefore, normally easy to distinguish. In a few cases, with certain hands, it can be confused with the letter *b*. In some cases, where the small *l* has a strong foot it can look very similar to a capital *L*.

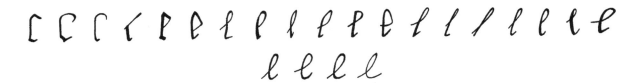

L

The capital *L* shows very little significant variation throughout the period. Some of the simpler forms can look similar to the small letter.

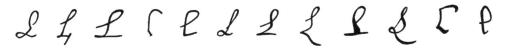

m n

The small letters *m* and *n* were often both made up from short down strokes or minims joined diagonally or, in early hands, not joined at all. As a result, in words where combinations of the letters *i, m, n, u* and *v* were written together and where the *i* was not dotted, it can be very difficult to interpret the minims and decide which letters were actually intended. Words such as *junior* (often written *iunior*) and *minor*, both comprising six minims followed by an *-or*, can only be interpreted from the context. In hands where the *i* was dotted, identification becomes easier (although the position of the dots does not always correspond precisely to the minims to which they relate), but it is only in later hands that the position of the cross-stroke as a means of distinguishing an *n* from a *u* can be relied upon. See also the examples given under the letter *u*.

M

The extra elaboration of the capital *M* helps to distinguish it from the small *m*. In a number of cases, the elaboration consisted solely of an extension to either the right or the left limb of the letter. This is a capital letter that is generally easily distinguished from other letters.

N

Rather unusual forms of the capital letter *N* may be met with from time to time, particularly in older manuscripts. Some forms of capital *N* have sufficient superficial resemblance to capital *H* to give rise to confusion.

o

Small *o* is generally formed in a way that leaves no doubt as to its identity, but there can, on occasion, be confusion with certain forms of the letter *e* and, in cursive hands where the letter is open-topped (the two examples on the right), with the letter *u*.

O

In spite of the various cross-strokes featured in some of the earlier examples, capital *O* is normally a clear and unambiguous letter.

p

Most forms of small *p*, especially the closed-loop forms made with three separate strokes of the pen, are generally easy to read. Later forms, made in a single stroke without taking the pen off the paper, can sometimes look very similar to contemporary forms of the letter *x*. The open-loop forms tend to appear in later manuscripts.

P

The capital letter *P* is normally quite distinct both from other capital letters and from the small *p*.

q

Small *q* is not generally a difficult character to recognise. The early form of the letter that appears on the extreme left of the line of examples may be unfamiliar at first sight and might, perhaps, appear to resemble a *y*, but in Latin documents (from which this example was taken) it is usually possible to distinguish it from the context. Forms of the small *q* where the down stroke curves up again in the form of a *g* can sometimes be mistaken for that letter.

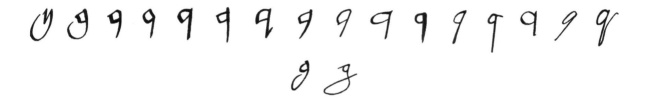

Q

The distinguishing feature of capital *Q* is the characteristic tail branching out to the right from the bottom of the letter.

r

The small letter *r* took a number of distinctly different forms as can be seen from the examples shown here. The 2-shaped *r* (most of the characters in the top line) often appeared in the same manuscripts as the long *r* (the first eight characters in the second line) or the *u*-shaped *r* (the remaining characters on that line). The 2-shaped *r*, however, was only used immediately following the letters *o* or *a*. Everywhere else, one of the other forms of *r* was used. Only the 2-shaped *r* appears to have had its use restricted in this way. The other versions of the letter were used more generally. There is some possibility of confusion between a tailed 2-shaped *r* and the letter *z* and between some forms of the *u*-shaped r and the letters *v* and *u*. Some forms of the 2-shaped *r* might also be misread as an *s*, especially when they appear at the end of a word.

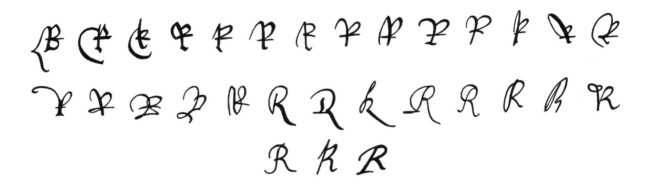

R

All the examples of the capital letter *R* here are really variations on the same theme, although some might appear more familiar to the modern reader than others. One or two of the shapes could, perhaps, be misread as a capital *B* or as a capital *K*.

S

Small *s* is another letter with a range of distinctly different forms, several of which were frequently used in the same manuscript, even in the same word. By convention, the long *s* was used in the middle of words and, in some scripts, also at the beginning. The form of *s* that provides the first nine examples illustrated was used exclusively as an initial letter. Equally, the 17 characters that come after the examples of the long *s* were used exclusively to terminate words. As a result, a single word in some documents could include examples of three different styles of *s*. The final six characters shown here represent the Italic influence and are taken from later texts.

In hands featuring the long *s*, there were two different ways of dealing with occurrences of a double *s*. Some scribes were happy to use the long form for both letters, but others insisted on the use of a short *s* for the second letter. Examples of both usages are given.

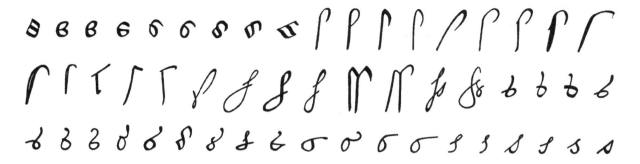

st sc and ft ligatures

When certain letters such as *st* and *sc*, written using the long *s*, were paired together, they tended to be treated as ligatures. That is, they were tied together and the form of each of the two letters involved was slightly modified. This also happened with the letters *ft*. The resulting ligatures are often extremely difficult to distinguish from each other and it is often only the context that enables the reader to discover what the scribe actually intended. Of the examples shown here, the first six were written as representations of *st*, the next three as *sc* and the three on the right as *ft*.

S

The capital form of the letter *S* may take a variety of different forms. Readers unfamiliar with the 'beaver-tailed' *S* (the first four examples) have been known to mistake it for the capital letter *M*. Some of the circular forms of the letter could be confused with capital *C* or even capital *E*. Several of the examples in the second row might also be misread as the letter *X*.

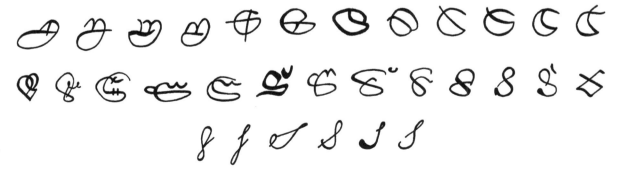

t

Most of the examples of small *t* given here are clearly identifiable. Where the style of handwriting features a straight-backed small *c*, however, that letter can sometimes be confused with a *t* and vice versa, especially when, in the latter case, the extension of the vertical stroke above the cross-stroke is vestigial or totally omitted. As can be seen from the last two examples, there was a tendency in some later cursive hands to forget to cross the *t*.

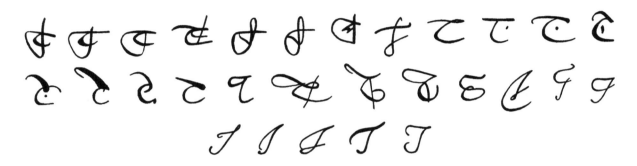

T

Capital *T* shows a wide range of variations, some more easily identified than others. Some of the later forms have, on occasion, been misread as forms of capital *I*, *J* or *S*.

u v

The Roman alphabet had only the single symbol *V* to represent both these letters. This led to a single symbol being used in medieval documents to represent both the vowel *u* and the consonant *v*. As can be seen, however, from the illustrations below, there were two distinct forms, one of which can only be described as *v*-like (the earlier examples) and the other as more *u*-like. There was a fairly rigid convention among medieval scribes that the *v*-like form should be used for the initial letters of words while the other form was to be used in the body of the word. In both cases, the letter could represent either a *u* or a *v*, depending on the requirements of the text.

Like the letter *n* referred to above, the *u*-like forms of these letters often consisted solely of two minims, making it difficult to decide whether an *n*, a *u* or a *v* was intended other than from the context or to determine how a succession of consecutive minims should be interpreted.

U V

Capital *U* and *V* usually took the form of enlarged versions of the small letters. Again, either a vowel *U* or a consonant *V* could be intended. Only the context can decide.

---

w

The letter *W* began by being literally a 'double *u*'. Early examples of the small letter *w* were identical with the capital letter and these are dealt with below in discussions on that letter, but in later writing a distinct form developed for the small letter. In appearance the general form closely resembled a *u* and a *v* joined together (see the notes relating to those two letters).

W

Many of the early forms of capital *W* were somewhat elaborate in their construction and, in almost all manuscripts where this form was used, the capital and small forms of the letter were identical. In most cases the basis of the letter as a 'double *u*' can clearly be seen. Even in later scripts, although the shape of the letters was much simpler, the small and capital forms were often similar or differed only in size, so that, again, it can be difficult to distinguish capital from small letters. It is sometimes possible to mistake the letters *lb* for a *W* or *w*, or vice versa as, for example, with the penultimate letter in the first line of the examples illustrated.

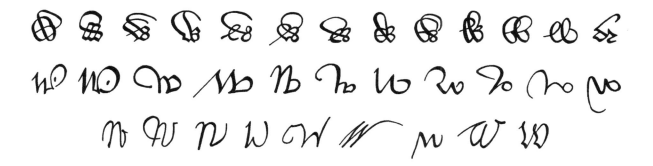

---

x X

The small letter *x* was very common in early documents owing to its extensive use in Roman numerals to represent a value of 10. Where it appears on its own, a small *x* can look very similar to some forms of ampersand. In early forms of the letter the crossed arms curved back to meet at both the top and the bottom leading, in some cases, to possible confusion with contemporary forms of the small letter *g*. In the more cursive hands, the letter *x* was sometimes written without taking the pen off the paper (see the examples to the right of the top line of letters illustrated) and this can sometimes lead to confusion with the small letter *p* which was frequently written in the same way (see the examples of *p* given earlier).

The capital letter X occurred only rarely as an English letter and when it did it was generally only a larger version of the small letter.

The Greek letter *chi* has a similar form to the English letter X and in that guise it appeared frequently in *chi rho*, the two Greek letters frequently employed in medieval documents to represent the word *Christ* (see, for example, plate 35).

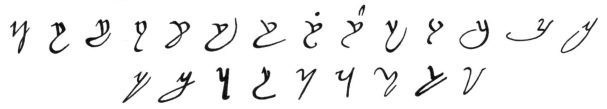

---

y

It should be noted that in some hands it was customary to place a dot over the letter *y*. The letter is simple and easily recognisable except, perhaps for the more cursive examples such as the last of the examples shown. A form of *y* was often used to represent the runic character *thorn*, which was used in many English documents in place of the letters *th* (see, for example, plate 2). It was a misreading of this character that originated such phrases as 'Ye Olde Teashoppe'.

Y

Most examples of capital Y resemble enlarged versions of the small *y*.

---

z

In documents of this period the letter *z* generally had a tail. It rarely appeared in Latin documents but was often used, in early English documents that were written in the days of phonetic spelling before dictionaries became generally available, in place of the letter *s*.

The same form was also sometimes used to represent the runic character *yogh*, used in some cases in place of *g* or *y* (see plate 35).

Z

The use of capital Z was not common. When it did occur, it tended to resemble an enlarged version of the small *z*.

Plates
Transcripts
Translations
Commentaries

1748

Octob.r 11. 1748 I Baptised Ann Draper, Daughter of —
George & —— Draper; Weaver, in the Dog-row. near
the three Colts, Bethnal-Green.

1750.

May. 1. 1750 Baptised Susanna Finch, Daughter of Peter & Ann
Finch, Weaver in Church Street in the Parish of St Matthew
Bethnal-Green.—

Feb. 5. 17$\frac{50}{51}$ Baptised Benjamin Cooke Son of Joseph & Jane Cooke
Weaver in St Johns Street in y.e Parish of St Matthew
Bethnal-Green, Middlesex.

1753.

April 26. 1753. Baptised John Draper son of George & ——
Draper, Weaver, & at y.e same time, being twins —

April 26. 1753. Baptis.d Daniel Draper son of George & —— Draper
Weaver. ~~in the Dog-row near the three Colts~~ in the work-
house at Bethnal Green—but formerly of the Dog-row near —
the three Colts

1754.

July 24. 1754. Baptis.d John Jemmeson, Son of David & Elizabeth
Jemmeson, Taylor, in the back lane; Bethnal-Green.

1755.

Mar. 17. 1755. Baptis.d Mary-Stringer Smith, Daughter of
of Vaughn & Elizabeth Smith. Barber, of St
Leonards. Shoreditch   By Will.m Sheffield

J.G

TRANSCRIPT

Non-conformist Register of Independents

(TNA:PRO ref: RG 4/4177)

1.	1748	
2.		Octob[e]r 11 1748 I Baptised Ann Draper Daughter of
3.		George & —— Draper, Weaver, in the Dog-row near
4.		the three Colts Bethnal-Green.
5.	1750	May 1 1750 Baptised Susanna Finch Daughter of Peter & Ann
6.		Finch, Weaver in Church Street in the Parish of S[ain]t Matthew
7.		Bethnal-Green.
8.		Feb[ruary] 5 1750/51 Baptised Benjamin Cooke Son of Joseph & Jane Cooke
9.		Weaver in S[ain]t Johns Street in [th]e¹ Parish of S[ain]t Matthew
10.		Bethnal-Green Middlesex.
11.	1753	April 26 1753 Baptised John Draper son of George & ——
12.		Draper, weaver, & at [th]e¹ same time, being twins
13.		April 26 1753 Baptisd Daniel Draper son of George & —— Draper
14.		weaver ~~in the Dog row near the three Colts~~ in the work-
15.		house at Bethnal Green but formerly of the Dog-row near
16.		the three Colts
17.	1754	
18.		July 24 1754 Baptisd John Jemmeson Son of David & Elizabeth
19.		Jemmeson, Taylor, in the back lane Bethnal-Green.
20.	1755	
21.		Mar[ch] 17 1755 Baptisd Mary Stringer Smith, Daughter of
22.		of Vaughn & Elizabeth Smith, Barber, of S[ain]t
23.		Leonards Shoreditch By Will[ia]m Sheffield
24.		JG

COMMENTARY

Document

These entries come from the register of Independents, Cambridge Road, Bethnal Green. Weavers were particularly numerous in this area due to Huguenot influence. Although it is noticeable here that George Draper's wife is unfortunately anonymous, non-conformist registers generally do give more personal information than their Church of England equivalents. The page has been chosen to exemplify the dual year frequently shown in the period 1 January to 24 March in the years immediately before 1752 when the beginning of the year changed from Lady Day (25 March) to 1 January. The date shown in the entry for 5 February would be in the historical year 1751.

Script

This writing, though cramped, does not present particular problems (though it is not nearly as simple to read as the entries for 1738 and earlier which are in a large round hand in an entirely different style and of extraordinary clarity).

Note

1. Note the use of thorn here for *th*.

1699

mo.
8. 3.

Abraham Gillet of y̍ Parish of Martins in y̍ ffields
Glazier, Son of W.ᵐ Gillet, of y̍ Parish of Giles's in y̍ ffields, Cutler.
And Sarah Ellard Daughter of J.ⁿ Ellard, of Giles's Parish aforesd
Tallow-Chandler. Having declared their Intentions of taking each
other in Marriage before several publick Meetings of y̍ people of
God called Quakers in London according to y̍ good Order used
among them, whose proceedings therein, after a deliberate Consideration thereof (with regard unto y̍ righteous Law of God, and
Example of his people recorded in y̍ Scriptures of Truth in y̍ case)
were approved by y̍ sᵈ Meetings, they appearing Clear of all others,
and having consent of parties & Relations concerned. Now these
are to Certify all, whom it may concern, that for y̍ full Accompli-
shing of their said Intentions, this Third day of y̍ Month called
October, in y̍ Year according to y̍ English Acco. 1699. They y̍
said Abraham Gillet and Sarah Ellard appeared in a publick
Assembly of y̍ aforesd people & others Met together for that
End, in their publick Meeting place at y̍ Savoy in y̍ Strand
and in a Solemn Manner he y̍ said Abraham Gillet, taking y̍ said Sarah Ellard by y̍ hand did openly declare
as followeth: Friends, in y̍ fear of y̍ Lord, and in y̍ presence
of this Assembly, whom I Desire to be my Witnesses, I take
this my friend Sarah Ellard to be my Wife, promising
through y̍ Lords Assistance to be to her a Loving and faithful
Husband, until it shall please y̍ Lord by Death to separate us.
And then & there in y̍ sd Assembly y̍ said Sarah Ellard did in
like manner declare as followeth ffriends, in y̍ presence of the
Lord, and before this Assembly (whom I desire to be my Witnesses) I take this my friend Abraham Gillet to be my
Husband, promising to be to him a faithful and loving wife, till
Death shall separate us. And y̍ sd Abraham Gillet and Sarah
Ellard, as a further Confirmation thereof, did then & there to these
presents set their hands. And wee whose Names are hereunto subscribed,
being present among others, at y̍ Solemnizing of their said Marriage
and Subscription in manner aforesd, as Witnesses hereunto
have also to these presents subscribed o.ʳ Names, y̍ Day & Year above
written.

Geo. Whitehead	Gerard Taylor	Isreal Golly	Abraham Gillet
Jno. Vaughton	Ri.ᵈ Hawkins	Ann Baker	Sarah Ellard
Geo. Bowles	Jno. Ball	Abigal Spurrier	Relations
Geo. ffolkes	Jno. Waters	Susana King	Wm Gillet
Jno. Golly	Jno. Litherington	Mary Derbe	Jane Gillet
Jacob Pullen jun.	Jno. Bradfield	Mary Roberts	Jno. Ellard
Matt. Hopkinson	Josiah Ellis	Eliz. Booby	Sarah Ellard
Isaac Page	Benj. Bealing	Eliz. Cuthbert	Jno. Ellard
Jos. Hayton			James Gillet
Jos. Taylor			Tho. Ellard
Isaac Miller			Jos. Ellard
			Eliz. Ladbrook
			Sarah Appling
			Eliz. Jenkins

73

Roger Judkins Sarah Appling
Eliz. ffolkes Wm Williams
Charl. Puppon.

TRANSCRIPT

Record of Quaker Marriage

(TNA:PRO ref: RG 6/825, p 35)

1. 1699
2. mo[nth]
3. 8[1] 3 **Abraham Gillet** of [th]e Parish of Martins in [th]e Fields
4. Glazier, Son of W[illia]m Gillet, of [th]e Parish of Giles's in [th]e Fields Cutler
5. And Sarah Ellard Daughter of Jo[h]n[2] Ellard of Giles's Parish afores[ai]d
6. Tallow-Chandler Having declared their Intentions of taking each
7. other in Marriage before several publick Meetings of [th]e people of
8. God called Quakers in London according to [th]e good Order used
9. among them whose proceedings therein after a deliberate Con-
10. sideration thereof (with regard unto [th]e righteous Law of God and
11. Example of his people recorded in [th]e Scriptures of Truth in [tha]t Case)
12. were approved by [th]e s[ai]d Meetings they appearing Clear of all others
13. and having Consent of parties & Relations concerned Now these
14. are to Certify all whom it may concern that for [th]e full Accompli-
15. shing of their said Intentions this Third day of [th]e Month called
16. October in [th]e Year according to [th]e English Acco[un]t 1699 They [th]e
17. Said Abraham Gillet and Sarah Ellard appeared in a publick
18. Assembly of [th]e afores[ai]d people & others Met together for that
19. End in their publick Meeting place at [th]e Savoy in [th]e Strand
20. and in a Solemn Manner he [th]e said Abraham Gillet ta-
21. king [th]e said Sarah Ellard by [th]e hand did openly declare
22. as followeth Friends in [th]e Fear of [th]e Lord and in [th]e pr[e]sence[3]
23. of this Assembly whom I desire to be my Witnesses I take
24. this my Friend Sarah Ellard to be my Wife promising
25. through [th]e Lords Assistance to be to her a Loving and Faithful
26. Husband until it shall please [th]e Lord by Death to separate us.
27. And then & there in [th]e s[ai]d Assembly [th]e said Sarah Ellard did in
28. like manner declare as followeth Friends in [th]e presence of the
29. Lord and before this Assembly (whom I desire to be my Wit-
30. nesses) I take this my Friend Abraham Gillet to be my
31. Husband promising to be to him a faithful and loving wife till
32. Death shall separate us And [th]e s[ai]d Abraham Gillet and Sarah
33. Ellard as a further Confirmation thereof did then & there to these
34. pr[e]sents set their hands And we whose Names are hereunto subscribed
35. being pr[e]sent among others at [th]e Solemnizing of their said Marriage
36. and Subscription in manner afores[ai]d as Witnesses hereunto
37. have also to these pr[e]sents subscribed o[u]r Names [th]e Day & Year above
38. written

Geo[rge] Whitehead	Gerard Taylor	Israel Gelly	Abraham Gillet
Jo[h]n Vaughton	Rich[ard] Hawkins	Ann Baker	Sarah Ellard
Geo[rge] Bowles	Jo[h]n Ball	Abigal Spurrier	Relac[i]ons
Geo[rge] Folkes	Jo[h]n Waters	Susan[n]ah King	W[illia]m Gillet
Jo[h]n Jelly[4]	Jo[h]n Lithergton	Mary Derbe	Jane Gillet
Jacob Pullen jun[io]r	Jo[h]n Bradfield	Mary Roberts	Jo[h]n Ellard
Matt[hew] Hopkinson	Josiah Ellis	Eliz[abeth] Beeby	Sarah Ellard
Isaac Page	Benj[amin] Bealing	Eliz[abeth] Cuthbert	John Ellard
Jos[eph] Hayton			James Gillet
Jos[eph] Taylor			Tho[mas] Ellard
Isaac Miller			Jos[eph] Ellard
			Eliz[abeth] Ladbook
			Sarah Appling
			Eliz[abeth] Appling
		Roger Judkin	Sarah Appling
		Eliz[abeth] Folkes	W[illia]m Williams
		Charl[es] Puppen	

[2]

COMMENTARY

Record of Quaker Marriage

(TNA:PRO ref: RG 6/825 p 35)

Document

This register (surrendered with many others, after initial reluctance by the Quakers, in 1841) begins in 1663, and is given as 'The Register Booke of the Marriages of the People of God in Scorn calld Quakers Belonging to the Meeting of the People of God aforesaid at Westminster'. The Quakers were very informative in their documents which are in extremely good order. Records of marriage in particular are valuable to the genealogist since so many relations tended to be congregated together and be recorded as witnesses. Until 1861 bride and groom, to participate in a Quaker marriage, had both to be members of the Society of Friends, but not so the witnesses.

Script

This document, being over 300 years old, is written in a remarkably legible hand. There is little to distinguish it from a modern hand other than the letter *e* written as though backwards, the long *s*, a few small abbreviations and the frequent instances of the character known as thorn, indicating *th*. There are two types of *h*: one harking back to that found in the secretary hand; the other of more recent appearance.

Notes

1. The Quakers, before 1752, named the months by numbers, beginning with March as the first month; thus month 8 is October (which of course owes its derivation to that number); thereafter January became the first month.
2. Here and subsequently Jnº (the curiously transposed abbreviation for John) has been transcribed with the letter *o* in the normal place.
3. This abbreviation is unusual for *re* following *p*. Normally after *p* a simple curved stroke (see p.22) is found.
4. The initial letter could be either *J* or *T*, but it seems more likely that Jelly (as variant of Gelly in the third column) is intended.

N.B. As the lines of names are irregular, no numbers have been assigned to them.

(Plate and transcript on previous spread)

COMMENTARY

Bounty Papers relating to a Revoked Administration
(TNA:PRO ref: ADM 106/3023)

Document

The Navy Board records of class ADM 106 (1658-1837) contain a wealth of miscellaneous and interesting personal documents such as letters, certain application papers and appointments to ships, and bounty papers (1675–1822) in which latter category this document appears. These papers may cite the deceased subject's widow and indigent condition, and children with their ages, or widowed mother, and nature of wounds and circumstances of their being received, surgeon's report, and date of death. Sometimes certificates of baptism and marriage (from the parish) are included. This document would seem to have been provoked by the administration of the goods of George Thomas of the ship *Rueport* granted (P.C.C.) in July 1678 to Sarah Thomas, described as his relict. The papers are in many individual hands and therefore are useful examples for transcribing.

Script

The letter *r* in some cases appears identical with some instances of *c* (v. in line 4: serv<u>ic</u>e aboa<u>r</u>d). The *t* is not always crossed. Notice the confusing though not unusual form of Arabic 8, described in Hector's *Handwriting of English Documents* as 'an exotic form, which suggests a recumbent capital S' occurring from time to time during the 17th and early 18th centuries.

Notes

1. This is an earlier spelling of proctor.
2. 8b[e]r: October; similarly may occur 7ber, 9ber and 10ber, reflecting the Latin origin of the names of those months.

(Plates and transcripts on following spread)

October the 24th 1678:

These are to certifye that the Administration
of George Thomas lately deceased slaine in his
Majesty's service aboard the Rupert, formerly
graunted vnto Sarah Thomas the pretended
Relict of the deceased was this day revoaked in
open Court by the Judge of the Prærogatiue
at the Motion of mer

        Thomas Pinfold Advocate
        Tho: Burt Proctor for
Margarett Thomas the lawfull
Relict

Rt Honoble   29. 9br 70.1
       I am informed by both partys that this Cert
is true   Tho: Marlow

---

ffebruary — 5 — in the yeare = 1663 —
George Thomas, and Margarit Coundall
were marryed, in St Samysson Church
in yorke

        by me Anthony Wright
        curate of St Sampsons
          in york

Herbert Jeffreys

TRANSCRIPT

Bounty Papers relating to a Revoked Administration

(TNA:PRO ref: ADM 106/3023)

First document

1.   October the 24th 1678

2.   These are to certifye that the Administration
3.   of George Thomas lately ~~deceased~~ slaine in his
4.   Majesty's service aboard the Rupert formerly
5.   graunted unto Sarah Thomas the Pr[e]tended
6.   Relict of the deceased was this day revoaked in
7.   open Court by the Judge of the Prærogative
8.   at the Motion of mee

9.   Thomas Pinfold Advocate &
10.   Tho[mas] Burt Procto[u]r¹ for
11.   Margarett Thomas his lawfull
12.   Relicte

13.   R[igh]t Hono[ura]ble 29 8ber² 78

14.   I am informed by both partys that this Cert[ificate]
15.   is true   Tho[mas] Marlow

Second document

1.   February 5 in the yeare 1663
2.   George Thomas and Margritt Coundall
3.   were marryed in S[ai]nt Sampson Church
4.   in Yorke

5.   by me Anthony Wright
6.   curate of S(ain)t Sampsons
7.   in York

8.   Herber Geffreys

June y^e 10th 1682.

These are to certify whom it may concern that
William Carew of the parish of St Botolph with=
out B^{ps}gate London was (as it is credibly reported)
drowned in the Gloucester Frigat (of which I
have formerly signed a Certificat) and that he
has left behind him a widdow and three children.
The name of his widdow is Bridgett Carew. Her
childrens names are Thomas, Richard, and Martha.
The first is aged about 17 years. The second about
11. And the daughter is about 8 years of age; so
that I suppose neither of them is married. The
ages of these Children appear to me by several
certificates of their baptisme, which I have de=
livered back to the widdow, that shee may shew
them to others as occasion may require; In testi=
mony of all which I have hereunto sett my hand
the day and year above written.

                    Tho: Pittis D.D. Rector
                      of the psh of St Botolph with=
                        out B^{ps}gate London.

        Haines Jonasse Church
        John James   wardens
        David Bell
        John Catlin

TRANSCRIPT

Certificate in Bounty Papers

(TNA:PRO ref: ADM 106/3023)

1.   June [th]e 10th 1682

2. These are to certify whom it may concern that
3. William Carew of the parish of S[ain]t Botolph with-
4. out B[isho]psgate London was (as it is credibly reported)
5. drowned in the Gloucester Frigat (of which I
6. have formerly signed a Certificat) and that he
7. has left behind him a widdow and three children
8. The name of his widdow is Brigett Carew Her
9. Childrens names are Thomas, Richard and Martha
10. The first is aged about 17 yeares The second about
11. 11 And the daughter is about 8 yeares of age Soe
12. that I suppose neither of them is married The
13. ages of these Children appear to me by several
14. Certificates of their baptisme which I have de-
15. livered back to the Widdow that shee may shew
16. them to others as occasion may require In testi-
17. mony of all which I have hereunto sett my hand
18. the day and year above written

19.   Tho[mas] Pittis D[octor] [of] D[ivinity] Rector
20.   of the p[ar]sh¹ of S[ain]t Botolph with-
21.   out B[isho]psgate London

22.   James Damaske Church
23.   John James   Wordenes
24.   David Bell
25.   John Tallis

COMMENTARY

Document

This is a further example of the useful genealogical material which may appear in bounty papers. See previous notes to plate 3.

Script

The letters *W* and *w* are similar, if not in some cases indistinguishable. An *e* of the Greek type is generally used, sometimes resembling a modern *r* and not always easily recognisable when joined (e.g. in *yeares* in ll. 10 and 11). A second type of *e*, however, is sometimes used (see the word 'these' in l. 13). Note the different hand, particularly the *r*, used for the signatures, perhaps in the writing of the churchwarden first named.

Note

 1. The abbreviation on the letter *p* does not include an *i*.

GEORGE the second by the Grace of God of
Great Britain France and Ireland King defender

Of the Faith and so forth To Our Right Trusty and
and wellbeloved Councillor Phillip Lord Hardwicke
Baron of Hardwicke Our Chancellor of Great Britain
Greeting We Will and Command that under our Great
Seale of Great Britain remaining in your Custody
You Cause these Our Letters to be made forth Patents
in Form Following GEORGE the second by the Grace
of God &c: To All to whom these Presents shall come
Greeting Whereas Our Trusty and wellbeloved
Michael Betton of Wellington in Our County of Salop
Gentleman and Thomas Betton of Shrewsbury in
Our said County Gentleman Have by their Petition
Humbly represented Unto Us That by much Study
Application and Great Expence they have found
Out and discovered an Oyl Extracted from a Flinty
Rocke which by Experience is found Greatly Beneficial
to some and an Entire Cure to most People who made
Tryal thereof in Rheumatic and Scorbutick and other
which they Apprehend and Believe will be of Publick
Use and Advantage That in Regard the Petitioners
are the first and Sole Inventors of the said Oyl and as
the same has never been put in Practice by any Others
they have most humbly Prayed Us to Grant to them
their Executors Administrators and Assignes the sole Use
and Advantage of their said Invention For the Term of Fourteen
Years according to the Statute in that Case made and
Provided We being willing to Give Encouragement to
all Arts and Inventions which may be for the Publick
Good Are Graciously pleased to Condescend to their Request

TRANSCRIPT

Part of Patent of Invention on Patent Roll

(TNA:PRO ref: C 66/3610)

1. **George** the second by the Grace of God of
2. Great Britain France and Ireland King defender
3. Of the Faith and so forth To Our Right Trusty and
4. And wellbeloved Councillor Phillip Lord Hardwicke
5. Baron of Hardwicke Our Chancellor of Great Britain
6. **Greeting We Will** and Command that under our Great
7. Seale of Great Britain (remaining in Your Custody)
8. You Cause these Our Letters to be made forth Patents
9. in Form Following **George** the second by the Grace
10. of God &c[eter]a **To All** to whom these Presents shall come
11. Greeting **Whereas** Our Trusty and wellbeloved
12. Michael Betton of Wellington in Our County of Salop
13. Gentleman and Thomas Betton of Shrewsbury in
14. Our said County Gentleman Have by their Petition
15. Humbly represented Unto Us That by much study
16. Application and Great Expence they have found
17. Out and discovered an Oyl Extracted from a Flinty
18. Rock which by Experience is found Greatly Beneficial
19. to some and an Entire Cure to most People who made
20. Tryal thereof in Rheumatic and Scorbutick and other <cases>
21. which they Apprehend and Believe will be of Publick
22. Use and Advantage That in Regard the Petitioners
23. Are the first and Sole Inventors of the said Oyl and as
24. the same has never been put in Practice by Any Others
25. they have most humbly Prayed Us to Grant to them
26. their Executors Administrators and Assignes the sole Use
27. And Advantage of their <said> Invention For the Term of Fourteen
28. Years According to the statute in that Case made and
29. Provided **Wee** being willing to Give Encouragement to
30. all Arts and Inventions which may be for the Publick
31. Good Are Graciously pleased to Condescend to their Request

COMMENTARY
Part of Patent of Invention on Patent Roll
(TNA:PRO ref: C 66/3610)

Document

The letters patent (temp. John to George VI) or open letters, i.e. *litterae patentes* as distinct from those which were closed (as enrolled on the close rolls q.v. commentary on plate 26) contain record of an immense variety of subjects including grants of offices, creations of peers and baronets, presentations to churches and chapels, denizations, grants of custody of lunatics and their estates and, as in this example, inventions (subjects which might appear on the rolls for only a limited period). The patents of invention, which ceased to be enrolled on the patent rolls in the 1850s, include a wonderful array of ingenuity. This can be tapped in brief detail in that most absorbing and fascinating book, the *Alphabetical Index of Patentees of Inventions* (1854, new edn. 1969) by Bennet Woodcroft, himself an inventor. This alphabetical list (covering the period 1617 to 1852, and around some 15,000 inventions) includes only a tiny scattering of female names and mostly relates to a very broad range of scientific inventions. This can add almost eccentric colour to the biographical side of family history and indeed can give some clues to tracing relationships, in that inventors of the same surname responsible for similar inventions may be worth investigating, and that a small number, as in this instance, involve more than one inventor of the same surname. Shown here is only the beginning of the enrolment, which was made in 1742.

Script

This hand is extremely clear but gives further practice in becoming accustomed to the letter *e* written as though backwards. The wealth of capital letters even outdoes the luxuriance of them found these days. A curiosity is the curved tail to be found attached to many of the final letters, similar to the abbreviation indicating *es* in other documents but here used apparently only as ornament.

(Plate and transcript on previous spread)

COMMENTARY
Will of John Horne
(TNA:PRO ref: PROB 11/760/86)

Document

Wills, well-known as one of the prime sources for family historians, are also useful to local historians in that they, giving the place of residence of the testator and often mentioning others living nearby, make a contribution to knowledge about the inhabitants of that place; and perhaps also about the houses, fields, etc. Not infrequently there were legacies for the repair of the fabric of the church or bequests of specific items for the church. With some printed indexes can be found an index locorum whereby it is easy to discover such relevant wills. It is worth noting the wording of English probate clauses since they give similar content to watch for when the clauses are in Latin (often following a will in English) before Lady Day 1733. See, for much useful information, pp. ix-xlvi of *Wills and Their Whereabouts* by Anthony Camp (1974); and *Prerogative Court of Canterbury and Other Probate Records* by Miriam Scott (1997).

Script

Being a registered copy of a will proved in the Prerogative Court of Canterbury, this record is in a hand usual to the massive volumes of such copies. There are still in existence (in the class TNA:PRO PROB 10) many of the originals of these wills which are written in more individual hands. The copies of course vary according to registration date, but the main noticeable feature to give problems is the form of the minims for the letters *i, m, n, u* and *v* (continuing to the 19th century). The dot accompanying the letter *i* is however there to help in this case, though often appearing over a subsequent letter.

Note

1. Marginal note gives the name as John.
2. The form of the apparent abbreviation after the letter *P* is not the usual form to denote *-re* after *p*.

(Plate and transcript on following spread)

John
Horne

In the Name of God Amen

I John Horne of Northstreet in the parish of Tilehurst in the County
of Berks Yeoman being sick and weak as to my Bodily health
but of sound and disposing Mind Memory and Understanding
do make this my last Will and Testament in manner and form
following that is to say first I give and bequeath unto my
eldest Son John Horne and to his heirs Executors and Assigns for
ever All my Estate whatsoever and wheresoever both Real and
personal Chargeable nevertheless and I do hereby Charge the
same with the payment of the Annual Sum of ten pounds to
my Son Richard Horne to be paid to him my said Son Richard
for and during the Term of his natural life by four quarterly
payments and the first payment to begin and be made
at the end of the first quarter next after my decease And I do
also Charge the same with the Sum of five pounds to be
paid to my — — Son Thomas Horne and with the payment of
the like Sum of five pounds to my Son Robert Horne and
of twenty Shillings to my Daughter Sarah Fenton And I do
also Charge my said Estate with the payment of all my debts
ffuneral and Testamentary Charges and Exposures And do constitute
and appoint my said Son full and sole Executor of this my last
Will and Testament revoking all former Wills by me at
any time heretofore made declaring this to be my last
Whereunto I have set my hand and Seal the eleventh day
of December in the Year of our Lord One thousand seven hundred
and forty six ./. The mark of the said John Horne the Testator ./.
Signed Sealed published and declared by the said John Horne
the Testator as and for his last Will and Testament in the presence
of us who at his request attested the same in his presence —
Edward Blackman ./. Richard Church ./. the Mark of Ann Cooke ./.

This Will

was proved at London before the Right Worshipful John
Bettesworth doctor of Laws Master Keeper or Commissary of the Prerogative Court of
Canterbury lawfully constituted the twenty ninth day of March 1748 by the Oath of
John Horne the Son of the deceased and Extor named in the said Will to whom
Admon was granted of all and singular the Goods Chattels and Credits of the
said deceased being first sworn by Commission duly to administer ✝ Exd.

Will of John Horne

(TNA:PRO ref: PROB 11/760/86)

In margin: John Horne

1. **In the Name of God Amen**
2. I John Horne of Northstreet in the Parish of Tilehurst in the County
3. of Berks Yeoman being sick and weak as to my Bodily health
4. but of sound and disposing Mind Memory and Understanding
5. do make this my last Will and Testament in manner and form
6. following that is to say First I give and bequeath unto my
7. Edest Son John Horne and to his Heirs Executors and Assigns for
8. ever All my Estate whatsoever and wheresoever both Real and
9. Personal Chargeable nevertheless and I do hereby Charge the
10. same with the Payment of the Annual Sum of ten Pounds to
11. my Son Richard Horne to be paid to him my said Son Rich[ar]d
12. for and during the Term of his natural life by four quarterly
13. Payments and the first Payment to begin and be made
14. at the end of the first quarter next after my decease And I do
15. also Charge the same with the Sum of five Pounds to be
16. paid to my —— Son Thomas Horne and with the Payment of
17. the like Sum of five Pounds to my Son Robert Horne and
18. of twenty Shillings to my Daughter Sarah Penton And I do
19. also Charge my said Estates with the Payment of all my Debts
20. Funeral and Testamentary Charges and Expences And do constitute
21. and appoint my said Son[1] full and sole Executor of this my last
22. Will and Testament revoking all former Wills by me at
23. any time heretofore made declaring this to be my last
24. Whereunto I have set my hand and Seal the eleventh Day
25. of December in the Year of our Lord One thousand seven hundred
26. and forty six The mark of the said John Horne the Testator
27. Signed Sealed Published and Declared by the said John Horne
28. the Testator as and for his last Will and Testament in the Pr[e]sence[2]
29. of us who at his request attested the same in his Presence
30. Edward Blackman   Richard Church   the Mark of Ann Cook

31. **This Will** was proved at London before the Right Worshipful John
32. Bettesworth Doctor of Laws Master Keeper or Com[m]issary of the Prerogative Court of
33. Canterbury lawfully constituted the twenty ninth Day of March 1748 by the Oath of
34. John Horne the Son of the deceased and Ex[ecu]tor named in the said Will to whom
35. Admin[istra]c[i]on was granted of all and singular the Goods Chattels and Credits of the
36. said deceased being first sworn by Commission duly to administer   Ex[amine]d

Here it is to be observed, that differences doe in noe waies
appertaine to Sisters, for that they are reputed to be
seperated and divided from the family whereof they
are descended, inasmuch as when they are once married, they doe loose theire owne surname, and doe
receive theire denomination from the family where
of theire husbands are descended, and so much doth
the word Soror notifie unto us as Sosinus saith: Soror
est quasi seorsim nata et à familia seperata.

To daughters it is permitted to beare the Armes of
theire fathers even as the elder brother after his
fathers decease without any scandall or challange of
their elder brother, for that to daughters never
were any differences allowed and that for three
causes: first, because their Coats are never, or very
seldome advanced in the field, for as much as to that
sex war is reputed odious. Secondly, for that the Coat
Armour is no longer borne by them than during
their life, for the same extendeth not to their Issue.
Lastly, because so long as Issue continueth of any
of the Brothers Lines, they are debarred from
the inheritance. yet in some cases they shall beare the
Coat=Armour to them and their Heires, as in example:
If all the Issue of the brothers happen to become
extinct, then the daughters shall inherit the Land
of their Auncestor. In which case they may therewith all assume his Coat Armour, and beare the same
by themselves & their Heires for ever. but betwixt
those Sisters be allowed no differences or badges of
Pedigrees: the reason whereof is, for that istheire
by the name of the house cannot be preserved;
therefore they are admitted to the inheritance
equally, & are adjudged but one heire to all in-
tents & purposes, in Lawes as well Martiall as Civill
without any eminent prerogative either of
honour or possession, betwixt elder & younger.

3

TRANSCRIPT

Document on Heraldry from State Papers
(TNA:PRO ref: SP 9/33, no 3)

1. Here it is to[1] be observed that differences[2] doe in noe waies
2. appertaine to sisters for that they are reputed to be
3. seperated and divided from the family whereof they
4. are descended in as much as when they are once mar
5. ried they doe loose theire owne surname and doe
6. receive theire denomination from the family wher
7. of theire husbands are descended and so much doth
8. the word Soror notifie unto us as Sosinus saith: Soror
9. est quasi seorsim[3] nata et a familia seperata[4]
10. To daughters it is permitted to beare the Armes of
11. theire fathers even as the elder brother after his
12. fathers decease without any scandall or challange of
13. their elder brother for that to daughters never
14. were any differences allowed and that for three
15. causes first because their Coats are never or very
16. seldome advanced in the field for as much as to that
17. sex war is reputed odious secondly for that the Coat
18. Armour is no longer borne by them than during
19. their life for the same extendeth not to their Issue
20. lastly because so long as Issue continueth of any ~~of~~
21. of the Bretherens Lines they are debarred from
22. the inheritance yet in some cases they sall beare the
23. Coat-Armour to them and their Heires as in example
24. If all the Issue of the bretheren happen to become
25. extinct then the daughters shall inherit the Land
26. of their Ancestor in which case they may there
27. with all assume his Coate Armour[1] and beare the same
28. by themselves & their Heires for ever but betwixt
29. those sisters be allowed no differences or badges of
30. Pedegrees the reason wherof is for that sithence
31. by the[m] [th]e name of the house cannot be preserved
32. therfore they are admitted to the inheritance
33. equally & are adjudged but one heire to all in
34. tents & purposes in Lawes as well Martiall as Civill
35. without any eminent prerogative either of
36. honour or possession betwixt elder & younger

COMMENTARY

Document on Heraldry from State Papers

(TNA:PRO ref: SP 9/33, no 3)

Document

This is an interesting little document, to be found in the wide-ranging class of SP 9. This section of the class includes papers, paintings etc. relating to genealogy, heraldry and other subjects thought to have belonged to the collection of William Ryley, Lancaster Herald (d.1667) which was bought by the diplomat Sir Joseph Williamson (1633-1701), Keeper of the State Papers and left by him to the State Paper Office. The document is endorsed in pencil 'Jac I' which, if correct, dates it in the period 1603-25. The text appears to be very similar to that of a passage in Guillim's *Display of Heraldrie* (1610).

Script

This hand is remarkably clear and straightforward and there is little to concern the reader except to become acclimatised to the long *s* (note the identical nature of the *f* and *s* in some cases, except for the bar on the former), *e* written, as noted before, as though backwards and *c* written as a right-angle with a small extension to the upright. The letter *c* written thus can easily be mistaken for a *t* in many hands but a considerable difference in the height of the ascender occurs here (v. the word extinct in l. 25). A feature of this hand is the extreme length of some of the descenders, many of which encroach well onto the line below.

Notes

1. Words here have been transcribed separately although apparently run together (perhaps due to subsequent addition to the text).
2. Differences: this word relates to the heraldic marks of cadency which sons might bear to differentiate their arms according to their position in the family, e.g. a crescent for the second son, a martlet (a small footless bird) for the fourth.
3. Apparently a form, often used erroneously, for *seorsum* (apart).
4. Translation: A sister is as though born apart and separated from the family.

(Plate and transcript on previous spread)

COMMENTARY

Entries from the Hallmote Court of Widnes
(TNA:PRO ref: DL 30/135/2075, rot 5r)

Document

This record is from a long series of Duchy of Lancaster manorial documents listed in the former P.R.O.'s *Lists & Indexes* VI which covers great numbers of such records in DL 30 and SC 2 (Special Collections). The various types of court rolls combine to give a wealth of superb detail about the manor (seldom co-terminous with the parish which might include parts of a number of manors) and its tenants. Of special interest to genealogists are the entries relating to surrender of copyhold lands and admission to copyhold (often after the death of a named relation). Rare cases of claims regarding fugitive villeins could give rise to much genealogical detail, one case being known to recite four generations (including 17 named relations) in a single entry. In addition many records add colour to those who lived on the manor insofar as tenants may have been fined for many interesting misdeeds such as not scouring their ditches (and thus perhaps causing flooding), encroachment, allowing animals to stray (with attendant damage), trespass, assault, allowing buildings to become ruinous, not belonging to a tithing, transgressions relating to the assize of bread and ale. There would also be elections of constables, tithing-men, ale-tasters etc. There is much to interest the local historian in the frequently precise description of land with names of fields and of tenants and occasionally of previous tenants (sometimes accounting for field names) and acreage, together with details of contiguous lands; also in manorial rentals and extents. The heading of this court record is dated Tuesday 25th April 1654. The document is therefore a useful example (being written during the Commonwealth when the use of Latin was discontinued for manor rolls and other legal documents) of the type of wording which might be expected from a Latin document in the same series written during the periods on either side of the Commonwealth. Further extracts from the records of this manor appear as plates 41 and 42. See, for much useful information, *Manorial Records* by Professor P.D.A. Harvey (1984).

Script

The second part of the *ff*, whether used as a capital letter or as two small letters, is somewhat unusual. Otherwise, though every hand requires to be examined individually for the eye to become accustomed to it, this appears to be written in a clear and straightforward script.

Notes

1. A hallmote (spelt variously) was a type of manor court, usually a court baron.
2. A small mark occurring here was perhaps an indication that a gap was to be filled.

(Plate and transcript on following spread)

And Sayt John Woodfall Batt one of the Customary Tenants of the manno:
of ... aforesaid Ayse Pure the Coppi Hould out of tho Pere held for the manno:
aforesaid being Seized of the Tyne of his death of and in Sundry Acres and
Acre parts of one Acre of land land Customary messuag aforesaid of the yearly
Rent of Seaven shillings Pynt Court whereupon the tene ffalleth out to the lord
of the manno: ... aforesaid Pynt Court whereupon to be theruppon Clad and Levened
And the Jury aforesaid furthe: Say and Present that Thomas Woodfall is Sonne
next heyre of the said John Woodfall all so that at the Age of ffifteene yeares at the
Tyme of the takinge of this Inquisition.

And Sayt Henry Greene geit hate one of the Customary tenants of the
manno: of ... aforesaid By Pine the late Moleno: of ... heret held
for the manno: aforesaid being Seized of the Tyne of his death of and in
Two Acres and the halfe of one Acre of land land Customary messuag
aforesaid of the yearly Rent of Two shillings Sixpence whereupon the tene ffalleth
out to the lord of the manno: aforesaid for a heryot to bee theruppon Clad and
Levened And the Jury aforesaid furthe: Say and Present that ... William
Greene the said Henry Greene ... Sonne ... is of the Age
of ... at the takinge of this Inquisition.

And Sayt Robert Mefro: Richard Winter and ... Woodfall are heyres
to this Court and being Called did not appeare therfore ... out of them ...
are amerced in by...

Entries from the Hallmote Court of Widnes

(TNA:PRO ref: DL 30/135/2075, rot 5r)

1. **And that** John Woodfall late one of the Customary Tenants of the manno[u]r
2. of Widnes afforesaid dyed since the laste Halmote Co[u]rt[1] heere held for the manno[u]r
3. afforesaid beinge Seized att the tyme of his death of and in Seaven Acres and
4. Fyve parts of one Acre of land land Customary in Widnes afforesaid of the yearly
5. Rente of Seaven shillings fyve pence wherupon theere Falleth due to the lords
6. of the manno[u]r afforesaid for a Herryott to bee therupon had and Receaved
7. And the Jury afforesaid Further saye and pr[e]sente That Thomas Woodfall is Sonne &
8. next heyre of the said John Woodfall dec[eased] And is of the Age of Fifteene yeares att the
9. tyme of the takeinge of this Inquisition

} v[s] iiij[d]

10. **And that** Henry Greene gent[leman] late one of the Customary tenants of the
11. manno[u]r of Widnes afforesaid dyed since the laste Halmote Co[u]rt heere held
12. for the manno[u]r afforesaid beinge Seized att the tyme of his Death of and in
13. Two Acres and the halfe of one Acre of land land Customary in Widnes
14. afforesaid of the yearly Rente of Two shillings Six pence wherupon theere Falleth
15. due to the lords of the manno[u]r afforesaid for a Herryott to bee therupon had and
16. Receaved
17. And the Jury afforesaid further saye and pr[e]sente That <Henry> Greene is Sonne and next
18. heyre of the said Henry Greene dec[eased] And is of the age of[2]   yeares att the
19. tyme of the takeinge of this Inquisition

} v[s] iiij[d]

20. **And that** Robert Ackers Richard Ducker and Mary Woofall owe suite
21. to this Co[u]rt and beinge Called did not appeare Therfore every one of them
22. are amerced in vj[d] in the whole

} xviij[d]

[8]

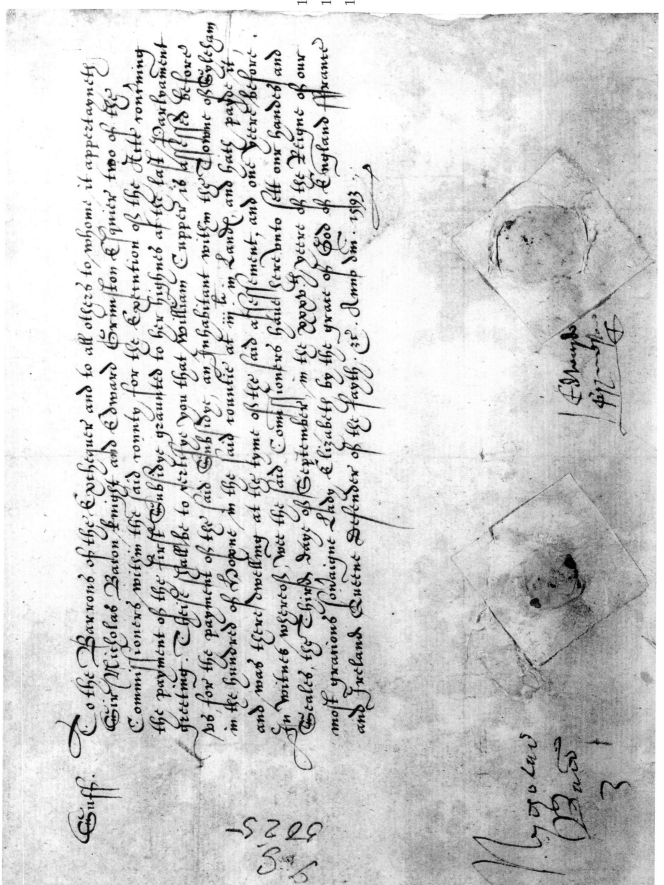

Suff.

To the Barrons of the Exchequer and to all others to whome it appertaynethe
Sir Nicholas Bacon knight and Edward Grimston Esquier two of the
Commissioners within the said county for the taxation of the Fiftenthe
the payment of the first Subsidye graunted to her highnes at the last Parliament
greeting. Theis shall be to certifie you that William Cupper is assessed before
us for the payment of the said Subsidye an Inhabitant within the Towne of Sylham
in the hundred of Hoxne in the said county at xiꝭ in Land, and hath payde it
and was there dwelling at the tyme of the said assessment, and one yere before ,
In witnes wherof wee the said Commissioners haue sett unto thes our handes and
Sealed, the thirde daye of September in the xxxv yeere of the Reigne of our
most gracious soueraigne Lady Elizabeth by the grace of God of England Fraunce
and Ireland Queene Defender of the Fayth .etc. Annb dm. 1593.

TRANSCRIPT

Certificate of Residence

(TNA: PRO ref: E 115/94/17)

1. In margin: Suff[olk]
   To the Barrons of the Exchequer and to all others to whome it appertayneth
2. Sir Nicholas Bacon knight and Edward Grimston Esquier two of the
3. Commissioners within the said county for the Execution of the Acte conc[er]ning
4. the payment of the first Subsidye graunted to her highnes at the last Parlyament
5. greeting Theise shall be to certifye you that William Cupper is assessed before
6. us for the payment of the said Subsidye an Inhabitant within the Towne of Syleham
7. in the hundred of Hoxne in the said countie at iij li[bre] in Land[es] and hath payde it
8. and was there dwelling at the tyme of the said assessement and one yeere before
9. In witnes whereof wee the said Com[m]issioners have here unto sett our handes and
10. Seales the Third daye of September in the xxxvth yeere of the Reigne of our
11. most gracious sov[er]aigne Lady Elizabeth by the grace of God of England France
12. and Ireland Queene Defender of the fayth &c Anno d[omi]ni 1593

    Edward
    Grymeston

13. Nycholas
14. Baco[n]
15.

COMMENTARY

Document

Certificates of residence (temp. Edward VI to Charles II) prevented a person who had moved from being taxed in more than one place. A brief note of payment made etc. (not here included) appears and the documents can with advantage be used with lay subsidies, and evidence from the pouches in which they had been placed, when available, as proof of change of residence. There is a helpful index.

Script

This document is beautifully written in an uncomplicated hand but in addition to the apparently inverted letter r and reversed e, note the long h which in other hands is often very poorly written, and even here takes different forms; also to be noted are the similarity of, and difference between, the x and v in small Roman numbers (l. 10) which can often appear confusingly alike. Signatures are notoriously difficult to read as there is seldom the chance for comparison of letters, but fortunately here the signatories are named in the document.

TRANSCRIPT

Final Concord

(TNA:PRO ref: CP 25/2/564/1658, Hil)

1. This is the finall Agreem[en]t made in the Co[u]rt of the Com[m]on Bench at Westm[inste]r in eight dayes of the Purificac[i]on of the
2. blessed Mary in the yeare of o[u]r Lord one thousand six hundred fifty eight Before Oliver S[t 1] John Edward Atkyns
3. Hugh Wyndham & John Archer Justices & others then & there pr[e]sent Betweene Christopher Harlock pl[ain]t[iff]
4. And Richard Goulding & Susanna his wife & Margery Goulding widow deforc[ian]t[es] of one messuage one
5. barne one stable one garden one orchard seaventeen acres of Land & one acre of wood w[i]th the appurtenanc[es] in
6. Benenden Whereupon a plea of Covenant was sum[m]oned betweene them in the said Co[u]rt that is to say that the
7. afores[ai]d Richard & Susanna & Margery have acknowledged the afores[ai]d tenem[en]t[es] w[i]th the appurtenanc[es] to be the
8. right of him the said Christopher As those w[hi]ch the said Christopher hath of the guift of the afores[ai]d Richard &
9. Susanna & Margery And those they have remised & quiteclaimed from them the said Richard & Susanna &
10. Margery & their heires to the afores[ai]d Christopher & his heires for ever And moreover the said Richard &
11. Susanna have granted for them & the heires of the said Richard that they will warrant to the afores[ai]d
12. Christopher & his heires the afores[ai]d tenem[en]t[es] w[i]th the appurtenanc[es] against them the said Richard &
13. Susanna & the heires of the said Richard for ever And further the said Margery hath granted for her &
14. her heires that they will warrant to the afores[ai]d Christopher & his heires the afores[ai]d tenem[en]t[es] w[i]th the
15. appurtenanc[es] against her the said Margery & her heires for ever And for this acknowledgm[en]t remise
16. quiteclaime warrant fine & agreem[en]t the said Christopher hath given to the afores[ai]d Richard & Susanna &
17. Margery sixty pound[es] sterlinge
18.

Kent

[10]

COMMENTARY

Final Concord

(TNA:PRO ref: CP 25/2/564/1658, Hil)

Document

The excellent series of final concords, spanning more than six centuries from the time of Henry II, comprises transfers of land in the form of small formal lawsuits, apparently so created for greater security. The plaintiff (often known as the querent in these documents) is the purchaser; the defendant (the deforciant) the seller. The original document was made in three joined parts embodying the same wording and irregularly divided so that the unique edges could be matched if necessary to prove authenticity. That part forming the base (as this example) of the original tripartite document is known as a foot of fine. The records are of similar form but with variations occurring according to legal background. It is not unusual, as in this case, to find the name of a man together with that of his wife (so often absent from records); and sometimes another or others of the same surname may appear, suggesting a relationship, however speculative. Until 1733 the documents were in Latin (for which see plates 45 and 48). A useful introduction to these records, by C.A.F. Meekings, appears in the Surrey Record Society's volume XIX, *Surrey Fines, 1509-1558*.

Script

This attractive hand is more consistent than most and has only simple abbreviations. The ligature joining *s* and *t* is used. Words are written very close together, so much so that, despite the formality of the hand, they are in some cases run together.

Note

1. This name has not been extended as it would always be contracted (St. John)

(Plate and transcript on previous spread)

COMMENTARY

Bounty Paper
(ref: TNA:PRO ADM 106/3023)

Document

For note on the bounty papers see plate 3. This is another paper exemplifying the abundance of useful detail in the class, in this case not only of strictly genealogical value, but also with special interest for family historians in giving some biographical particulars.

Script

The main part of this document is in reasonably legible handwriting, albeit with somewhat exuberant capital letters. The remainder has some of the usual (though here not too extreme) problems of transcribing signatures, as there is no chance of comparing letters. Further difficulties occur with the numbers in different hands. In particular the examples of the figure 8 are deceptive (see note on document 3). In some instances the letter which has been transcribed as a final *s* bears a close resemblance to the abbreviation for *-es* etc.

Notes

1. Seaman: this word appears to have been written over a now illegible word, and crossed out.
2. Some imperfections appear in this paragraph. Postulated letters for what appears to have been intended are in italics.
3. 167½: This year would more commonly be written as 1671/2 i.e. the period, by English computation, 1 January to 24 March 1671 (the historical year 1672).
4. This, as in other documents in this class, is followed by unidentifiable initials.

(Plate and transcript on following spread)

Wee whose names and Subscribed aswell the Mayor and
Burgesses of the Burrough of Christchurch within
the pish of Christchurch in the County of South: as
other Inhabitants of the same pish, Doe hereby certifie
all whome it shall or may concerne, that the bearer
hereof John Rogers of Hinton within the same pish
Seaman, was the naturall and lawfull Son of Edward
Rogers late of Hinton aforesaid Seaman husbandman
deceased & of Alice his wife, & that he was the naturall
& lawfull brother by the whole blood to Richard
Rogers late whilest he lived of Hinton aforesaid Seaman
who (as wee are credibly informed) was Imprest
into his Maties Shipp Royall James frigott, & was
either killed or burnt or otherwise distroyed when
the said frigott was distroyed In Testimony whereof
wee have hereunto putt o[ur] hands & Comon Seale of
the Corporaton of the Burrough aforesaid the
Seaventh day of September in the Six and Twentith
yeare of the raigne of o[ur] Soveraigne Lord King
Charles the Second of England &c: Annoq[ue] Dni 1674

Edw: Oldor Mayor   Hen: Godwyne Visar

Robert Stokes
Henry tuppin
He: Rogers   There are to certifie y[t] Rich: Rogers
John wolfhman   able Seaman entord on bord his Ma[ts]:
Fran: Slade.   Shipp Roy James &c: y[e] 12 march
                        1671 & said to be burned y[e] 29 th
    Tho Coffin   May 72

    william Carle   17 Iune 74
                          Henry Rogers   Church
    Jo: Blake   Richard Buggey   wardens

I Doe certifie that there was one Rich: Rodgers
entord on his Ma[ties]: late Ship Royll James book on y[e]:
12 march 71 & was sayd to be Slayne 29 may 72:

R Haddock   Jo Godwin   Henry Tulse

[11]

TRANSCRIPT

Bounty Paper

(ref: TNA:PRO ADM 106/3023)

1.   Wee whose names are Subscribed aswell the Mayer and
2.   Burgesses of the Burrough of Christchurch within
3.   the p[ar]ish of Christchurch in the County of South[amp]t[on] as
4.   others Inh[ab]itants of the same p[ar]ish Doe hereby certefie
5.   all whome it shall or may conc[er]ne that the bearer
6.   hereof John Rogers of Hinton within the same p[ar]ish
7.   Seaman was the naturall and lawfull Son of Edward
8.   Rogers late of Hinton aforesaid Seaman[1] husbandman
9.   (dec[eas]ed) & Alice his wife & that he was the naturall
10. & lawfull brother by the whole blood to Richard
11. Rogers late whilest he lived of Hinton aforesaid Seama[n]
12. who (as wee are credibly informed) was Impressed
13. into his Ma[jes]ties Shipp Royall James Frigott & was
14. either Killed or burnt or other wise distroyed when
15. the said Frigott was distroyed In Testimony whereof
16. wee have hereunto putt o[u]r hands & Com[m]on Seale of
17. the Corporac[i]on of the Burrough aforesaid the
18. Seaventh day of September in the Six and Twentith
19. Yeare of the raigne of o[u]r Sov[er]aigne Lord King
20. Charles the Second of England &c An[n]oq[ue] D[omi]ni 1674

21. Edw[ard] Odber Mayor
22. Robert Stokes   Henry Goldwyre Vicar
23. Henry Hopkins
24. He[nry] Rogers   [2]These are to Certifie [tha]t Rich[ar]d Rogers
25. John Welshman   able-Sea*man* enterd on bord his Maj[es]t[es]
26. Fran[cis] Slade   Shipp Roy*al* James on [th]e 12 March
27. Tho[mas] Coffin   167½[3] & Said to be *slaine* [th]e 28th
28. William Earle   May 72
29. Jo[hn] Blake   Ex[amine]d[4] 17 Jan[ua]ry 75
30.   Henry Rogers } Church
31.   Richard Buggly } Wardens
32. I Doe certifie that there was one ~~John Rogers~~ Rich[ard] Rodgers
33. entred on his Ma[jes]ti[es] late Ship Roy[a]ll James's book on [th]e
34. 12th March 71 & was Sayd to be Slayne 28 May Foll[owing]

35. R Haddock   Jo[hn] Godwin   Henry Tulse

Touching Woods
neere Clapham

TRANSCRIPT

Entry in the Privy Council Registers concerning Woods at Clapham

(TNA:PRO ref: PC 2/48, p 633)

In margin: Touching Woods neere Clapham

1. Wheras the Board was this day informed that Edw[ard] Cox and
2. John Wells have taken of one M[r] Worthfield the Owner
3. certaine Coppis Woods contayneing aboute 30 Acres lyeing neere
4. Clapham in the County of Surrey W[hi]ch they are now aboute to
5. grubb and stock upp contrary to the lawes in that Case p[ro]vided <to>
6. the detrim[en]t of the publique and the decay of fuell It was
7. by theire Lo[rdshi]pps for pr[e]venc[i]on therof thought fitt & ordered
8. that the said M[r] Worthfield Edw[ard] Cox & John Wells should attend
9. the Board at Whytehall on Wednesday next in [th]e after-
10. noone to answer the same and should lykewise hereby bee
11. straightly required & enjoyned to for beare grubbing or stocking upp
12. of any of the said Woods in the meane tyme & untill farther order
13. from this Board

[12]

COMMENTARY

Entry in the Privy Council Registers concerning Woods at Clapham

(TNA:PRO ref: PC 2/48, p 633)

Document

The Privy Council was a small body of advisers to the king. Its duties included giving counsel on many issues including the numerous and very varied petitions to him and on difficult cases of controversy. Though its powers diminished, the registers of its minutes span the period 1540-1920 (with some gaps). The volumes thus contain a great variety of matters and, being indexed throughout, references are easy to locate. The entries recorded in the above registers embrace (in addition to the many relating to petitions and controversies, as in the case here and in plate 19) many references to prisons, ecclesiastical affairs, ship money, licences to travel abroad, musters, buildings and fens, as well as to soap, tobacco, plague, pirates, assault and abduction. The heading for this page is 'At Whytehall the last of Feb^r 1637'.

Script

As so often, the *W* and *w* appear to be interchangeable. The inital *f* has a rather unusual long tail bending back upon itself. There are two forms of *h* of which one looks quite modern; the other an advanced form of the typical secretary version, with no curve above the line and a large loop below the line.

TRANSCRIPT

Bill in Court of Requests

(TNA:PRO ref: REQ 2/1/45)

1.   To the king o[u]r moost Dreade sov[er]aigne lorde
2. In their moost lamentable wyse beshechen and shewen unto yo[u]r moost excellent highnes yo[u]r pou[er] subject[es] and true bedefolk[es] John Hughson of Feltwell in yo[u]r Countie
3. of Norff[olk] and Johan his wyff oon of the Doughters and heires of Richard Selven brother and heire of Thomas Selven deceassd and Elizabeth Humble wedowe
4. an other of the Doughters and heires of the said Richard That where the said Thomas Selven by the space of xx[ti] [1] yeres past or therabout[es] in consideracion
5. that oon Thomas Blaknall shuld marye and take to his wyff oon   [2]   Basterdoughter of the said Thomas Selven gave unto the said
6. Blaknalle and   [2]   his wyff his Mano[u]r of Sherington graunge w[i]t[h] thapp[u]rtena[u]nt[es] in the p[ar]isshe of Silverston in yo[u]r Countie of Sussex being of the
7. clere yerely value of xli[bre][3] and above And after that the said Blaknall deceassed w[i]t[h]out any suche heires of his bodie lauffully begotten and then the said
8.   [2]   basterdoughter Maried and toke to her husbond oon Anthonye Dryland and deceassed also w[i]t[h]out any heire of her bodye lauffully begotten
9. Whiche Dryland after that bargayned and sold the said Mano[u]r and other the p[re]misses to oon Will[i]am Walsingham Esquyer Whiche Walsingham p[er]ceyvyng no

[13]

1

2

3

4

5

6

7

8

9

10

11

12

13

14

15

16

17

18

19

20

10. good title that he had in the said Mano[u]r and other the p[re]misses shortley after that bargayned and sold alle the said Mano[u]r and other the p[re]misses to oon s[ir]

11. Edward Bray knight And after that the said s[ir] Edward Braye by the space of vj monethes now last past bargayned and sold alle the said Mano[u]r and

12. other the p[re]misses to oon Nich[ol]as Mascall who now inhabitethe w[i]t[h]in the said Mano[u]r and other the p[re]misses and the same wrongfully w[i]t[h]holdeth from yo[u]r said

13. subject[es] and intendeth so to do as it is to suppose to the utter undoing and disenhereting of yo[u]r said pou[er]e subject[es] and their heires forev[er] oonles yo[u]r

14. moost excellent highnes moved w[i]t[h] petie to them the sonner[4] be shewed in this behalf In consideracion wherof and for asmuche as the said Mascall

15. is a Riche man and greatly frended and alied in those p[ar]ties and that yo[u]r subject[es] be but verye pou[er]e Folk[es] not hable to sue ayenst[5] hym for their right

16. and remedie in the p[re]misses by the due Course of yo[u]r moost gracious Comen lawes nor other <wyse> It may therfore please yo[u]r Majestie of yo[u]r moost blyssed

17. dysposicion to cause the said Mascall to com before you or the lord[es] of yo[u]r moost honorable Counceill attendaunt uppon yo[u]r Roiall p[er]sone he their

18. to make anonswhere to the p[re]misses and then yo[u]r majestie or yo[u]r said Counceill to sett suche order and direccion theirin as you or they

19. shall thynk to stond and be according to right equytie and good consciens And yo[u]r said subject[es] during their lyff[es] shall specially pray

20. to almyghtie Je[s]u[6] for the p[ro]sperous p[re]s[er]vacion of yo[u]r moost roiall p[er]sone and excellent estate long to endure

COMMENTARY

Bill in Court of Requests
(TNA:PRO ref: REQ 2/1/45)

Document

Although many cite their poverty in cases in chancery proceedings, the purpose of the Court of Requests (proceedings temp. Henry VII-Charles I, though mentioned earlier) was to enable the poor to obtain justice without difficulty. Women found this a useful court, and it is perhaps worth observing that not all litigants lacked substance. The records include material of interest to both genealogists and local historians. Cases include such subjects as marriage under age, legitimacy, ancient demesne and customs, bondage, poor relief, highways, forgery, trespass and wrongful impounding of cattle, bigamy and detention of dower. As with the records of chancery proceedings, the bill, with any answer, rejoinder etc., and depositions, are in English. The parish in question appears to be Selmeston.

Script

This has the appearance of a typical piece of well-written, regular secretary hand. Although there are many genuine abbreviation marks, there are also many final abbreviation marks of no significance. As in other documents it is difficult to distinguish between capital and small letters *k*, *w* and *h* and in some cases the letter *d*.

Several forms of *B* occur (see Basterdoughter and, differently, two forms for the initial of Bray). The marks resembling x at the end of some lines are merely line fillers (see p.10).

Notes

1. There is some redundance in expressing 20 in this way.
2. Here and subsequently the gaps are presumably for an unknown name.
3. i.e. £10.
4. From the writing (since, as so often, *n* and *u* are written identically) this word could equally be souner. The *O.E.D.* quotes both old forms but prefers sonner and suggests that instances of souner are probably due to error.
5. This is an obsolete form of 'against'.
6. Ihu: the letters are from Greek; that in the form of *h* here reflects the Greek *H* (i.e. the letter eta, the long *E*).

(Plate and transcript on previous spread)

COMMENTARY

Part of Rental of the Manor of Dacre in Cumberland

(TNA:PRO ref: SC 12/27/8)

Document

The manor generated documents other than the actual record of the court proceedings, e.g. custumals, surveys, accounts, estreats (see plate 17) and rentals, of which this is an example. Two further lists against place-names appear to complete this document below the part shown, and then the total which includes turnsilver (described by the *O.E.D.* as a 'local payment of uncertain nature', quoting a single example, from Whellan's *History of Cumberland and Westmorland*). The rental is listed as of 17 James I (1619-20).

Script

This, albeit sloping to the right rather more than usual, is a typical secretary hand. However, there can be many small variations of the hand. To be noted are the low crossing of the letter *t*; and the diagonal line across the top of many instances of the letter *a*, a feature of some secretary hands. The often capricious use of capital initial letters in documents tends to result in many appearing in places considered unsuitable by the modern writer. Here, however, the scribe appears to have been rather too parsimonious with his capitals. There seems no doubt of the surnames sisson, allinson and, in one instance, marke being so written without a capital letter. Surnames beginning with a possible *W* and *H* have been given the benefit of the doubt since the capital and small versions of these letters can be indistinguishable.

For Roman figures, see p.15.

Notes

1. i.e. Manor of Dacre.
2. Where the sum against Edward Sisson is struck out, the amount is not wholly legible. The line which appears between the second and third *x* seems to have been the end of the original line intended to come before the amount of rent, but ignored due to the number of digits.
3. Thus apparently, but there is little doubt that this should be the local surname Threlkeld.
4. yng: presumably for *ing*, given in the *O.E.D.* as a 'common name in the north of England, and in some other parts, for a meadow; esp. one by the side of a river and more or less swampy and subject to inundation.' The parish of Dacre is situated on the river Dacre.

(Plate and transcript on following spread)

Maner de
Dacre

A perfect Rentall of all the Rents
w(i)thin the Manner of Dacre aforesaid
for one whole year ended at
Michaelmas last past.

Dacre.

 Edward Sisson rent p annu(m)   xxxiij s xiij d

 Richard Markes   xxvij s j d

 Gerland Thirlkeld   xxvij s viij d

 William Mattinson   xxvij s viij d

 Thomas Davies   xxvij s viij d

 Andrew Norby   xxvij s viij d

 Robert Hodgson   xxvij s viij d

 Robart Norby   x s

 John Todde   x s

 Thymart Codle   v s vij d

 Andrew Norby for a Cottage   iij d

 for Rent of Chappell guy   iiij d

 John Burret   iiij s

Sowlby Robert Hodgson   xxiiij s iiij d

 Thomas Holland   xxiiij s iiij d

 Henry Thorgrasson   xxiiij s iiij d

 Henrie Paulinson   xxiiij s iiij d

 Dorithie Samson   xxiiij s iiij d

 Thomas Johnson   xxiiij s iiij d

 Thomas Markes   xxiiij s iiij d

 Edward Holling   xxiiij s iiij d

 Nicholas Dawson   xxiiij s iiij d

 Christofer Atkinson   xxiiij s iiij d

 John Wharton   xxiiij s iiij d

[14]

Part of Rental of the Manor of Dacre in Cumberland

(TNA:PRO ref: SC 12/27/8)

1.	Maner[ium] de	A p[er]fect Rentall of all the Rents	
2.	Dacre[1]	w[i]thin the Manner of Dacre aforesaid	
3.		for one wholle year ended at	
4.		Michaellmes last past	
5.	Dacre		
			< xxxviij^s viij^d>
6.		Edward sisson rent p[er] an[n]um	~~xxxix^s viij~~^{d} [2]
7.		Richard Marke	xvij^s j^d
8.		Gerard Shrelkeld[3]	xvj^s viij^d
9.		Will[ia]m Mattinson	xvj^s viij^d
10.		Thomas Davies	xvj^s viij^d
11.		Andrew Wray	xvj^s viij^d
12.		Robert Hodgson	xvj^s viij^d
13.		Robart Wray	x^s
14.		John Todde	x^s
15.		Thomas Todde	v^s xj^d
16.		Andrew Wray for a Cottage	ij^d
17.		For Rent of Chappell yng[4]	iiij^d
18.		John Turner	iiij^s
19.	Sowlby	Robert Hellinge	xiiij^s iiij^d
20.		Thomas Helling	xiiij^s iiij^d
21.		Henry Langcaster	xiiij^s iiij^d
22.		Henrie Rainoldson	xiiij^s iiij^d
23.		Doratie Cannon	xiiij^s iiij^d
24.		Thomas Cannon	xiiij^s iiij^d
25.		Thomas marke	xiiij^s iiij^d
26.		Edward Hellinge	xiiij^s iiij^d
27.		Nicholas Dawson	xiiij^s iiij^d
28.		Christofor allinson	xiiij^s iiij^d
29.		John Barton	xiiij^s iiij^d

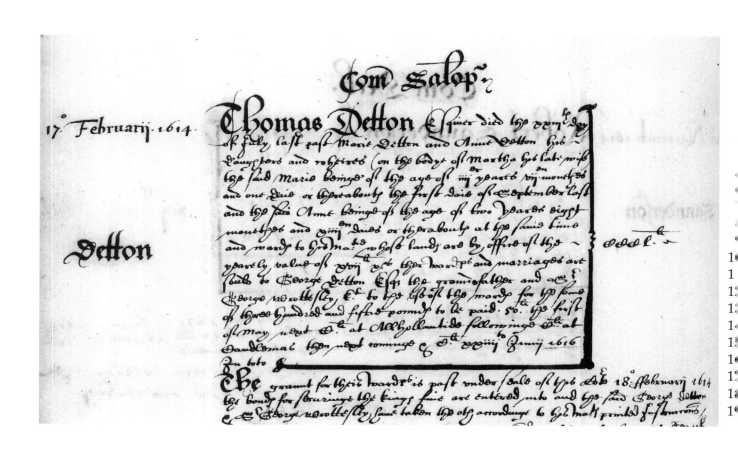

Com Salop

17° Februarij 1614

Thomas Detton Esquier died the [xx]th day of July last past. Marie Detton and Anne Detton his daughters and heires on the body of Martha his late wife. the said Marie beinge of the age of iiij yeares vij monthes and one die or thereabouts the first daie of September last and the said Anne beinge of the age of twoe yeares eight monthes and viij daies or thereabouts at the said time and wardes to the Ma[tie] whose lands are by office of the yearely value of [viij] o[l] the wardes and marriages are sould to George Detton Esq the grandfather and [&c] George Wrottesley, Es[q] to the vse of the wardes for the some of three hundred and fiftie pounds to be paid &c the first of May next &c at Allhallomtide followinge &c at Candlemas then next comynge &c xxiij Junij 1616 In toto £

Detton   cccl l

The grant for theis wardes is past vnder seale of &c date 18° Februarij 1614 the bonds for secureinge the kings fine are entered into and the said George Detton & George Wrottesley haue taken the oth accordinge to his Ma[ts] printed Instruccons

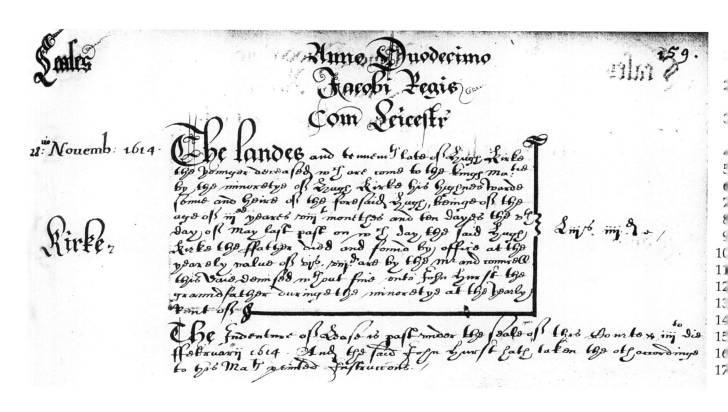

Anno Duodecimo
Jacobi Regis
Com Leicestr

59.

28° Nouemb: 1614

The landes and tenem[t] late of [Hugh] Kirke the yonger deceased w[ch] are come to the kings Ma[tie] by the minoritye of Hugh Kirke his [sonne] and warde sonne and heire of the foresaid Hugh beinge of the age of iij yeares viij monthes and ten dayes the [xv]th day of May last past on w[ch] day the said Hugh Kirke the father died and sonne by office at the yearely value of vijs. viijd ar by the m[r] and counsell this [vse] demised w[thout] fine vnto John Hurst the grandfather duringe the minoritye at the yearly rent of £

Kirke   [&c] iijd

The Indenture of Lease is past vnder the seale of this Courte x iiij die Februarij 1614. And the said John Hurst hath taken the oth accordinge to his Ma[ts] printed Instruccons.

TRANSCRIPT

Entries Relating to Wardship

(TNA:PRO ref: WARD 9/204, pp 67, 159r)

Com[itatus] Salop'[1]

2.	17º [2] Februarii 1614	**Thomas Detton** Esquier died the xxiij[th 3] day	
3.		of July last past Marie Detton and Anne Detton his	
4.		Daughters and coheires (on the bodye of Martha his late wife)	
5.		the said Marie beinge of the age of iiij[er] yeares vij[en] monethes	
6.		and one Daie or thereabout[es] the first daie of September last	
7.		and the said Anne beinge of the age of two Yeares eight	
8.		monethes and xiiij[en] daies or therabout[es] at the same time	
9.	**Detton**	and ward[es] to his Ma[jes]tie whose land[es] are by office of the	} CCCL[li 4]
10.		yearely value of xvij[li] x[s 5] ther Ward[shi]ps and marriages are	
11.		sould to George Detton Esq[uie]r the graundfather and S[i]r	
12.		George Wrottesley K[nigh]t to the use of the ward[es] for the som[m]e	
13.		of three hundred and fiftie pound[es] to be paid 50[li] the first	
14.		of May next C[li 6] at Allhollowtide followinge C[li] at	
15.		Candlemas then next cominge & C[li] xxiiij[to] Iunii 1616	
16.		In toto ———————	

17. **The** graunt for theis Ward[shi]ps is past under seale of this Co[u]rte 18º [7] Februarii 1614
18. the bond[es] for securinge the king[es] fine are entered into and the said George Detton
19. & S[i]r George Wrottesley have taken the oth according to his Ma[jes]t[es] printed Instrucc[i]ons

---

1.	**Leases**	**Anno Duodecimo**	
2.		**Jacobi Regis**	
3.		**Com[itatus] Leicestr'[7]**	

4.	28[vo] Novemb[ris] 1614	**The landes** and tennem[en]t[es] late of Hugh Kirke	
5.		the Younger deceased w[hi]ch are come to the King[es] Ma[jes]tie	
6.		by the minoretye of Hugh Kirke his highnes Warde	
7.		sonne and heire of the foresaid Hugh, beinge of the	
8.		age of iij[ee] yeares viij[t] monethes and ten dayes the v[th]	
9.		day of May last past on w[hi]ch day the said Hugh	} Liij[s] iiij[d 8]
10.	**Kirke**	Kirke the Father died and found by office at the	
11.		yearely value of vj[s] viij[d 9] are by the M[aste]r and councell	
12.		this Daie demised w[i]thout fine unto John Hurst the	
13.		graundfather duringe the minoretye at the Yearly	
14.		Rent of ———————	

15. **The** Indenture of Lease is past under the seale of this Courte iiij[to] die
16. Februarii 1614 And the said John Hurst hath taken the oth accordinge
17. to his Ma[jes]t[es] printed Instrucc[i]ons

COMMENTARY

Entries relating to Wardship

(TNA:PRO ref: WARD 9/204, ff 67v, 158r)

Document

Wardship was a great benefit to the monarch, being exploited to his financial advantage. The Court of Wards and Liveries dealt with the financial side of wardship. If at his death a tenant in chief of the king left an heir who was a minor, then the king exacted rights over the marriage of that minor, and over the profits from the land until the minor's majority or earlier marriage. He could, however, sell those rights and these documents record such sales, in both cases naming one of the grandfathers of the heirs.

Script

This small but neat hand should not give many problems. Noted below is the scribe's somewhat idiosyncratic method of using superscript letters reflecting Latin and English endings. It seems that there are two forms of *K*. For Roman figures, see p.15, and below.

Notes

1. This is the second entry on a page with the heading on the left: 'Wardes'; and in the centre: '*Anno Duodecimo Jacobi Regis*' (in the twelfth year of King James). Translation of the sub-heading here: County of Shropshire.
2. The superscript *o* is a legacy from the ending of what the Latin ordinal number would be in the ablative case: *septimo decimo*, to agree with the unwritten *die* (day). Similarly, in subsequent dates on the page, the superscript letters for ordinal numbers reflect the Latin: *vicesimo quarto, duodevicesimo, vicesimo octavo* and *quarto*. February of 1614 would be in the historical year 1615.
3. This is a curious and not very logical way of writing twenty-third (though the intention is perhaps three and twentieth); and in a different way, four (and other numbers subsequently).
4. The sum is £350. Here and subsequently *li* stands for *libre* (pounds).
5. £17 10s. The letter *s* stands for *solidi* (shillings).
6. £100.
7. Translation: County of Leicester.
8. 53s. 4d. The letter *d* stands for *denarii* (pence).
9. 6s. 8d. This amount occurs frequently in documents, being half a mark.

(Plates and transcripts on previous spread)

COMMENTARY

Part of Estreat Relating to the Manor of Drakelow and Rudheath
(TNA:PRO ref: SC 2/155/82, rot 1)

Document

An estreat is an extract from a record and may particularly relate to amercements. This document has one more paragraph and a sum total, is signed by Raphe Mainwaring and addressed to Hugh Beckett and John Symcock, his bailiffs.

Script

This is a good typical example of secretary hand, and as such does not have any particular exceptions to the usual form.

Notes

1. The mark following these words, in appearance like a double letter s, merely introduces a paragraph. According to L.C. Hector, in *The Handwriting of English Documents*, it was considered by later writers that this mark had indicated the word *scilicet*, which error caused the words *to wit* to be inserted at the beginning of some documents.
2. Amercement: fine payable by one in the mercy of the lord of the manor.
3. Fines: payments e.g. for admission to customary tenancy.
4. 1626.
5. Do his suit: attend the manorial court.
6. The scribe appears to have added a small ornament here.
7. Pain: penalty.

(Plate and transcript on following spread)

Drakelowe   The vewe of ho churiam frfastures —
Rudheath   fynes due to his Mat'ie at the Leet
             and Court Baron of his highnes mannor
             of Drakelowe and Rudheath holden there
             the furth daie of October in the second
             yeare of the raigne of o'r soueraigne
             Lord Charles by the grace of God
             kinge of England Scotland
             ffraunce and Ireland defend'r of the
             faith &c Before Rayph Mainwaring
             Deputie to Robert Davenport gent.

Of the righte ho:ble Robert Viscount
Cholmondely for that he appeared   } iij s. iiij d.
not to doe his suyte & servise

Of Michaell Oldfeild Esq'r for the lyke — iij s. iiij d.
Of John Anderton gen for the lyke ——— vj d.
Of william vernon gen for the lyke ——— vj d.
Of Hugh Dawson for the lyke ——— iij s. iiij d.
Of Thomas Barber for the lyke ——— vj d.
Of John Brundrett for the lyke ——— vj d.

Of m'ris Marie Wilbraham wid &
John Holland & Thomas Steven
for not laying open the waies   } iij d.
making it passeable that leadeth
throughe Drakelowe, acording to a
payne sett in that behalfe, euir
one of theym a peece

Of Robert Rowe for not repayring
his building, and for not pauinge   } vj s. iiij d.
acording to a payne sett in that
behalfe

Of Jeffrey Gulregt for not
laying open th'incrochem't   } vj d.
meere vnto his howse acording
to a payne sett in that behalfe

Of John Woynyngton of Rudheath
for not repayring his building   } vj d.
acording to a payne sett in that
behalfe

TRANSCRIPT

Part of an Estreat relating to the Manor of Drakelow and Rudheath in Cheshire

(TNA:PRO ref: SC 2/155/82 rot 1)

1.	Drakelowe	¹	Thextreate of the Am[er]ciam[en]t[es]² forfaytures	
2.	& Rudheath		& fynes³ due to his Ma[jes]tie at the Leete	
3.			and Co[u]rt Baron of his highnes manno[u]r	
4.			of Drakelowe and Rudheath holden there	
5.			the fourth daie of October in the second	
6.			yeare of the raigne of o[u]r sov[er]aigne	
7.			lord Charles⁴ by the grace of God	
8.			kinge of England Scotland	
9.			France and Ireland defendo[u]r of the	
10.			faith &c Before Raphe Mainwaring	
11.			deputie to Robert Davenport gent[leman]	

12.	Of the right Ho[noura]ble Robert Viscount	
13.	Kilmorey for that he appeared	iij⁵ iiijᵈ
14.	not to doe his suyte⁵ & service	
15.	Of Michael Oldfeld Esq[uie]r for the lyke	iij⁵ iiijᵈ
16.	Of John Anderton gen[tleman] for the lyke	vjᵈ
17.	Of William Vernon gen[tleman] for the lyke	vjᵈ
18.	Of Hugh Amson for the lyke	iij⁵ iiijᵈ
19.	Of Thomas Carter for the lyke	vjᵈ
20.	Of John Brundrett for the lyke	vjᵈ

21.	Of M[ist]ris Marie Wilbraham wid[ow]⁶	
22.	John Holland & Thomas Steven	
23.	for not laying open the waie &	
24.	making it passeable that leadeth	iiijˡⁱ
25.	through Drakelowe acording to a	
26.	payne⁷ sett in that behalf ev[er]ie	
27.	one of theym a peece	

28.	Of Robert Rowe for not repayring	
29.	his building and for not paveing	iij⁵ iiijᵈ
30.	acording to a payne sett in that	
31.	behalf	

32.	Of Geffrey Culchet for not	
33.	laying open thincrochm[en]t	
34.	neere unto his howse acording	xˢ
35.	to a payne sett in that behalf	

36.	Of John Wynyngton of Rudheath	
37.	for not repayring his building	
38.	acording to a payne sett in that	xˢ
39.	behalf	

TRANSCRIPT

Hearth Tax of Wentworth in Cambridgeshire

(TNA:PRO ref: E 179/244/22, f 205)

1.	Wentworth Paid	
2.	M[r] Tho[mas] Rippington	6
3.	And[rew] Gunton	3
4.	Tho[mas] Sabarton	1
5.	M[r] Yennis	4
6.	Rob[er]t Houghton	1
7.	Jo[h]n[1] Goutes	1
8.	W[illia]m Linford	1
9.	Rob[er]t Watson	2
10.	Wid[ow] Smith	1
11.	Tho[mas] Tompson	1
12.	Wid[ow] How	1
13.	Widd[ow[Scotterell	3
14.	Widd[ow] Meakes	2
15.	Moses Nix	1
16.	M[r] Burchill	3
17.	Widd[ow] Draper	2
18.	W[illia]m Gundon	2
19.	Nath[aniel] Martin	1
20.	Jer[emiah][2] Gunton	1
21.	Tho[mas] Gunton	1
22.	Jos[eph][3] Meakes	2
23.	Mich[ael] Hall	1
24.	Geo[rge] Lunferd	2
		___
25.		43
26.	Wentforth unpaid	
27.	Widd[ow] Rich	4
28.	Widd[ow] Searle Rob[ert] Healy	2
29.	Nat[haniel] Martin Jo[h]n Barwick	2
30.	M[r] Rippington	6
		___
31.		14

32.		Hearth[es]	Li[bre]	s[olidi]
33.	Rec[eive]d for	43	02	03
34.	unpaid	14		
		___		
35.	[th]e Tottall	57		

COMMENTARY

Hearth Tax of Wentworth in Cambridgeshire
(TNA:PRO ref: E 179/244/22, f 205)

Document

The Hearth Tax was levied from 1662 to 1689. Although included with the lay subsidy documents, it does not strictly come within that category. As with other taxes, it links a name, place and date and gives, by way of the number of hearths, the relative standing of the inhabitants, imparting this information in a more interesting way than by an impersonal sum of money. The hearths listed in this return (for Lady Day 1666) were charged at the rate of 1s. each.

Script

This hand distinguishes well between the letters *u* and *n*. Its main hazard is in the long descenders and ascenders e.g. the very long *p* and *G* and tall *M* which interfere with the legibility of the words below or above. The letter *c* is a short vertical line with the second stroke either at right angles or emerging from the base of that line, sometimes faded out, or nearly so.

Notes

1. The spelling of the extension of Jn° has been regularised.
2. This name could otherwise be Jeremy or even another name beginning Jer-.
3. This name could otherwise be Josiah.

concerning the —
brewery of
Reading about
the Corne mills
there.

Whereas a petition was this day pnted to the Board in
the name of Elinor Gibbons, Eliz: Crowe widdowe, Thomas Harison
William Jerman, Edward Andrewes, William Sandy Tho: Worsley &
Richard Welbeck, his Matis Tennantes & incorporated Brewbers
of the Towne of Reading Shewing amongst other thinges that
the Crowne & farme of the water Corne Mills in Reading paying
only a small farme Rent to his Matie for the same doth
vnder colour of a decree obtayned by them in the Court
of Excheqr in 20. Jacobj for the suppressinge of the horse
mills of one widdow Harrison, John Crowne & Richard
Winch all since deceased endeavour to withdrawe the
Petrs. likewise, who are farmers to his Matie at a very
great fyne & Rent, from settinge by theire Mill. for theire
owne private vse, withoute wch they are not able to keepe
theire trades. The said decree as the Petitionrs. alledge
being to withdrawe only the aforsaid three persons & no others
And therefore humble besought theire Lopps to take such
order therein as that the Petrs. may not be any further molested
concerninge the same. Theire Lopps hereupon having had thereof
doe hereby recommend it to the Lord cheife Baron & the
rest of the Barons of the Excheqr to take the said decree
of 20: Jacobj into consideration, & thereupon to settle such
order therein as they shall finde rather agreeable to the
trewe intention of the said decree.

TRANSCRIPT

Entry in the Privy Council Registers concerning the Brewers of Reading
(TNA:PRO ref: PC 2/48, p 637)

In margin: *Concerning the Brewers of Reading about the Corne Mills there*

1. Whereas a Petic[i]on was this day p[rese]nted to the Board in
2. the name of Elinor Gibbons Eliz[abeth] Grove widdowes Thomas Harison
3. Will[ia]m Jerman Edward Andrewes Will[ia]m Gawdy Tho[mas] Worsley &
4. Richard Welbeck his Ma[jes]t[es] Lycenced & incorporated Beerbrew[e]rs
5. of the Towne of Reading Shewing amongst other things that
6. the Own[e]rs & Farm[e]rs[1] of the water Corne Mill[es] in Reading paying
7. only a small Farme Rent to his Ma[jes]tie for the same[2] Doe
8. under pretence of a decree obtaynd by them in the Co[u]rt
9. of Excheq[ue]r in 20 Jacobi[3] for the suppressing of the Horse
10. mills[4] of one Widdow Harrison John Grove & Richard
11. Winch all since deceassed endeavour to restraine the
12. Pet[icione]rs likewise who are Farm[e]rs to his Ma[jes]tie at a very
13. great Fyne & Rent from setting up such Mills for theire
14. owne private use w[i]thout w[hi]ch they are not able to keepe
15. up theire Trades The said Decree as the Peticon[e]rs[5] alleadge
16. being to restraine only the aforesaid three p[er]sons & no others
17. And therefore humbly besought theire Lo[rdshi]pps to take such
18. order therein as that the Pet[icione]rs may <not> be any further molested
19. concerning the same Theire Lo[rdshi]pps upon advise had thereof
20. Doe hereby recomend it to the Lord cheefe Baron & the
21. rest of the Barons of th[e] Excheq[ue]r to take the said Decree
22. of 20 Jacobi into considerac[i]on & thereupon to settle such
23. order therein as they shall finde cause agreeable to the
24. scope & intenc[i]on of the said Decree

COMMENTARY

Entry in the Privy Council Registers concerning the Brewers of Reading
(TNA:PRO ref: PC 2/48, p 637)

Document

For notes on the Privy Council registers see plate 12. The document on p. 637 comes under the earlier general heading: 'At Whytehall the last of Feb^r 1637'.

Script

The writing in the volume is clearly in different hands, most of it more easily read than in this entry which is in a good, typical secretary hand, but has the complication of having in many cases extensive descenders which the eye needs to distinguish from the writing on the line below. There is, as so often, some ambiguity over the difference between capital and small letters, here in the case of *d* and *w*. The letter *s*, particularly in the initial position, is not unlike the letter *h* in other secretary hands; the final *s* resembles the abbreviation sign for *es*; and the *c* often resembles an *i* as in, for example, 'Jacobi', 'considerac[i]on'. Some abbreviations do not accord with normal expectations, e.g. over the word 'presented'.

Notes

1. Farmers appears to be used here, as often, with the meaning of lessees.
2. Here and subsequently the transcript shows as separate the words which seem to have been run together in haste.
3. 20 *Jacobi* (i.e. 20th year of reign of King James I): 1622-23.
4. Horse mill: a mill driven by a horse.
5. The word appears to be written thus, though it would seem that an extra letter *i* would have been intended.

(Plate and transcript on previous spread)

COMMENTARY

Deposition of John Thompson
(TNA:PRO ref: E 134/1653/East13)

Document

Many depositions include (as does this one) information about properties, useful to the local historian. Their great strength for the genealogist is usually the description of the deponent which gives his or her name, place of residence, occupation (frequently) and age, the last being a piece of rare good fortune even if the age given is sometimes in rounded figures. Although this document (dated in 1653) is of the period of the Commonwealth when many legal documents were not for the time being written in Latin, depositions were in any case in English at this period. The background to this case is that the plaintiffs Sir George Allen, Bt., and his wife Frances (through Robert Thompson their guardian) and Francis Thompson brought the case relating to the possession by Henry Gent, grandfather of the plaintiff Frances, of land in Bumpstead at the Tower, Steeple Bumpstead and Birdbrook, in Essex. Steeple Bumpstead and Birdbrook were adjoining parishes, the latter on the borders of Cambridgeshire. The case was brought against George Gent, Thomas Jagger (Jaggard in the deposition) and his wife Dorothy. Many exchequer and chancery depositions can be located through the Bernau index on microfilm at the Society of Genealogists.

Script

This is a normal form of secretary hand, if a little unruly. The scribe demonstrates two quite different forms of the letter *h*, used at whim only it would seem, being both to be seen in the same environment e.g. both in the word 'the'. Ascenders and descenders are long, but not as inconveniently so as in some documents as the lines are well spaced.

Notes

1. The county is Essex.
2. Herbage: the right to feed cattle on the ground of another.
3. 1635.
4. As previously noted, signatures are particularly hard to decipher with certainty, since they are very idiosyncratic and there is not the usual so useful facility of comparison with other similar letters in a known context.

(Plate and transcript on following spread)

TRANSCRIPT

Deposition of John Thompson

(TNA:PRO ref: E 134/1653/East13)

1. *On* the pl[ain]t[iff]s behalfe **John Thompson** Rector of the p[ar]ish Church of Birdbrooke in the said County[1] aged

2.   forty six yeares or thereabouts sworne & exa[m]i[n]ed the day & yeare aboves[ai]d deposeth as followeth (vi[delice]t)

3. 1 **To** the First Int[errogatory] he saith hee knoweth & did know all the p[ar]ties in the Int[errogatory] named save onely the Def[endan]t Jaggard

4. 3 **To** the third hee saith that the Def[endan]t George Gent hold[es] in his hand[es] the Feild called Pricefeild in the Int[errogatory] menc[i]o[n]ed &

5.   Pricefeild meadow also And this Dep[onen]t conceiveth the yearely value of the same Pricefeild to bee about twelve pound[es] p[er]

6.   annu[m] For that he *finds* by the Notebookes of M[r] John Gent his p[re]cedent Incumbent in the s[ai]d Rectory (being the Def[endan]t George

7.   his naturall Brother) that the s[ai]d Def[endan]t George paid to his said brother severall yeares together foure & twenty shilling[es]

8.   p[er] annu[m] for the Herbage[2] of the same feild[es] And this Dep[onen]t likewise conceiveth that the meadow in the Int[errogatory] menc[i]o[n]ed called

9.   Pricefeild meadow doth conteine tenn acres for [tha]t at this Dep[onen]ts first comeing to bee Recto[u]r of the s[ai]d p[ar]ish hee found [tha]t

10.   one acre of the same meadow had bene formerly & usually assigned to the s[ai]d former Incumbent by agreem[en]t in kinde

11.   for & <in> leiwe of the tithe of the residue of the same & this Dep[onen]t hath hitherto soe continued the enjoym[en]t of the same accordingly

12.   And this Dep[onen]t conceiveth every acre of the said ten acres to bee worth five & twenty shillings by the yeare which he the

13.   rather beleiveth in respect of the p[ro]ffitt w[hi]ch he hath made of that his said assigned acre and further saith not

14. 4 **To** the fourth he saith that the Def[endan]t Jaggard in the Inter[rogatory] named holdeth in his hand[es] the Farme & land[es] in the Inter[rogatory]

15.   menc[i]oned And this Dep[onen]t conceives the same to bee worth five & thirty pound[es] p[er] annu[m] & offered so much therefore &

16.   is still willing to give soe much for the same & desired Thomas Rogers servant to the s[ai]d Def[endan]t Jaggard to acquaint

17.   his said Master M[r] Jaggard therewith but the said Rogers after retorned answere to [th]e Dep[onen]t that his said Master would not

18.   lett it under forty pound[es] p[er] annu[m] And further saith not

19. 6 **To** the sixt hee saith that he did see Henry Gent and Thomas Gent in the Int[errogatory] named seale & as theire Act & <Deed>

20.   deliver the Indenture now shewed to this Dep[onen]t beareing date the eleventh day of May in the eleventh yeare of

21.   the Reigne of the late King Charles[3] and that this Dep[onen]t did then subscribe his name as a witnes to the sealeing

22.   & delivery thereof with his owne hand as the same appeares to bee indorsed on the same Indenture And that the

23.   names of Henry Gent & Thomas Gent <subscribed to [th]e same Indenture are [th]e p[ro]pp[er] hand writing[es] of the s[ai]d Henry & Thomas Gent> &

24.   the names of the other witnesses to the same Deed are also the sev[er]all

25.   p[ro]pper hand wrighting[es] of the said other witnesses And further to this Inter[ogatory] he cannot Depose To the rest of

26.   the Interr[ogatories] hee is not to bee exa[m]i[n]ed by any direcc[i]on

George Aleyn   Edm[und] Plum[m]e[4]

[20]

To the Kynge our soveraigne lord

TRANSCRIPT

Bill in Court of Requests

(TNA:PRO ref: REQ 2/1/10)

1.   To the kynge oure sov[er]aign lorde

2.   Complaynyng shewyth unto youre Excellent majestie yo[u]r true subject & pore Orato[u]r Robert Robyns s[er]va[u]nt to the

3.   knyght marschall that where youre seid Orato[u]r fo[u]r the some of xxvij[li]bre] xiijs[olidi] viijd[enarii] paide to one Nicholas Blewet lorde

4.   of the man[er] of Kyddysforde youre seid Orato[u]r hade of the seyd Nicholas serten tenement[es] to holde by Coppye of corte

5.   Roll of the seid maner for t[er]me of his lyffe after the Custome of the said man[er] v[ide]licet] one Cotage w[i]th a Curtylage

6.   ij acres of lande & medue a p[ar]cell of lande betwen ludlowe brygg & [th]e myll and also ij water mylles one beyng

7.   a Corne Myll & thothyr a Fullen Myll of the whiche p[ar]cellz youre seid pore Orato[u]r was peasablye seased

8.   in his demesne as of free holde after the Custome of the seid maner by the space of iij yere[s] & more & toke

9.   therof the p[ro]ffitez as lauffull was for hym to do so yt is mooste g[r]acyus sov[er]aign lorde that nowe of late youre

10.   saide pore Orato[u]r beynge in youre g[r]acius s[er]vyce in Fraunce The seide Nicholas Blewet of his greate malles &

11.   Frowarde mynde towarde yo[u]r seide pore Orato[u]r hathe not onelye dysturbbed youre seid Orato[u]r of thoccupacion

12.   of the seid p[ar]cell[es] but also hathe Clerely turned the water Cowrse frome the seid Mylles so that yo[u]r seyde

13.   Orato[u]r Can take no p[ro]fytt[es] of the seid myll[es] Cont[r]arie to Ryght & Consciens <and> to <h[is]> uttyr undoyng & because yo[u]r

14.   seid Orato[u]r is a pore ma[n] & the seid Nicholas of greate abilite & beynge lorde of the seid man[er] youre said

15.   Orato[u]r is w[i]thowte remedie oneles youre g[r]acyus helpe be hade in the p[re]miss[es] Therfo[u]r the same moste g[r]acyuslye

16.   Consyd[er]et by youre moste excellent highnes it may pleas youre hyghnes to graunte yo[u]r moste g[r]acius l[ett]res

17.   of p[ri]ve seale to be dyrected to the seid Nicholas Commaundyng hym by the same under a s[er]ten

18.   payne & at s[er]ten day p[er]sonally to apere before youre g[r]ace ys Counsayle attendyng on yo[u]r majestie To

19.   Answer to the p[re]miss[es] & there to abyde suche order as shall stande w[i]l[t]h] Justice Equyte & Consciens

20.   and youre said pore Orato[u]r will daylie p[r]aye for the p[re]s[er]vacion of youre moste Royall Estate longe

21.   to Enduer

COMMENTARY

Document

For notes on the Court of Requests, see plate 13.

Script

This document contains many final abbreviation marks which are purely a formality. In some cases in this hand the superscript *r* (e.g. in 'for', 'maner', 'after', 'water') appears to have no significance. Some ambiguity occurs about the small *s*, the size of which appears to vary.

108

To the Revd. Dr Richard West Arch-deacon
of Berks The Petition of the Minister & Churchwardens
of Speenhurst in the County of Berks humbly
sheweth viz:

Whereas the Parish Church of Speenhurst aforesaid is
not large enough conveniently to contain the Congregation therein Assembling to hear & perform Divine
service. And Whereas the most proper & least
expensive way to remedy the said Inconvenience will
be by Building or erecting a Galery in the said Parish Church
to contain part of the said Congregation. We therefore the
said Minister & Churchwardens of Speenhurst aforesaid
(A Vestry being first called for this very purpose) Do humbly
petition that a faculty may be granted to impower the
said Churchwardens to build or erect a Galery for the
purpose aforesaid at the West end of the said Parish Church
it being the most convenient place for the same And that
the Gallery may contain in length twenty two foot in
Breadth eight foot & in Height eight foot
And for the Grant of the Petition we shall (as bound in duty)
Pray &c

                    Witness our hands July 9th 1712:

Tho: Gloucher Rect:

Richard Barnes
                              } Church Wardens
Richard Loader

                                              Proclamavit
22 July 1712 ffiat ffacult

Jos: Woodward offic:

[22]

TRANSCRIPT

Letter

(Berkshire Record Office ref: D/A2/C161 f 108)

1. To the Rev[eren]d D[octo]r Richard West Arch-Deacon
2. of Berk*shire* [th]e Petition of [th]e Minister & Churchwardens
3. of Tylehurst in [th]e County of Berk*shire* humbly
4. sheweth vi[delicet]

5. Whereas [th]e Parish Church of Tylehurst afores[ai]d is
6. not large enough com[m]odiously to contain [th]e Congre-
7. gation therein Assembling to hear & perform Divine
8. Service And Whereas [th]e most proper & least
9. expensive way to remedy [th]e s[ai]d Inconvenience will
10. be by Building or erecting a Galery in [th]e s[ai]d Parish-Church
11. to contain part of [th]e s[ai]d Congregation We therfore [th]e
12. s[ai]d Minister & Churchwardens of Tylehurst afores[ai]d
13. (A Vestry being first calld for this very purpose) Do humbly
14. petition [tha]t a Faculty may be granted to impower [th]e
15. s[ai]d Church Wardens to build or erect a Galery[1] for [th]e
16. purpose afores[ai]d at [th]e West end of [th]e s[ai]d Parish Church
17. [tha]t being [th]e most convenient place for [th]e same And [tha]t [th]e
18. s[ai]d Gallery may contain in Length Twenty <Two> Foot in
19. Breadth eight Foot & in Height ~~two~~ <eight> Foot
20. And for [th]e Grant of [thi]s Petition we shall (as becometh us)
21. Pray &c
22.   Witness our Hands July 7th 1712

23.   Tho[mas] Walker Rect[or]
24.   Richard Barnes   }
25.   Richard Loader   } Church Wardens

26.   22° Julii 1712 Fiat ~~Facul~~ <Proclamac[i]o>[2]

27.   Jos[eph][3] Woodward Offi[cia]lis[4]

[22]

COMMENTARY

Letter
(Berkshire Record Office ref: D/A2/C161 f 108)

Document

Unlike most of the other documents in this book, this was not composed as a record and the writing is therefore of a very informal nature. Although dated in 1712, it has very little of the problems usually associated with palaeography, but nonetheless needs the kind of observation required for more formal documents.

Script

The Greek type of letter *e*, easily read near the start of the letter, is less easily detected in a surname. The writer uses a second *e* which does not have the reversed appearance which is still noticeable elsewhere at this time. The writer appears to be in haste and economises on crossing the *t*. The *o* tends to be very narrow; the *a* is sometimes open (note the similarity of the words 'as' and 'us' in l. 20). An equivalent of the old rune thorn, symbolising *th*, continues to be used.

Notes

1. It would seem that *e* has been overwritten with *a* or *vice versa*.
2. Translation: Let there be a proclamation.
3. This name could be Josiah.
4. Translation: official (n).

(Plate and transcript on previous spread)

COMMENTARY

Bill of Complaint from Chancery Proceedings
(TNA:PRO ref: C 1/1443/78)

Document

Chancery proceedings, spanning some five centuries from the time of Richard II, are among the most fertile and interesting sources for family and local history. They can produce information about several generations of a family and give insight into the motives and characters of ancestors. Very considerable numbers relate to disputes about land. Usually consisting of a bill of complaint and the defendant's answer and sometimes a replication (plaintiff's response) and rejoinder (defendant's further response) and perhaps depositions, they often provide a wealth of information. A litigious ancestor can be a genealogical blessing. Except for quite early ones in Anglo-Norman French, they are written in English. Of the notoriously varied indexes, that of one of the two Elizabethan series (C 2 Eliz.) is particularly valuable in that it (with a file of addenda) indexes plaintiffs and defendants and gives a brief resumé of cases and, of special use to local historians, includes an index locorum. A huge project has been started at the National Archives to produce a systematic index. *Chancery Equity Records and Proceedings 1600-1800* by Henry Horwitz (1998) gives excellent information on these records. See also the useful booklet *Chancery and Other Legal Proceedings* by R.E.F. Garrett (1968.) The Bernau Index at the Society of Genealogists identifies many cases.

Script

W and *w* appear to be identical in this document, as also *H* and *h*. There are not many actual abbreviations, but the scribe makes use of a number of apparent abbreviation marks which are no more than a formality and do not generally indicate an omission (although there might sometimes be an argument for a final *e*). These have therefore been ignored in the transcript. This peculiarity, found in many documents of the period, seems likely to be a legacy from earlier days when documents were more heavily abbreviated.

Notes

1. Many chancery bills have no more indication of date than this type of address. The only Nicholas who was an archbishop of York at a suitable period shows this bill to be within the period 1556-1558 (v. *Handbook of British Chronology*, ed. Fryde, Greenway, Porter and Roy).
2. This is an obsolete form of 'against'.
3. It seems the contraction mark has been omitted.
4. Similarly a contraction might have been expected here.
5. Normally the second of two consecutive letters *m* is taken as omitted by abbreviation, but here it seems the first is intended.
6. For *sub poena*.

(Plate and transcript on following spread)

Bill of Complaint from Chancery Proceedings

(TNA:PRO ref: C 1/1443/78)

1. To the Rev[er]end father in god Nych[ol]as Archebusshop
2. of Yorke lorde Chauncello[u]r of Englonde[1]

3. In mooste humble wise schewen & Complaynen unto youre grace youre dayly orators John Jurden & Johan his wyfe oonly doughto[u]r & sole heir
4. of John Hamond deceassed That where oon Nych[ol]as Hamond late of Dagnall in the Cou[n]tie of Buck[ingham] yoman was seysed in his demeane
   as of
5. Fee Among[es] other land[es] & ten[emen]t[es] of & in oon Mease oon Cotage threscore Acres of lande Meadowe pasture & wood with thapp[u]rtenanc[es]
   sett liyng &
6. beyng in Dagnall aforeseyd And the seyd Nych[ol]as Hamonde so beyng seysed of the p[re]myssez of suche Estate dyed therof seysed After
7. whose deceas the seyd Mease & other the p[re]myssez w[i]t[h] thapp[u]rtenanc[es] discendyd & cam and of right ought to discende & com unto the
8. seyd John Hamond as son & heire of the seid Nych[ol]as Hamond Byforce wherof the seyd John Hamonde entred into the seid Mease
9. & other the p[re]myssez w[i]t[h] thapp[u]rtenanc[es] & was therof seysed in his demeane as of fee And the seid John Hamond so beyng therof seysed
10. dyed therof seysed After whose deceas the seid mease & other the p[re]myssez with thapp[u]rtenanc[es] discendyd & cam and of right ought to
11. discende & com unto the seid Johan nowe youre oratrice as doughto[u]r & heire of the seid John Hamonde And so it is good lord that
12. certen Evydenc[es] ded[es] writyng[es] & M[y]nyment[es] conc[er]nyng the p[re]myssez & of right belongyng to youre seid orato[u]rs be comen to the
13. hand[es] & possession of Thomas Wynchecombe Esquyer & Crystian his wife Henry White Esquyer & Brigett his wife Byforce
14. wherof the seyd Thomas Wynchecombe & Cristyan Henry Whyte & Brigett have wrongfully entred into the seid Mease and
15. other the p[re]myssez w[i]t[h] thapp[u]rtenanc[es] & deteyn & kepe the same from yo[u]r seid orato[u]rz ayenst[2] all right & Conscience And bycause
    youre
16. seyd orato[u]rz do not knowe the certen nombre ne Content[es] of the seid Evydenc[es] ded[es] & writyng[es] ne wherin they be conteyned in bagg
17. boxe or Chest sealyd or lockyd or not they ar therfore w[i]t[h]out remedy to obteyne the same by the co[m]en[3] lawe And also
18. youre orato[u]rz ar not Able to maynteyn any Acc[i]on[4] ayenst the seid Thomas Wynchecombe & Cristyan Henry Whyte &
19. Brigett for the p[re]myssez at the co[m]men[5] lawe for lacke of the seid Evydenc[es] ded[es] & writyng[es] And so ar lyke to lose the same
20. onles yo[u]r grac[es] favo[u]r be to them herin schewed. Maye yt therfore please youre grace the p[re]myssez considered to graunte the
21. Kyng[es] & quen[es] writt of Suppen[a][6] to be dyrectyd to the seid Thomas Wynchecombe & Crystian Henry Whyte & Brygett
22. co[m]mandyng them & ev[er]y of them by the same p[er]sonally to Apere before youre grace in the Kyng[es] & quen[es] highe Court of
23. Chaunc[er]y at A certen daye & under A payne by yo[u]r seyd lordschip to be lymettyd then & there to Answer to the p[re]myssez and to be
24. further ordred therin accordyng to right & Conscience And youre seid orato[u]rz wyll dayly p[r]aye to god for the p[ro]sp[er]ous Estate of youre
25. seyd grace long in hono[u]r to endure

Moseley

[23]

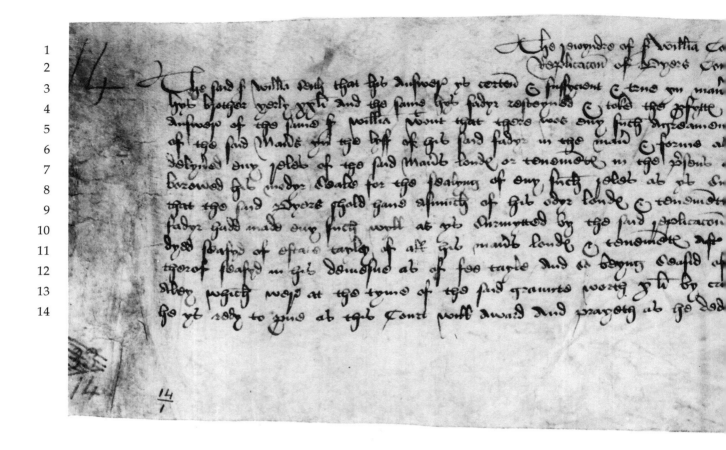

TRANSCRIPT

Rejoinder in Case in the Court of Star Chamber
(TNA:PRO ref: STAC 1/1/14)

1.   The rejoyndre of s[ir] Willia[m] Courteney to the
2.   Replicac[i]on of Pyers Courteney

3. The said s[ir] Willia[m] seith that his Answer ys certe[i]n & suffycient & true yn man[er] & forme as ys
supposed by the same And Also seyth that his fadyr[1] payed to the said Pyers

4. hys brother yerly xxli[bre] And the same hys fadyr resceyved & toke the p[ro]fytt[es] of the said Man[er]s
specyfied in the said byll & therof dyed seasyd as ys alleyed[2] yn the

5. Answer of the same s[ir] Willia[m] w[i]t[h]out that[3] there wos eny such Agreament made bytwene hys said
fadyr & hys said Brother Pyers for the takyng of the p[ro]fytt[es]

6. of the said Man[er]s yn the lyff of his said fadyr in the man[er] & forme as ys surmytted by the said
replycac[i]on And w[i]t[h]out that the said s[ir] Willia[m] sealyd or

7. delyv[er]ed eny reles of the said Man[er]s lond[es] or teneme[n]t[es] in the p[re]sens of his said fadyr &
modyr or yn eny other wise And w[i]t[h]out that the same s[ir] Willia[m]

8. borowed his modyr seale for the sealyng of eny such reles as ys surmytted by the said replicac[i]on And
w[i]t[h]out that his said fadyr made eny suche wyll

9. that the said Pyers shold have Asmuch of his odyr lond[es] & teneme[n]t[es] as w[i]t[h] the said Man[er]s
shold make uppe the value of xl li[bre] And how be yt his said

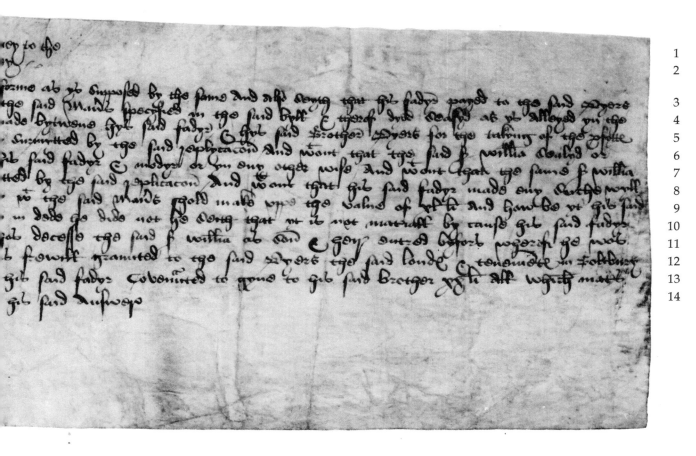

1
2
3
4
5
6
7
8
9
10
11
12
13
14

10. fadyr hadd made eny such wyll as ys surmytted by the said replicac[i]on as in dede he dide not he seith that yt is not mat[er]iall by cause his said fadyr

11. dyed seasyd of estate tayley[4] of all his man[er]s lond[es] & teneme[n]t[es] Aft[er] whos decesse the said s[ir] Willia[m] as son & heir entred byfors wherof he wos

12. therof seasyd in his demesne as of fee tayle And so beyng seasid of his frewill graunted to the said Pyers the said lond[es] & teneme[n]t[es] in Boltbury

13. Aley which were at the tyme of the said graunte worth x li[bre] by cause his said fadyr Covena[u]nted to gyve to his said brother xx li[bre] All which mat[er]s

14. he ys redy to p[ro]ve as this Court will Award And prayeth as he dede in his said Answer

COMMENTARY

Rejoinder in Case in the Court of Star Chamber
(TNA:PRO ref: STAC 1/1/14)

Document

This court (temp. Henry VII-Charles I) dealt frequently with cases of riotous behaviour, assault etc. which appear to some extent to have been a cloak for matters at variance relating to property. Cases might include such topics as alleged proposed murder, ejectment, false imprisonment, affray, forcible entry and unlawful assembly, but also less violent subjects such as shipping leather without licence, and defamation. The curious name of the court is apparently derived from the room in the old Palace of Westminster where it met (the *camera stellata*) the ceiling of which was decorated with stars. The rejoinder, as in chancery proceedings, was the defendant's answer to the plaintiff's replication, itself a response to the defendant's initial answer. This case, dated in 1500, relates to Somerset and concerns forcible entry and ouster. It gives further genealogical material, mentioning the intended marriage between Piers Courteney and Joan (in some instances called Jane) daughter of Sir Thomas Beaumount; and Margaret, daughter of Sir William Bonvyle, the wife of the younger Sir William Courteney. A useful volume on these records is *The Court of the Star Chamber and its Records to the reign of Elizabeth I*, by J.A. Guy (1985).

Script

Note the apparent abbreviation over final *ll* (e.g. byll, mat[er]iall). *W* and *w* appear largely indistinguishable. The letter *a* in many instances appears similar to *o*. The small letter *s* is used in three forms, in some cases on account of its position in the word, and otherwise perhaps to some extent dependent upon the following letter.

Notes

1. The letter *d*, rather than later *th*, appears in 'fadyr', 'modyr' (obsolete forms of father, mother) and in this document one might have expected 'broder' which can similarly occur as an early form. The text is here not wholly consistent since 'other' (l. 7) and 'odyr' (l. 9) both appear.
2. This is an obsolete form of alleged.
3. The expression 'without that' (sometimes with a second word 'that') is a usual form introducing denial.
4. Here the letter *y* appears to have been added, perhaps reflecting the Scottish *tailye* or the Anglo-French *taylé*, relating to entail.

(Plate and transcript on previous spread)

COMMENTARY

Order for Annuity for Joan Lovell

(Richmond-upon-Thames Local Studies Collection no 2346)

Document

This document, with its mention of local land, a husband and wife, the former's office and the latter's widowhood, exemplifies the fact that, however the larger record offices, with national, county or diocesan coverage, provide the immediate hunting ground for manuscripts which may afford material for local and family history, there are also many much smaller collections of documents held at libraries etc. which can be worth trawling for additional good material of a perhaps miscellaneous but rewarding nature. See *British Archives – A Guide to Archive Resources in the United Kingdom* by Janet Foster and Julia Sheppard (3rd edn., 1995).

Script

The writing is in a very consistent hand and is similar in form to the entries from the close rolls of similar period (v. plates 26 and 40). As in those documents the letter *w* is written so large that on immediate impact it appears to be the capital letter and is indeed identical with it; the *L* appears identical with *l*; there is more than one form of *v,* as also of *r* (the long *r* of which has a very fine up-stroke, in some cases almost undetectable); *M* is very similar to *m* but is differentiated by the descender from the third stroke (cf. Mannor and Richmonde in l. 6); and a formal abbreviation appears over a final *ll* e.g. in Lovell, Michaell, usuall etc.

Notes

1. A number of definitions for 'sue' are given in the *O.E.D.* the most likely of which appears to be the obsolete use as 'to follow in the sequence of events'.
2. This was the year 1591.

(Plate and transcript on following spread)

Order for Annuity for Joan Lovell

(Richmond upon Thames Local Studies Collection – document 2346)

1. **Elizabeth** by the grace of god Quene of England Fraunce and Ireland defender of the faith &c **To** the Treasorer
2. and Chamberlaynes of our Exchequire at Westm' for the tyme beinge or which hereafter shalbe Greetinge **whereas** by our l[ette]res
3. patent[es] bearing equall date with these p[re]sent[es] have given and graunted unto our welbeloved subject Jone Lovell wydowe late
4. wife of John Lovell the office of overseer and keeper of our Orcharde within our Mannor of Richmond in our County of Surrey
5. together with the office of keeper of the garden called the Quenes garden and lodge to the same garden belonginge within the said
6. Mannor and towne of Richmonde which said offices the said John Lovell her late husband helde and enjoyed duringe his life And the
7. said Jone Lovell widowe Overseer and keeper of the said Orcharde and keeper of the said garden and lodge we have made ordeyned
8. and appoynted And also have given and graunted by the said l[ette]res patent[es] unto the said Jone Lovell and her deputies or assignes free
9. ingresse egresse and regresse to and from the said garden att all tymes at their will and pleasure by the path comonly called the by
10. pathe throughe the fryers grounde To have houlde occupy and enjoye the said offices And likewise to have enjoye and yerely to
11. receave an an[n]uitye or yerely fee of six poundes and twenty pence for exerciseinge of the said offices to the said Jone Lovell and
12. her assignes from the death of the said John Lovell her late husband during her naturall life oute of the treasure of us our heires and
13. successors at the Receipt of the Exchequire of us our heires and successors by the handes of the Treasorer and Chamberlaynes
14. there for the tyme beinge at fower termes of the yere that is to saye at the feastes of S[ain]t Michaell the Archaungell the birthe of
15. our lord god thanunciac[i]on of the virgyn Marye and the Nativitie of S[ain]t John Baptiste by even porc[i]ons with all other wages
16. fees p[ro]fitt[es] com[m]odities easement[es] advauntages allowances rightes and emolument[es] whatsoev[er] to the said offices or either of them
17. belonginge or app[er]teyninge **And** whereas also by our said l[ette]res patent[es] for weedinge sandinge soylinge and other necessaries
18. yerely to be done in the said garden and orcharde of Richmond from tyme to tyme as occasion shall sue[1] have given and graunted
19. to the said Jone Lovell a c[ler]ten an[n]uitye or yerely fee of fower poundes of lawfull money of England To have and yerely receave
20. the said an[n]uitye or yerely fee of fower poundes to the said Jone Lovell at fower usuall feastes of the yere that is to saye
21. at the feaste of S[ain]t Michaell tharchaungell the birth of our lord god thanunciac[i]on of the virgyn Marye and the Nativitye of
22. S[ain]t John Baptist by even porc[i]ons out of the treasure of us our heires and successors at the Receipt of the Exchequire of us
23. our heires and successors by the handes of the Treasorer and Chamberlaynes there for the tyme beinge duringe the life of the
24. said Jone Lovell as by our said l[ette]res patent[es] more playnly appereth **Wee** therefore com[m]aunde you not onely to paye unto the
25. said Jone Lovell soe muche of the said an[n]uitye or yerely fee of six poundes and twenty pence from the death of the said
26. John Lovell her late husband that is behinde and unpaide But also that from henceforth ye paye unto her every yere duringe her
27. naturall life from tyme to tyme at the feastes aforesaid bothe the said an[n]uitye or yerely fee of six poundes and twenty pence
28. and likewise the said yerely fee of foure poundes accordinge to the tenor of our said l[ette]res patent[es] receavinge of the said Jone
29. Lovell her l[ette]res of acquitaunce testifienge your payment therein which shalbe for us sufficient in this behalf **Witnes** our self
30. att Grenewich the sixtenthe daye of July in the thre and thirteth yere of our raigne[2]

Powle

TRANSCRIPT

Indenture on Close Roll

(TNA:PRO ref: C 54/921)

In margin: D[e] Indentur[a] int[er] Hannes & Hannes[1]

1. This Indenture made the xxiij[th] daye of Maye in the fifte[e]nth yere of the reigne of o[ur][2] sov[er]ainge ladie
2. Elizabeth by the grace of god Quene of England Fraunce and Ireland defendor of the faythe &c
3. Betwene Rob[er]te Hannes of Witney in the Countie of Oxon' Shomaker Cosen and heire of
4. Richard Hannes late of Witney aforeseid deceassed that is to witt sonne of Henrye Hannes
5. the eldest sonne of the seid Richard Hannes on thone partie And Jerome Hannes of Witney
6. aforesaid uncle unto the seid Rob[er]te Hannes on thother partie Witnesseth that the seid Rob[er]te
7. Hannes for and in considerac[i]on of a c[er]ten som[m]e of money by the seid Jerome to hym the seid Rob[er]te
8. well and truly contented and payed before thensealinge of this p[re]sent Indenture hathe b[ar]gayned
9. and sould gyven and graunted and by thes p[re]sent[es] dothe b[ar]gayne and sell gyve and g[r]aunt unto
10. the seid Jerome Hannes all those houses gardens orchard[es] land[es] and tenement[es] with their
11. app[ur]tena[u]nc[es] in Witney aforeseid which were the aforenamed Richard Hannes graundfather of the
12. seid Rob[er]te and arnowe in the tenures and occupac[i]ons of Henry Tackley Will[ia]m Dunford[3] and
13. Richard James or their assignes or any others and the rev[er]c[i]on of all and ev[er]lye the p[re]mysses and
14. all his right title int[er]est and clayme unto the same houses gardens orchard[es] and land[es] or any
15. parte of them or to the rev[er]sion or rev[er]syons of them or any parte of them To have and to hould
16. all and singuler the p[re]misses unto the seid Jerome his heyres and assignes forev[er] of the cheif
17. lord or lord[es] of the Fee therof by the rent[es] and s[er]vic[es] therof dewe and of right accustomed
18. to thonly p[ro]per use and behouf of the seid Jerome his heires and assignes forev[er] absolutlye and
19. without any mann[er] of condic[i]on In witnes wherof the seid parties to thes Indentures
20. ent[er]chaungeably have putt their Seales yeven[4] the daye and yere abovewritten
21. **Et memorand[um] q[uod] quarto die Iunii Anno suprascript[o] venit p[re]dict[us]**
22. **Rob[er]tus Hannes coram dict[a] d[omi]na Regina in Cancellar[i]a sua apud**
23. **Westm' & recognovit Indenturam p[re]d[i]c[t]am ac om[n]ia & singula in eadem**
24. **contenta & sp[ec]ificat[a] in forma supradict[a]**

TRANSLATION

Marginal Heading   Concerning the indenture between Hannes & Hannes

Additional Note at Foot   And it is to be remembered that on the fourth day of June in the abovewritten year the aforesaid Robert Hannes came before the said Lady Queen in her chancery at Westminster and acknowledged the aforesaid indenture and all & singular the things contained and specified in the same in the abovesaid form.

[26]

COMMENTARY

Indenture on Close Roll

(TNA:PRO ref: C 54/921)

Document

Close rolls (temp. John-Edward VII) contain the enrolments of letters close, as distinct from letters patent (open). They comprise a very wide and miscellaneous range of topics, including a number which are of interest to genealogists and local historians, such as a variety of types of private deeds, conveyances of estates of bankrupts, recognizances and bonds, certificates of naturalisation, deeds of settlement of ecclesiastical districts and parish boundaries, surrenders of monasteries to the Crown and trust deeds granting sites for churches, chapels and schools. However, such subjects appear on the rolls (sometimes endorsed) for limited and differing periods only. Close rolls also appear amongst the records of the Palatinates of Durham and Lancaster. This indenture is rich in genealogical detail.

Script

As with many scripts, there appears to be no difference between *W* and *w,* or between *H* and *h.* The usual letters are largely represented by minims and the letter *i* is undotted. Three types of *u* are noted: the initial of uncle (l. 6) could be a capital letter, but the same form appears medially in l. 9. The shape of the abbreviation indicating an absent *er* is a little deceptive. As so often, some abbreviation marks, including the deceptive line through *ll,* occur with no obvious purpose.

Notes

1. Due to the four minims in this name, it could, in the absence of additional evidence, be otherwise interpreted.
2. The superior *r* takes various forms and in some cases is taken as a sign of abbreviation. The variants are somewhat ambiguous (and thus give rise to possible differences in transcription i.e. o[u]r or o[ur]).
3. This is a somewhat unusual letter *D.* The section on letters would solve this. However, a clue to its identity occurs in the second line of the following entry where there is mention of a John Drywood (beginning with a more conventional *D*) who was of a place beginning with a similar curious letter. The place-name can be investigated with the help of a gazetteer.
4. This is an obsolete form of the word given.

(Plate and transcript on previous spread)

COMMENTARY

Part of an Act Recorded on a Parliament Roll
(TNA:PRO ref: C 65/739, m 41)

Document

The Parliament Rolls (temp. Edward III-Elizabeth II) contain varying amounts of information during this period, but much detail of interest to the local historian. This part is the beginning of an enrolment of 1 George III, some 30 feet long and ending *Le Roy le Veult*. The terrain to which the entry refers is flat and perhaps liable to problems, being juxtaposed to Sunk Island, a large piece of land which apparently emerged as an island, two miles from the shore, in the 1600s and was gradually recovered from the Humber.

Script

This is an unusual and, on first impact, difficult hand (known as 'Parliament' hand). However, it is an excellent challenge for practising the so important palaeographer's skill of determining puzzling letters by comparison with other like letters which, by their context, are incontrovertible, and so building up a recognition of the forms of those letters. Thus it is perhaps best to draft a transcript of the document without spending too much time on the more obscure letters and then work through it again, and perhaps again. It is worth observing that the letter *w* is of curious form (and identical whether capital or small); that the *r* is sometimes no more than a straight stroke which goes below the line; that the *o* frequently resembles the *e* and that sometimes the *e* resembles the *o* (see for instance the similarity of the *o* in 'County' and the *e* in 'cleansing' in l. 5, and the apparent transposition of forms in 'other' in l. 19). There are frequent small ornamentations at the end of words. Despite these idiosyncrasies, however, it is a remarkably regular hand in most ways and interesting to unravel.

Note

1. Thus it seems, but the word appears uncertain, having evidently been altered.

(Plate and transcript on following spread)

An Act

TRANSCRIPT

Part of an Act Recorded on a Parliament Roll

(TNA:PRO ref: C 65/739, m 41)

1. **An Act** for amending the road from Sacred
2. Gate in the parish of Thorngumbald to Pattington Creak
3. or Haven and from the guide post in Winestead to
4. Frodlingham Gate in or near Widow Brantons Farm in
5. the County of York and for scouring and cleansing the
6. said Creek or Haven

7. **Whereas** the road leading from Sacred Gate in the parish of Thorngumbald
8. in Holderness in the County of York to Pattingdon Haven through Thorngumbold Ryhill
9. Keyingham Ottringham Winestead and Pattington in Holderness aforesaid being about
10. ten miles in length and also the road branching out of the same in Winestead afores[ai]d
11. and leading from thence through Winestead lanes to a gate called Frodingham gate
12. near Widow Brantons Farm in the lordship of Frodingham in Holderness aforesaid being
13. About ~~ten~~ <two> miles in length are from the nature of the soil and by reason of the many
14. heavy Carriages passing through the same become so deep[1] and ruinous that they
15. are in many ~~places~~ parts thereof utterly impassable in the winter season for
16. Waggons Carts and Wheel Carriages and are very dangerous and troublesome
17. for laden horses and travellers on horseback who have occasion to pass to and
18. fro in and upon the same And whereas there is a Creek or Chanel navigable for
19. keels sloops boats and other vessels between the river Humber and the town of
20. Pattrington aforesaid and which is called or known by the name of Pattrington
21. Haven and which was formerly of great benefit and advantage for the carriage or
22. Conveyance by Water of Corn and Grain and other Goods Wares and Com[m]odities in

Most Humbly complaynynge Shewith vnto y^r moste excellen[t]
[C]ambridge of Este Coker in the Comtie of Soms[ett] gent, [he]
and Gyles Cambridge of Est Coker aforesaid beinge [t]enured
[C]ambridge, John Sawtrell Elizabeth Sawtrell and oth[er] againste
[ ] daye of Aprill last past gave evydence vppon their o[the]
said Comtie, and moreouer ot[h] thinge saide y that ye said Subiect[es]
armes at Este Coker aforesaide, And th[at] ye did assalt and be[at]
evydence so geven was vtterlye of their owne free will and
large offers and great gyfte to them to be geven [a]s Willm Cambr[idge]
Myddleton Willm Myddleton, Nicholas Trueke, Richard Dyb[ble]
Subiect[es] vtterlye t[e]mt[ed]   So yt is mw y^t please y[r]
[C]ambridge not hauinge the feare of god before their eyes
God vnde[c]tifully corruptlye and wilfully contrarye to y[r] Ch[urch]
manifeste and wilfull iniurye to the great losse and hyndraun[ce]
of dyvers oth[er] like bonde despute and ill dysposed p[er]sons vtter[ly]
spea[ca]ble offence of p[er]iurye The said estate vpon ye se[ ] In Con[ ]
[si]nister occasions of witnesses to testifie to y[ou]r their knowledge
before god. but also such an evell example and indirect practize by w[hich]
many y^r subiect[es] may be by the testimonye and evidence of such [ ]
[b]ut also that the same vnhonest doinge and practizes tend[ith]
lett and hyndraunce of the dewe execuion and administraion of J[ustice]
tenderly considered to grante to y^r said Subiect[es] ye most [ ]
Gyles Cambridge, Willm Cambridge Anthony Cambridge John C[ambridge]
Nicholas Trueke Richard Dibble the elder Richard Dybble [ ]
onye more from and eu[er]ye of them by vertue of the same [to be]
Starre Chamber at a certaine day and vnder a certaine [ ]
[ ] to and also ye seuerall premisses [ ]
[ ]te and complaynt [ ] And y^r said
[ ] to god for ye p[ ]s p[ ]s[er]vaion of y^r Royall [ ]

a dreade Sovraigne Ladye

to youe excellente majestie

... the poore humble faithefull and obediente subiecte Richard ...
... one Robert Webbe of Est Coker aforesaid husbandman ...
witnesses on the ... and behalfe of William Hambridge, Anthony ...
... said subiecte, at Ilchester in the said Countie of Somersett the ...
... to the Grand Jurye then sworne by the iustice of peace of the ...
... and others dyd breke and enter in to a howse with force and ...
... the said Robert Webbe and one Richard Tyball the yonger, ...
... by the subornacion and sinister persuacions, fauoure promisses ...
... Anthony Hambridge, John Bamfeild, Elizabeth Turstell, John ...
... William Ingram, John palmer and others as ...
... moste excellent ma... that the said Robert Webbe ... Tyball ...
... regardinge youre ma... lawes, have to the highe displeasure of ...
... lawes in that behalfe made and ordeyned therein committed ...
... and impoverishment of the said subiecte and to the greate ...
... to committ the lyke offence yf that most abhominable and ...
... whereof and for as muche as thiese unlawfull subornacion and ...
... more then twentye is not onely a ... ... and ...
... and ... reproofe, the ... ... and goode of ...
... false and corrupte witnesses be taken from them unjustly, And for ...
... to the maintaynaunce of vice and wickednesse and to the greate ...
... and lawes ... May yt therefore please youre highenes the ... ...
... writtes of Sub pena, to be directed to them the said Robert Webbe ...
... Elizabeth Turstell, John Middleton, William Middleton ...
... yonger William Ingram and John palmer commaundinge and ...
... to appeare before your ma... and ... Counsell in the highe Courte of ...
... by your ma... to be lymyted and appoynted, then and ... to answere ...
... sworne as to your highenes said Counsell ... shall ...
... subiecte accordinge to ... most bounden dewtie shall daylye ...
... bounde to praye ...

Dale

TRANSCRIPT

Bill in the Court of Star Chamber
(TNA:PRO ref: STAC 5/H6/9)

1.   To owre moste Drede Sov[er]aigne Ladye
2.   the Quenes moste execellente magestie

3. Most humbly complayninge sheweth unto yo[u]r moste execellent Ma[gest]i[1] yo[u]r poore humble faithefull and obediente subjecte Richarde
4. Hambridge of Este Coker in the Countie of Som[er]s[et][2] gent[leman] that where one Robert Webbe of Est Coker aforesaid husbondman
5. and Gyles Hambridge of Est Coker aforesaide beinge p[ro]duced as witnesses on the p[ar]te and behalfe of Will[ia]m Hambridge Anthony
6. Hambridge John Gawtrell Elizabeth Gawtrell and oth[e]r[es] againste yo[u]r said Subjecte At Ylchester in the said Countie of Som[er]s[et] the
7.   daye of Aprill last past gave evydence uppon their othes to the Graund Jurye ther sworne by the justic[es] of peace of the
8. said Countie and amongeste oth[e]r thing[es] saide that yo[u]r said subjecte and oth[e]r[es] dyd breke and enter in to a howse w[i]th force and
9. armes at Este Coker aforesaide And th[e]r dyd assalt and beate the said Robert Webbe and one Richard Dybbell the yonger
10. w[hi]ch evydence so geven was p[ar]telye of their owne free will and p[ar]telye by the subornac[i]on and sinister p[er]swasions fayre p[ro]myses
11. huge offers and great gyft[es] to them to be geven of Will[ia]m Hambridge Anthony Hambridge John Gawtrell Elizabeth Gawtrell John
12. Myddleton Will[ia]m Myddleton Nicholas Traske[3] Richarde Dybble thelder Will[ia]m Yngram John Palmer and others as yo[u]r saide
13. Subjecte verilye thinkethe So yt is may yt please yo[u]r most excellent ma[ges]ti that the said Robert Webbe & Gyles
14. Hambridge not having the feare of god before their eyes nor regardinge yo[u]r ma[ges]t[es] lawes have to the highe dyspleasure of
15. God undewtifully corruptelye and wilfully contrary to yo[u]r highenes lawes in that behalfe made and p[ro]vyded therin commytted
16. manifeste and wilfull p[er]jurye to the great losse ~~and~~ hyndrance and impoverishement of yo[u]r said Subjecte and to the great incoridgment

17. of dyvers oth[e]r lyke lewde desp[er]ate and ill dysposed p[er]sones attemptinge to com[m]ytt the lyke offence yf that most abhomynable and

18. execrable offence of p[er]jurye should escape unponyshed In Considerac[i]on whereof and for as muche as such unlawfull subornac[i]on and

19. sinister p[er]swasions of witnesses to testifie be yonde their knowledge and more then truthe is not onely a thinge verye p[er]nicious and detestable

20. before god but also such an evell example and indirecte practize by reason and meanes whereof the lyves land[es] lyving[es] and good[es] of

21. any yo[u]r subjectes may be by the testimonye and evidence of such lyke falce and corrupte witnesses be taken from them unjustly And for

22. that also that the same unhonest sleight[es] and practizes tende onely to the mayntaynance of vyce and wickednesse and to the gret

23. lett and hinderance of the dewe execuc[i]on and administrac[i]on of Justice and lawe May yt th[e]rfore please yo[u]r highenes the p[re]misses[4]

24. tenderly considered to graunt to yo[u]r said Subjecte yo[u]r most Gracious writes of Sub pena to be directed to them the said Robert Webbe

25. Gyles Hambridge Will[ia]m Hambridge Anthony Hambridge John Gawtrell Elizabeth Gawtrell John Myddleton Will[ia]m Myddleton

26. Nicholas Traske Richard Dibbell the elder Richard Dybbell the yonger Will[ia]m Yngram and John Palmer comaundinge and

27. enjoyninge them and every of them by vertue of the same p[er]sonally to appeare before yo[u]r ma[ges]ti or yo[u]r ma[ges]t[es] Counsell in yo[u]r highe Court of

28. Starre Chamber at a certeine day and under a certeine payne by yo[u]r ma[ges]ti to be lymyted and appoynted then and th[e]r to answere

29. *to the p[re]misses and furth[er]* to stand to and abyde suche order and direcc[i]on therein as to yo[u]r highenes said Counsell <in the said Court> shall ~~seme~~

30. be thoughte mete and convenyent And yo[u]r said subjecte according to his most bounden dewtie shall dayly

31. pray to god for the p[ro]sperous preservac[i]on of yo[u]r Royall ma[ges]ti longe to Raigne over us

Dale

[28]

COMMENTARY

Bill in the Court of Star Chamber
(TNA:PRO ref: STAC 5/H6/9)

Document

For a brief description of this court and records, see commentary on plate 24. This case of assault etc. is typical of the subject matter often dealt with by this court, and is rather more outspoken than most.

Script

This is a further example of secretary hand. The letters *d*, *p* and *w* appear to have indistinguishable small and capital initial letters. The medial and final *d* is sometimes at such an angle that it crosses other ascenders, e.g. in the word 'should' in l. 18; the letter *h* varies in form (see for instance 'thinkethe' in l. 13) and in legibility; and the *a* is rather flat and has in many cases a diagonal line above it to a greater or smaller extent and in some cases an introductory line for extra confusion. As in some of the other documents there are abbreviations which are probably no more than a formality.

Notes

1. Magesti: abbreviation as it appears is uncertain in form but is normally Matie. The transcript spells extensions with the letter *g* to conform with the spelling in line 2. Note also the later examples of the word ending in *i*.
2. A slightly curious abbreviation appears here and subsequently but the meaning is clear.
3. In fact there appears to be part of another letter after the *a* in this name though insufficient to be *e*; cf. Traske in l. 26.
4. Premisses: (otherwise premises) i.e. (here and subsequently) in this context means what has been previously mentioned (from Latin *premittere* which equally gives rise to the meaning of land etc. previously mentioned).

(Plate and transcript on previous spreads)

COMMENTARY

Part of Interrogatories and Depositions Made in Respect of a Theatre
(TNA:PRO ref: E 133/10/1521, ff 1r, 1v, 2r, 4r)

Document

For a note on depositions and their use to both genealogists and local historians see commentary on plate 20. In this case interrogatory 11 mentions Cuthbert the son of James Burbage. These documents are of particular interest due to the information about the early theatre built by James Burbage (for whom see an article in the *D.N.B.*). The single interrogatory, descriptions of two deponents and parts of their depositions have been extracted from their original positions in the documents and here combined.

Script

The deplorable hand in which the depositions are written is typical of a great many documents of this kind. Abysmal as the writing seems, a little practice in recognising certain shapes, such as the perfunctory versions of the words 'the', 'to' and 'be', and the horizontal line suppressing the form of several minims in combination, such as *im* or *in* (not unknown in modern handwriting) will gradually enable the eye to identify most words. However, it is not always possible to be fully confident of the exact letters intended by the scribe and for this reason it has seemed best here to transcribe by putting in brackets the letters which are indicated by actual or omitted abbreviation marks, and otherwise postulating in some cases what general scrutiny of this hand suggests is intended.

Notes

1. A usual word then for 'since'.
2. 25th October 44 (i.e. in the reign of Elizabeth, so in the year 1602).
3. The scribe has departed into Latin for the date and apparently also for the county (hence the apparently Latin county name has not been extended).
4. This curious mark seems, in view of the very brief indication of the word later in this deposition, the letter *t* with small abbreviation mark in the deposition of Henry Johnson, and the wording of the interrogatory, to stand for 'tenaunt' (to use the scribe's spelling elsewhere).
5. The third letter is ambiguous.
6. Thus it appears from the beginning of the word and the context.

(Plates and transcripts on following spread)

Part of the Interrogatories and Depositions made in Respect of a Theatre

(TNA:PRO ref: E 133/10/1521, ff 1r, 1v, 2r, 4r)

9

1. **Item** Whether did one James Burbage as Tena[u]nte to the defend[an]t builde a playing place called
2. the Theatre uppon p[ar]te of the saide voide grounde letten unto him by the saide defend[an]t lying w[i]thin the
3. Lower gate of the saide Priorye and whether did the defend[an]t lett som[m]e other p[ar]te of the saide voide grounde
4. unto his tena[u]nt[es] to be imployed for garden plott[es] and whether were the same imployed accordinglie and
5. by whome and howe long sithence[1]

25° die octobr[is] 44[2]

6. John Goburne of Chesson in com[itatu] Hertf[r3] <late citizen &> merch[an]t taylo[u]r of the citty of lo[ndon]
7.
8. aged 44 yeres &c

9

9. that ~~one~~ James Burbage & in the Int[errogatory] named & <one> John Braynes <as t[enaunt][4] &> under the
10. title of the s[ai]d def[endant] caused a playing ~~howse~~[5] place calld the theatre to be build
11. uppon p[ar]te of the s[ai]d void ground letten unto him by the s[ai]d def[endant] lyeing w[i]thin the
12. lower gate of the <s[ai]d> priory & that the def[endant] ~~let~~ did also let to the s[ai]d Burbage
13. some other p[ar]te of the s[ai]d void ground ~~unto the s[ai]d Burbage~~ who did let
14. the same in sev[er]all p[ar]cells to sundry t[en]a[untes] dwelling there to be imployed for
15. garden plots & some of them were so imployed accordingly ~~atl~~ w[hi]ch
16. hathe bene so done synce this d[e]p[on]e[ntes] knowledge thereof both by the s[ai]d
17. def[endant] & Burbage

18. Henrie Johnson of Shortditch in the cou[nty] of Midd[lesex] ~~brick citizen~~ <tyler> & bricklayer of lo[ndon] aged 55 yeres
19. or th[ere]ab[outs]

9

20. that James Burbage as t[enaunt] to the def[endant] did about 25 or <26> yeres last past build a playing
21. place calld the theatre uppon p[ar]te of the s[ai]d void ground letten unto him by the s[ai]d def[endan]t
22. lyeing w[i]thin the lower gate of the s[ai]d priory & that the def[endant] <about the time[6] afores[ai]d> did let some other p[ar]te of the
23. s[ai]d void ground unto his tena[u]nt[es] dwelling in the howses w[i]thin the ~~priory~~ lower gate of the
24. priory to be used by them ~~for garden plots or~~ <to> what other uses they thought fitt & more to that int[errogatory] *he*
25. canot depose

[29]

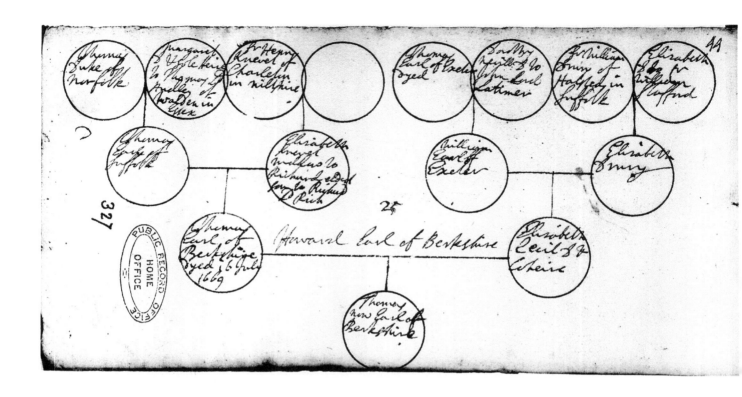

TRANSCRIPT

Pedigrees from State Papers

(TNA:PRO ref: SP 9/32, nos 327 and 328)

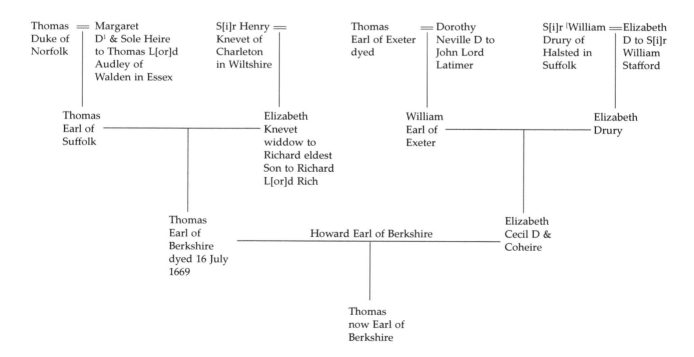

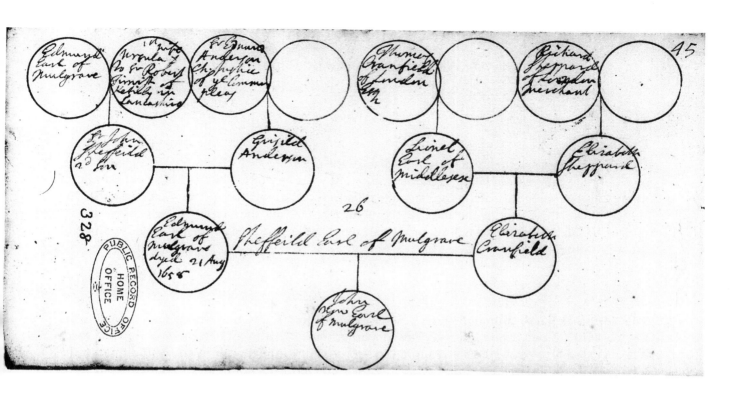

PUBLIC RECORD OFFICE HOME OFFICE

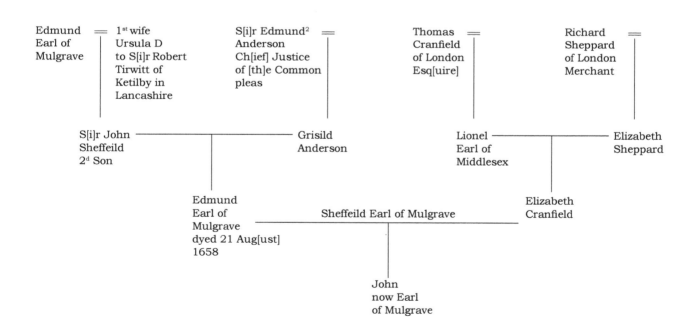

| Edmund Earl of Mulgrave | = | 1ˢᵗ wife Ursula D to S[i]r Robert Tirwitt of Ketilby in Lancashire | | S[i]r Edmund[2] Anderson Ch[ief] Justice of [th]e Common pleas | = | | Thomas Cranfield of London Esq[uire] | = | | Richard Sheppard of London Merchant | = |

S[i]r John Sheffeild 2ᵈ Son ——————————— Grisild Anderson

Lionel Earl of Middlesex ——————— Elizabeth Sheppard

Edmund Earl of Mulgrave dyed 21 Aug[ust] 1658 —————— Sheffeild Earl of Mulgrave

Elizabeth Cranfield

John now Earl of Mulgrave

[31]

COMMENTARY

Pedigrees from State Papers

(TNA:PRO ref: SP 9/32, nos 327 and 328)

Documents

These pedigrees of peers are shown in the list for the class SP 9 (which has much of genealogical and heraldic interest) as being compiled apparently about 1687. They belong in a bundle of many similar pedigrees of the aristocracy, illustrating the ancestry of the holder of the title shown above the name at the base of the pedigree. Despite the layout (in which the circles appear to have been made with compasses) none of the pedigrees appears to show all eight great-grandparents.

Script

This informal hand, although fairly uncomplicated, has a few awkward characteristics: the letter *o* tends to be written in a very open manner, thus often resembling *u*, and in some cases *a* is also similarly open; the *t* is seldom crossed so that it appears to resemble *l*, although the latter can generally be distinguished as it tends to be looped; capital and small letters in some instances, markedly in the case of *s* and *w*, appear indistinguishable, and have been transcribed as seems best.

Notes

1. To retain the original format, D (standing for Daughter) has not been extended.
2. In the rather cramped space the scribe appears to have omitted a minim.

(Plates and transcripts on previous spread)

COMMENTARY

Examination in the State Papers

(TNA:PRO ref: SP 12/167 p 78)

Document

The state papers (in varying forms temp. Henry VIII-Victoria) contain reference to a vast variety of topics giving rise in many cases to information on family matters which can include material for two or more generations. See notes on genealogical matters in particular in SP 9 (commentaries to plates 7, 30 and 31). The state papers include also much that is useful for local historians. This document is from the State Papers Domestic for a good part of which series there is a run of informative indexed calendars.

Script

See the note on plate 29 on similar writing. This hand is unfortunately very cursive and as in the case of many modern hands the formation of the letters cannot in parts fully justify what the scribe clearly intends. However the depositions will have given some insight to help with the reading of this document. Although one does gradually become accustomed to this kind of writing, it remains important to compare letters as, despite the difficulties, the hand is fairly consistent. The letter *a* tends to be very open, sometimes resembling *u*; superscript *c* and *t* are similar; *h* is often minimal, and final *r* negligible.

Notes

1. Note the elision.
2. By comparing this word with 'sayethe' (ll. 9 and 14) and with 'remaynethe' (l. 12), it seems that this spelling is intended. The year is 1583/4, the historical year 1584.
3. Possibly there is a second *o* in this word.
4. Thus apparently from the writing, but because the scribe's *o* sometimes resembles *e*, it may well be that Genova, i.e. Genoa, is intended.
5. A cousin german: a first cousin.

(Plate and transcript on following spread)

... of John Norton taken ... the ... of Denmarke in the ... of the Queenes mate Reignes.

27

He confesseth that he was borne at a place in Kent called (Westwell) neere the towne of Chylesnode. & was sonne to one Christopher Norton a gentleman who dwelt in the same place. And there dyed aboute fyfe yeres past. of the plague /

78

He sayeth that at the tyme of his fathers deathe, there were left alyve him self, and ij of his bretheren more, namelye Thomas Norton the eldest, who at this present ys at Roome, and Raphe Norton the yongest, who at this present remayneth at Geneva, as farr as this ex(aminate) ynte knoweth.

And he sayeth that his eldest Brother (Thomas Norton) hathe bene beyonde the seas best thing yeres & his second Brother Raphe Norton went also thither aboute one halfe yere after. And that the landes & leases w.ch his father left behynde him after his deceasse be esteemed worthe neere Twoo hundred & fyftye li. the yere: wherof his ij eldest bretheren are answered the profitt of the whole ... to the ... out of the landes, dwe onlye ... in ... dwellinge at (...) neere ... who hathe the yerelye profitt of the same landes & leases and doth answere the same to his sayd bretheren, sins theyre sayd theyre fathers deceasse /

He further confesseth that his father was often tymes to ... Christopher Norton the Rebell & was borne in Yorkeshyre /

... & he sayeth that his

[32]

TRANSCRIPT

Examination in the State Papers

(TNA:PRO ref: SP 12/167 p 78)

1.   Thexamynacyon[1] of John Norton taken the
2.   xvj[th] daye of Januarye in the xxvj[th] yere
3.   of the Quenes ma[jes]t[es] Raygne[2]

4. He Confessethe that he was borne at a place in Kent
5. Called (Westwell) neere the towne of Ashefurde & was soon[n]e
6. to one Chrystopher Norton a gentellman who dwelt in the
7. same place and there dyed abowte five yeres past of the
8. plauge

9. He sayethe that at the tyme of his Fathers deathe there were
10. left alyve him self and ij of his brotherne more namelye
11. Thom[a]s Norton the eldest who at this present ys at Rome[3]
12. and Richard Norton the seconde who at this present remaynethe
13. at Geneva[4] as farr as this examyn[an]te knowethe

14. It[e]m he sayethe that his eldest Brother (Thom[a]s Norton) hathe
15. bene beyonde the seas these viij yeres & his second Brother
16. Richard Norton went allso thether w[i]t[h]in one half yere after and
17. that the lands & leases w[hi]che his father left behynd him after
18. his deceasse be estymated wurthe neere Twoo hundrethe pounds
19. by the yere wherof his ij eldest bretherne are answered the
20. profitt of the whole joynctelye togeather this examyn[an]te havynge
21. onlye Tenn pounds by the yere pencyon owt of the lands And
22. that one Mr Bygg[es] dwellynge at (Fordyche) neere Canterburye
23. Dothe receave the yerelye profitt[es] of the same lands & leasses and
24. dothe answere the same to his sayed bretherne And hathe so done
25. ever sithence his fathers deceasse

26. He further Confessethe that his Father was Cosen Jermyne[5] to
27. Chrystopher Norton the Rebell & was borne in Yorkesheere

Anno Domini, 1636.
Anno RR. Caroli. 12.

27. die Martij, baptizata erat Margareta Arden, filia
Georgij Arden, et Sibilla Ux. eius: Ano et sup.ᵃ

ult.º die Martij, baptizatᵘˢ erat Richardᵘˢ Rowdon, f.º
Eduardi Rowdon (gen.), et Anna Ux. eius: Ao et sup.ᵃ

9. die Aprilis, bapt.ᵃ erat Maria Burrhopp, f.ᵃ
Johis Burrhopp, et Dorothea Ux: eius: Ao et sup.ᵃ

19. die Aprilis, baptizatᵘˢ erat Eduardᵘˢ Filor, filius
Richardi Filor, et Anna Ux. eius: Ano et sup.ᵃ

29. die Aprilis, bapt.ᵘˢ erat (ap. Barton) Philippᵘˢ Finch, fil.º
Antonij Finch, et Jocosa Ux. eius: Ano et suprà.

4. die Maij, baptizata erat Jana Hooper, filia
Thoma Hoop (iun.), al̃s. Jennings, et Margareta Ux. eius: ao. ut.

15. die Maij, baptizata erat Jana Michill, filia
Johis Michill, et Gratia Ux. eius: Ano et suprà.

eod. tempore, baptizata erat Jana Budget, filia
Walteri Budget, et Margareta Ux. eius: ao et sup.ᵃ

29. die Maij, bapt.ᵃ erat (ap. Pencombe) ffrancisca Galdoe, f.ᵃ
Ægidij Galdoe, et Alicia Ux. eius: Ano et sup.ᵃ

5. die Junij, baptizata erat Elizabetha Davis, f.ᵃ
Humfredi Davis, et Jocosa Ux. eius: Ao et supra.

26. die Junij, baptizatᵘˢ erat Richardᵘˢ Rowles, filius
Johis Rowles, et Alicia Ux. eius: Ano et suprà.

[33]

TRANSCRIPT AND TRANSLATION

Baptisms in the Parish Register
of Bromyard, Herefordshire

(Herefordshire Record Office ref: AH21/1)

1	Anno Domini 1636
	In the year of the lord 1636
2	Anno R[egni] R[egis] Caroli 12
	In the 12[th] year of the reign of King Charles
3	27 die Martii baptizata erat[1] <u>Margareta</u> Arden filia
4	Georgii Arden et Sibillæ ux[oris] eius An[n]o ut sup[er]a
	On the 27[th] day of March was baptized Margaret Arden daughter
	of George Arden and Sibyl his wife in the year as above
5	ult[im]o die Martii baptizat[us] erat <u>Richard[us]</u> Rowdon f[ilius]
6	Eduardi Rowdon (gen[erosi]) et Annæ ux[oris] eius A[nn]o ut sup[er]a
	On the last day of March was baptized Richard Rowdon son
	of Edward Rowdon (gentleman) and Anne his wife in the year as above
7	9 die Aprilis bapt[izat]a erat <u>Maria</u> Burrhopp f[ili]a
8	Joh[ann]is Burrhopp et Dorotheæ ux[oris] eius A[nn]o ut sup[er]a
	On the 9[th] day of April was baptized Mary Burrhopp daughter
	of John Burrhopp and Dorothy his wife in the year as above
9	19 die Aprilis baptizat[us] erat <u>Eduard[us]</u> Tiler filius
10	Richardi Tiler et Annæ ux[oris] eius An[n]o ut sup[er]a
	On the 19[th] day of April was baptized Edward Tiler son
	of Richard Tiler and Anne his wife in the year as above
11	29 die Aprilis bapt[izatus] erat (ap[u]d Wacton) <u>Philipp[us]</u> Finch fil[ius]
12	Antonii Finch et Jocosæ ux[oris] eius An[n]o ut supra[2]
	On the 29[th] day of April was baptized (at Wacton) Philip Finch son
	of Anthony Finch and Joyce his wife in the year as above
13	4 die Maii baptizata erat <u>Jana</u> Hooper Filia
14	Thomæ Hoop[er] (jun[ioris]) al[ia]s Jen[n]ings et Margaretæ ux[oris] eius a[nn]o etc
	On the 4[th] day of May was baptized Jane Hooper daughter
	of Thomas Hooper (junior) otherwise Jennings and Margaret his wife in the year etc.
15	15 die Maii baptizata erat <u>Jana</u> Michill Filia
16	Joh[ann]is Michill et Gratiæ ux[oris] eius An[n]o ut supra
	On the 15[th] day of May was baptized Jane Michill daughter
	of John Michill and Grace his wife in the year as above
17	eod[em] tempore baptizata erat <u>Jana</u> Budget Filia
18	Walteri Budget et Margaretæ ux[oris] eius a[nn]o ut sup[er]a
	At the same time was baptized Jane Budget daughter
	of Walter Budget and Margaret his wife in the year as above
19	29 die Maii bapt[izat]a erat (ap[u]d Pencombe) <u>Francisca</u> Caldoe f[ili]a
20	Ægidii Caldoe et Aliciæ ux[oris] eius An[n]o ut sup[er]a
	On the 29[th] day of May was baptized (at Pencombe) Frances Caldoe daughter
	of Giles Caldoe and Alice his wife in the year as above
21	5 die Junii baptizata erat <u>Elizabetha</u> Davis f[ili]a
22	Humfredi Davis et Jocosæ ux[oris] eius A[nn]o ut supra
	On the 5[th] day of June was baptized Elizabeth Davis daughter
	of Humphrey Davis and Joyce his wife in the year as above
23	26 die Junii baptizat[us] erat <u>Richard[us]</u> Rowles filius
24	Joh[ann]is Rowles et Aliciæ ux[oris] eius An[n]o ut supra
	On the 26[th] day of June was baptized Richard Rowles son
	of John Rowles and Alice his wife in the year as above

Anno Domini · 1625 ·———

Anno RR· Jacobi· 23·, et Caroli primo

4· die Junij, matrimonium fuit Cñolommizatu, intèr Johanem Hughes, als, Reynolds, et Jorosa Dauis: Añō Bt sup̃.

16· die Junij, matrimonium fuit Solommizatum, intèr Richardu Hallowas, et Alicia Arton: Añō Bt sup̃.

eod· die Junij, matrimonium fuit Solommizatu, intèr Thoma Brooks, et Elizabetha Asido, vid·: Añō Bt sup̃.

29· die Junij, matrimonium fuit Solommizatum, intèr Humfredu Gyttoos, et Maria Hawkins: Añō Bt sup̃.

23· die Julij, matrimonium fuit Solommizatum, intèr Johanem Millard, et Mariam Morris: Añō Bt sup̃.

7· die Dec·, matrimoniũ fuit solommizat· (ap̃ dlingoworks), intèr Christophorũ Capper, et Maria Mason: Añō Bt sup̃.

2· die ffebruarij, matrimoniũ fuit Solommizat·, intèr Eduardu Bucknam, et Johama ffronts, vid·: Añō Bt sup̃.

21· die ffebruarij, matrimonium fuit Solommizatu, intèr Johanem Stenard, et Elizabetha Berry: Añō Bt sup̃.

TRANSCRIPT AND TRANSLATION

Marriages in the Parish Register of Bromyard, Herefordshire

(Herefordshire Record Office ref: AH21/1)

1. Anno Domini 1625
   In the year of the Lord 1625
2. Anno R[egni] R[egis] Jacobi 23 et Caroli <u>primo</u>
   In the 23[rd] year of the reign of King James and in the first of Charles
3. 4 die Junii matrimonium fuit Solemnizatu[m][3] inter
4. Johan[n]em Hughes al[ia]s Reynold[es] et Jocosa[m] Davis A[nn]o ut sup[er]a
   On the 4[th] day of June a marriage was solemnized between
   John Hughes otherwise Reynoldes and Joyce Davis in the year as above
5. 16 die Junii matrimonium fuit Solemnizatum inter
6. Richardu[m] Halloway et Alicia[m] Acton An[n]o ut sup[er]a
   On the 16[th] day of June a marriage was solemnized between
   Richard Halloway and Alice Acton in the year as above
7. eod[em] die Junii matrimonium fuit Solemnizatu[m] inter
8. Thoma[m] Brooke et Elizabetha[m] Fido vid[uam] An[n]o ut sup[er]a
   On the same day of June a marriage was solemnized between
   Thomas Brooke and Elizabeth Fido widow in the year as above
9. 29 die Junii matrimonium fuit Solemnizatum inter
10. Humfredu[m] Gyttoes et Maria[m] Hawkins A[nn]o ut sup[er]a
    On the 29[th] day of June a marriage was solemnized between
    Humphrey Gyttoes and Mary Hawkins in the year as above
11. 23 die Julii matrimonium fuit Solemnizatum inter
12. Johannem Millard et Mariam Morris A[nn]o ut sup[er]a
    On the 23[rd] day of July a marriage was solemnized between
    John Millard and Mary Morris in the year as above
13. 7 die Dec[embris] matrimoniu[m] fuit solemnizat[um] (ap[u]d Ullingewicke)
14. inter Christophoru[m] Capper et Maria[m] Mason A[nn]o ut sup[er]a
    On the 7[th] day of December a marriage was solemnized (at Ullingewicke)
    between Christopher Capper and Mary Mason in the year as above
15. 2 die Februarii matrimoniu[m] fuit Solemnizat[um] inter
16. Eduardu[m] Bucknam et Johanna[m] French vid[uam] A[nn]o ut sup[er][4]
    On the 2[nd] day of February a marriage was solemnized between
    Edward Bucknam and Joan French widow in the year as above
17. 21 die Februarii matrimonium fuit Solemnizatu[m] inter
18. Johannem Steward et Elizabetha[m] Berry An[n]o ut sup[er]a
    On the 21[st] day of February a marriage was solemnized between
    John Steward and Elizabeth Berry in the year as above

COMMENTARY

Baptisms and Marriages in the Parish Register of Bromyard, Herefordshire
(Herefordshire Record Office ref: AH21/1)

Documents

Parish registers are the backbone of the proof for much genealogical deduction and a family historian would be pleased to find registers in such good condition as these. It is only in the last few decades that, due to the strictures laid upon their preservation, they have now mostly been deposited in county record offices etc. rather than being kept in their parishes. Where they are defective, however, a search for bishops' transcripts may fill the gap (and in some cases in fact enhance the information which is available in the parish register). Useful books are *The Parish Chest* by William E. Tate (1969), and *The History of Parish Registers in England* by John Southerden Burn (1976 reprint from edn. of 1862).

Script

For clarity of writing these pages of baptisms and marriages compare extremely well with many of the period. Some of the methods of abbreviation are not of a regular nature (e.g. *fᵃ*), but what is intended is unquestionable and slight variations have not here been distinguished by italics. Note the use of the abbreviation resembling a superscript 9 and representing *-us*.

Notes

1. The tense here is curious, being an exact translation for the English for 'was baptized' but strictly being in Latin the passive pluperfect. The wording in the translation is as the writer appears to have intended.
2. Note how the words *supera* and *supra* (having the same meaning) appear to be used indiscriminately. This seems to be purely at whim, since there are no constraints of space as in the following entry.
3. Here also the writer has avoided a normal Latin past tense with words that nonetheless convey the intended meaning.
4. *Super* is yet another adverb with the meaning of 'above', but perhaps a superscript letter *a* is omitted.

(Plates, transcripts and translations on previous two spreads)

COMMENTARY

Lay Subsidy of Yeadon in the Wapentake of Skyrack, W.R. Yorkshire
(TNA:PRO ref: E 179/207/200, rot 5)

Document

Lay subsidies (of which surviving records run from the 13th to the 17th centuries) were intermittent taxes raised for the monarch. The records of particular use show lists of names under place-name headings which are often the names of tithings (for identifying which the E 179 data-base is a useful tool) within a larger area such as a hundred, wapentake or lathe. Taxation (shown in right column) was levied on assessed value (shown in left column). Entries may give the value in goods, i.e. possessions, but sometimes indicate it in lands or wages. Generally, the more substantial people are named at or near the beginning of the lists. It is only for a small number of individuals that any extra information is forthcoming e.g. here several are shown as widows, and sometimes a rank, descriptions as senior and junior (not necessarily indicating father and son) or occasionally occupations are found, but the lists are very useful both for genealogists and local historians in giving names of inhabitants at a certain place at a certain time. It has to be remembered, however, that differing proportions of the inhabitants occur in the periodic subsidies and that, though the presence of a name is very interesting, the absence of a name does not indicate its non-existence there. The poll taxes of the late 14th century are particularly valuable. There were separate subsidy records for clerics.

Script

This is a fairly informal but regular form of secretary hand. The letter *m* appears the same whether capital or small. It is interesting to note instances of *yogh* – a late use of this character; and that some of the abbreviations appear one above the other (in *Willelmus*).

Notes

1. In this line and in ll. 3 and 19 the character *yogh*, rather than *Y* or *y*, is used.
2. The Greek letters χ, *chi* (for *ch*) and ρ, *rho* (for *r*) appear here (as in churches etc.) to indicate Christ as the first part of the name.
3. Swayn: it is possible that the apparent mark of abbreviation here is a formality without significance, but the writer does not in this section add any such flourish to other names ending in the letter *n*. It is not an orthodox abbreviation, but an ending of *s* or *er* may have been intended.
4. The writing indicates ij^d, but the tax for others against xx^s is only j^d, and the total at the end is not right if this is taken as ij^d.

(Plate, transcript and translation on following spread)

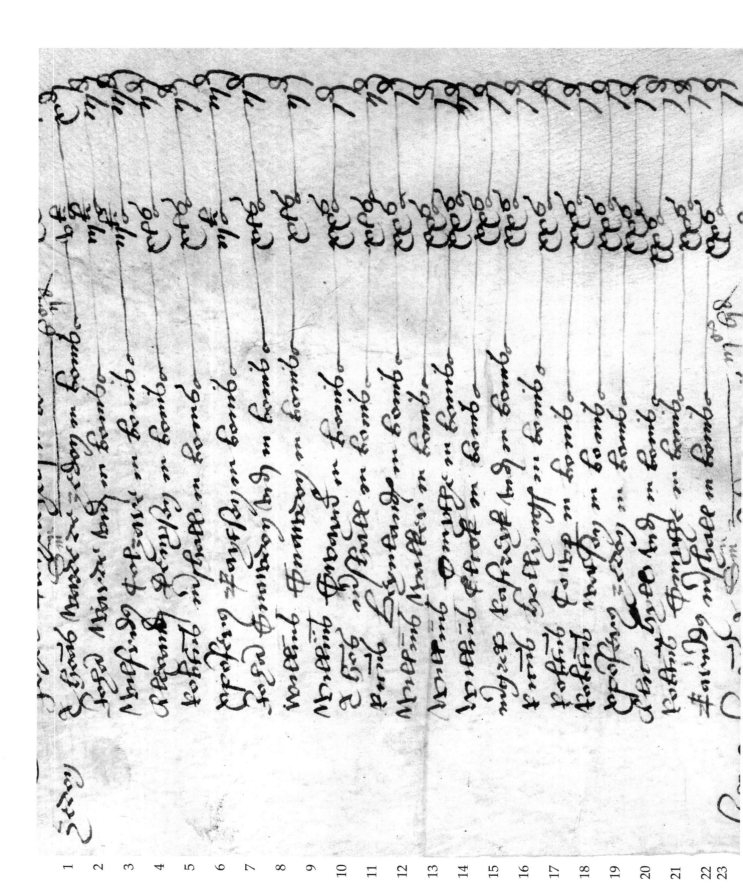

[35]

Lay Subsidy of Yeadon in the Wapentake of Skyrack, W.R. Yorkshire

(TNA:PRO ref: E 179/207/200, rot 5)

TRANSCRIPT

[Yedon][1]

1.	Tho[m]as Warde de [Y]edon in bonis	v^{li} x^{d}
2.	Joh[ann]a Warde vid[ua] in bonis	iij^{li} iij^{d}
3.	Wilfrid[us] Coll[y]are in bonis	iij^{li} iij^{d}
4.	Alexand[er] Denyson in bonis	xl^{s} ij^{d}
5.	Rob[er]tus M[ar]shall in bonis	xl^{s} ij^{d}
6.	[Christ]ofer[us][2] Baytson in bonis	iij^{li} iij^{d}
7.	Joh[ann]a Snawdon vid[ua] in bonis	xl^{s} ij^{d}
8.	Will[el]m[u]s Snawdon in bonis	xl^{s} ij^{d}
9.	Will[el]m[u]s Swayn[3] in bonis	xx^{s} j^{d}
10.	Tho[m]as M[ar]shall in bonis	xl^{s} ij^{d}
11.	Ric[ard]us Beynland[es] in bonis	xx^{s} j^{d}
12.	Will[el]m[u]s Walker in bonis	xx^{s} j^{d}
13.	Will[el]m[u]s Smythe in bonis	xx^{s} ij^{d4}
14.	Will[el]m[u]s Elcok in bonis	xx^{s} j^{d}
15.	M[ar]gret[a] Rastreyk vid[ua] in bonis	xx^{s} j^{d}
16.	Ric[ard]us Hollyng[es] in bonis	xx^{s} j^{d}
17.	Rob[er]tus Cowp[er] in bonis	xx^{s} j^{d}
18.	Rob[er]tus Watson in bonis	xx^{s} j^{d}
19.	[Christ]ofer[us] [Y]edon in bonis	xx^{s} j^{d}
20.	Alic[ia] Hyll vid[ua] in bonis	xx^{s} j^{d}
21.	Rob[er]tus Smythe in bonis	xx^{s} j^{d}
22.	Barn[ar]d[us] M[ar]shall in bonis	xx^{s} j^{d}
23.	S[u]m[m]a	iij^{s} vj^{d}

TRANSLATION

1. Yedon

1.	Thomas Warde of Yedon in goods	£5	10d.
2.	Joan Warde widow in goods	£3	3d.
3.	Wilfrid Colyare in goods	£3	3d.
4.	Alexander Denyson in goods	40s.	2d.
5.	Robert Marshall in goods	40s.	2d.
6.	Christopher Baytson in goods	£3	3d.
7.	Joan Snawdon widow in goods	40s.	2d.
8.	William Snawdon in goods	40s.	2d.
9.	William Swayn[3] in goods	20s.	1d.
10.	Thomas Marshall in goods	40s.	2d.
11.	Richard Beylandes in goods	20s.	1d.
12.	William Walker in goods	20s.	1d.
13.	William Smythe in goods	20s.	2d.[4]
14.	William Elcok in goods	20s.	1d.
15.	Margaret Rastreyk widow in goods	20s.	1d.
16.	Richard Hollynges in goods	20s.	1d.
17.	Robert Cowper in goods	20s.	1d.
18.	Robert Watson in goods	20s.	1d.
19.	Christopher Yedon in goods	20s.	1d.
20.	Alice Hyll widow in goods	20s.	1d.
21.	Robert Smythe in goods	20s.	1d.
22.	Barnard Marshall in goods	20s.	1d.
23.	Total	3s.	6d.

London Walk   March 173⅔

ffrancisca Andrews alias Mootham... Decimo quinto die em Com̃ Nathanieli uc̃ Septembrij Andrews Marito ultim̃ Francisca Andrews als Mootham nuper paroc̃ St Dionisij Backchurch London defc̃ā hentij &c̃ ad adfrandum bona jura et credita dict̃ā defc̃ō de bene &c̃ Jurat ult Martij 1734

Sarah Bowers otherwise Crowder... On the thirtieth day Admcon of the Goods Chattels and Credits of Sarah Bowers otherwise Crowder late of the parish of St Leonard Shoreditch in the County of Midx Widow deced having Goods in divers Jurisdicons was granted to John Crowder the natl and lawfull Son of the sd deced being first sworn duly to administer - - - - September March 1734

John Zouch Baker On the twenty ninth day Admcon of the Goods Chattels and Credits of John Zouch Baker late of the parish of St Leonard Shoreditch in the County of Midx Batchelor deced having Goods in divers Jurisdicons was granted to Samuel Baker The natural & lawfull Brother (and next of kin of the sd deced being first sworn duly to administer - - - - September March 1734

Sara Brush Vicesimo primo die em Com̃ Johanni Brush Patri natꝰ et ultimo Sara Brush nuper paroc̃ St Jacobi Clerkenwell in Com̃ Midx Soluta defc̃ā hen &c̃ ad adfrand bona jura et credita dict̃ā defc̃ō de bene &c̃ Jurat - - uc̃ Sept ult Martij 1734

Elizabetha Beaumont Decimo sexto die em Com̃ Elizabetha Beaumont Soluta filia natꝰ et ultima Elizabetha Beaumont nuper paroc̃ St Andreæ Holborn London Vidua defc̃ā hentij &c̃ ad adfrandum bona jura et credita dict̃ā defc̃ō de bene &c̃ Jurat uc̃ Septembrij ult Martij 1734

TRANSCRIPT AND TRANSLATION

Grants of Administration

(TNA:PRO ref: PROB 6/109, f 47v)

1.   **London Walk**[1]   **March 1732/3**

2. **Francisca Andrews**   Decimo quinto die em[anavi]t Com[missi]o Nathanieli

    Frances Andrews   *On the fifteenth day a commission was granted to Nathaniel*

3. **alias Mootham**   Andrews Marito l[egi]timo Franciscæ

    otherwise Mootham   *Andrews the lawful husband of Frances*

4.   Andrews al[ia]s Mootham nuper paro[chi]æ

                       Andrews otherwise Mootham late of the parish

5. S[anc]ti Dionisii Backchurch London def[unc]tæ h[ab]entis &c ad

    of Saint Dionis Backchurch London deceased having &c. to

6. ad[mini]strandum bona iura et credita dictæ def[unc]tæ de bene &c Iurat[o]

    administer the goods rights and credits of the said deceased for well &c. he
    having been sworn

ult[imus] Septembris[2]
last [day] of September

ult[imus] Martii 1734[2]
last [day] of March 1734

7. **Sarah Bowers**   On the thirtieth day Adm[inistrat]ion of the Good[es]

8. **otherwise Crowder**   Chattels and Credits of Sarah Bowers

9.   otherwise Crowder late of the parish of

10. S[ain]t Leonard Shoreditch in the County of Midd[lese]x Widow

11. dec[eas]ed (having Goods in divers Juris[di]c[i]ons) was granted to

12. John Crowder the n[atu]ral and lawfull Son of the s[ai]d dec[eas]ed

13. being first sworn duly to administer

September

March 1734

14. **John Zouch Baker**   On the twenty ninth day Adm[inistrat]ion of

15. the Goods Chattels and Credits of John Zouch Baker late

16. of the parish of S[ain]t Leonard Shoreditch in the County

17. of Mid[dlesex] Batchelor dec[eas]ed (having Goods in divers Juris[di]c[i]ons)

18. was granted to Samuel Baker the natural & lawfull

19. Brother and next of kin of the s[ai]d dec[eas]ed being first

20. sworn duly to administer

September

March 1734

21. **Sara Brush**   Vicesimo primo die em[anavi]t Com[missi]o Johanni Brush Patri

    Sarah Brush   *On the twenty first day a commission was granted to John Brush*

22. n[atu]rali et l[egi]timo Saræ Brush nuper paro[chi]æ S[anc]ti Jacobi

    the natural and lawful father of Sarah Brush late of the parish of Saint James

23. Clerkenwell in Com[itatu] Mid' Solutæ def[unc]tæ h[ab]en[tis] &c ad

    Clerkenwell in the county of Middlesex spinster deceased having &c. to
    ad[mini]strand[um]
    administer

24. bona iura et credita dictæ def[unc]tæ de bene &c Iurat[o]

    the goods rights and credits of the said deceased for well &c. he having been sworn

ult[imus] Sept[embris]
last [day] of September

ult[imus] Martii 1734
last [day] of March 1734

25. **Elizabetha Beaumont**   Decimo sexto die em[anavi]t Com[missi]o

    Elizabeth Beaumont   *On the sixteenth day a commission was granted*

26. Elizabethæ Beaumont Solutæ filiæ n[atu]rali et l[egi]timæ

    to Elizabeth Beaumont spinster the natural and lawful daughter

27. Elizabethæ Beaumont nuper paro[chi]æ S[anc]ti Andreæ

    of Elizabeth Beaumont late of the parish of Saint Andrew

28. Holborn London Viduæ def[unc]tæ h[ab]entis &c ad ad[mini]strandum

    Holborn London widow deceased having &c. to administer

29. bona iura et credita dictæ def[unc]tæ de bene &c Iurat[æ]

    the goods rights and credits of the said deceased for well &c. she having been sworn

ult[imus] Septembris
last [day] of September

ult[imus] Martii 1734
last [day] of March 1734

[36]

COMMENTARY

Grants of Administration
(TNA:PRO ref: PROB 6/109, f 47v)

Document

Letters of administration could be granted (by, at this period, one of many ecclesiastical probate courts, generally depending on the place of residence) in the absence of a will. Although the information given is usually much less useful than that found in a will, it is nonetheless valuable. It was usually the case that the administrator was a wife, husband or relation and, of course, the discovery of an administration can at least terminate a fruitless search for a will. This page of entries has been chosen to illustrate the change from Latin to English on 25th March 1733. The entries do not appear chronologically, but those dated before the 25th (then computed as 1732, and sometimes shown as 1732/33) are in Latin, and those from 25th March (the first day of 1733) in English. For further information see, as for wills, *Wills and Their Whereabouts* by Anthony Camp (1974), and *Prerogative Court of Canterbury Wills and Other Probate Records* by Miriam Scott (1997).

Script

This is a very cramped hand and some of the abbreviated words seem initially rather obscure. However, since the wording is very similar in each entry, transcription should gradually prove less difficult. The somewhat curious sign of abbreviation mainly used, e.g. over *'ltimo'* in l. 3, is, though not unique, fairly unusual. Care should be taken to disentangle the ascenders and descenders. It would be worth transcribing the English entries before tackling those in Latin.

Notes

1. The London walk or seat was one of five areas dealing with administrations granted in the Prerogative Court of Canterbury. It covered the City of London and parts of Middlesex.
2. The days or months shown to the right of the entries show the time by which the inventory was to be submitted; and (below) the time by which the account was to be submitted.

(Plate, transcript and translation on previous spread)

COMMENTARY

Entries of Burial in the Parish Registers of Kingston, Surrey
(Surrey History Centre ref: P33/1/1)

Document

Parish registers began in 1538 so this page of burials is early and, since there are two hands mingled throughout the page, it thus appears not to have been one of those transcribed following the approval in 1598 by Elizabeth I of an order for parish registers to be copied (there being an option of copying from the year 1558). Although the page has a muddled appearance, it is nonetheless better than in many early registers in which the baptisms, marriages and burials occur together in indiscriminate order.

Script

It is noticeable that the use of capital letters for Christian names and surnames is so very erratic that in some cases there remains uncertainty. The letter *d* is particularly ambiguous. The entries made by the two scribes differ in that one scribe appears to use Roman numerals and to consider the day (*dies*), which can be masculine or feminine, to be generally feminine; the other to prefer Arabic numerals and to consider the day to be masculine. The former appears somewhat absent-minded, entering a rather unfortunate '*fui sepulta*' (translated as apparently intended) and on the bottom line beginning with an entry of a sum of money rather than a date. The tenses *sepultus/sepulta fuit* (generally preferred by the first scribe) and *sepultus/sepulta erat* (favoured by the second scribe) do not follow normal classical usage for the perfect passive tense (*sepultus/sepulta est*).

Notes

1. The superscript *a* (and in subsequent lines *ta* and *o*), the ablative endings of Latin ordinal numbers, are in this document found attached to both Roman and Arabic numbers, thus representing *tertia, quarto* etc. according to whether *dies* is taken to be m. or f.
2. Thus apparently, though faint, the only Roman numeral in this hand (so perhaps ambiguous).
3. Uncertain amount of first part of line evidently expunged.
4. The letter *i* appears to be interpolated, not superscript.
5. The symbol at the end of the word indicates, among other possibilities, *-is*, where *-i* would be expected here to fit the grammar.
6. Possibly expunged.
7. Annys: a form of Agnes. According to the *Oxford Dictionary of English Christian Names* (edn of 1977) Joan, Elizabeth and Agnes were the three most usual English feminine names in the 16th century. They make up nine of the 13 girls' names on this page of burials.
8. This scribe appears to have reverted to English here.

(Plate, transcript and translation on following spread)

1 ... die mensis decembris sepultus fuit Jacob ...
2 eodem die ... eiusdem mensis ... Katerina ...
3 ... die Elyzabeth Robynson
4 v. die mensis decembris sepulta erat Johanna torrence
5 14° sepultus erat nicholas wylson eod. die ...
6 15 die sepultus erat ...
7 ...a die eiusdem mensis Jacob ...
8 ... eiusdem mensis Jacob ... sepulta
9 ... die mensis decembris ...
10 ... sepultus erat
11 ... die eiusdem mensis Jacob ...
12

Januarij

13 ... die eiusdem mensis sepultus fuit
14 ...
15 ... die eiusdem mensis ... sunt sepulti fuit
16 ... die eiusdem mensis ... harden
17 sepultus fuit
18 14. die mensis Januarij Clemens ... sepult... erat
19 eodem die Anna ... A° d\[omi\]ni 1545
20 ... Allwrigane sepultus erat 15° die mensis ... in f...
21 ... die eiusdem mensis Jacob ... infan...
22 Margareta Coke sepulta erat 18 die mensis Januarij
23 eod die Elisabeth ... sepulta erat
24 Agneta heyward sepulta erat 19. die mensis Januarij d\[omi\]ni vt \[supra\]
25 ...a die Januarij ... ...
26 ...a die eiusdem mensis Elysabeth ... sepulti
27 ... sepulta   sepulta
28 ... die mensis februarij margareta lybb...
29 eodem die eiusdem mensis ... lybbat sepult...
30 ... die ... filia ... sepulta
31 sepulta ... die Jacob ... erat sepulta

1. December
2. iij[a] [1] die mensis decembris sepult[us] fuit Joh[ann]es Vale
   On the 3rd day of the month of December John Vale was buried
3. eodem die & eiusdem mens[is] Helena feriman
   On the same day & of the same month Helen Feriman
4. iiij[to] die Elysabethe Robynson
   On the 4th day Elizabeth Robynson
5. v[o] [2] Die me[n]s[is] Decembris Sepulta erat Johanna towrner
   On the 5th day of the month of December Joan Towrner was buried
6. 14[o] Sepult[us] erat nichola[us] wylson eod[em] Die q[u]id[am] Allinigena
   On the 14th Nicholas Wylson was buried   On the same day a certain stranger
7. 15 Die Sepult[us] erat nycholas Wylson
   On the 15[th] day Nicholas Wylson was buried
8. xviij[a] die eiusd[e]m mensis Joh[ann]a Thomas
   On the 18th day of the same month Joan Thomas
9. [3] xxj[a] die eiusdem mens[is] Joh[ann]a ley sepulta
   On the 21st day of the same month Joan Ley [was] buried
10. xxvj[a] die mens[is] decembris stephan[us]
11. Rosyar sepult[us] erat
    On the 26th day of the month of December Stephen Rosyar was buried
12. xxx[ta] die eiusdem mens[is] Joh[ann]es luttman
    On the 30th day of the same month John Luttman
13. January
14. iiij[ta] die eiusd[e]m s mens[is] sepult[us] fu[i]t[4]
15. Robertus powre
    On the 4th day of the same month Robert Powre was buried
16. x[a] die eiusd[e]m mens[is] Ricard[us] Hunt sepult[us] fuit
    On the 10th day of the same month Richard Hunt was buried
17. xj[a] die eiusd[e]m mensis Thurston Harden
18. sepult[us] fuit
    On the 11th day of the same month Thurston Harden was buried
19. 14[o] Die me[n]s[is] Ianuarii Clemens munday sepult[us] erat
    On the 14th day of the month of January Clement Munday was buried
20. Eodem die Anna Jenkyns   A[nn]o D[omi]ni 1545[o]
    On the same day Anne Jenkyns   In the 1545th year of the Lord
21. q[u]id[am] Allinegena sepultus erat 15[o] Die me[n]s[is] sup[r]a Dict[is][5] & A[nn]o ut s[upr]a
    A certain stranger was buried on the 15th day of the month abovesaid & in the year as above
22. eod[e]m die & eiusdem mensis Joh[ann]es Justyce <infans> puer[6]
    On the same day & of the same month John Justyce <an infant> a boy
23. Margareta Cooke sepulta erat 18 Die me[n]s[is] Ianuarii
    Margaret Cooke was buried the 18[th] day of the month of January
24. Eod[em] die Elisabeth[a] Robynson[6]   Sepulta erat
    On the same day Elizabeth Robynson   was buried
25. Agneta Heyward sepulta erat 19 Die me[n]s[is] Ianuarii A[nn]o ut s[upr]a
    Agnes Heyward was buried on the 19[th] day of the month of January in the year as above
26. xxj[a] die Ianuarii lawrence munday sepult[us] fuit
    On the 21st day of January Lawrence Munday was buried
27. xxjx[a] die eiusdem mensis Elysabethe Waremare
28. fui sepulta
    On the 29th day of the same month Elizabeth Waremare was buried
29. iiij[ta] die mensis februarii Margareta lybsothe sepulta
    On the 4th day of the month of February Margaret Lybsothe [was] buried
30. eod[e]m die & eiusd[e]m mens[is] Will[ia]m Tybert sepult[us]
    On the same day & of the same month William Tybert [was] buried
31. v[ta] die annys smyth filia Myls smyth erat
32. sepulta
    On the 5th day Annys[7] Smyth daughter of Miles[8] Smyth was buried
33. vjd vj[ta] die Joh[ann]a lurchen erat sepulta
    6d on the 6th day Joan Lurchen was buried

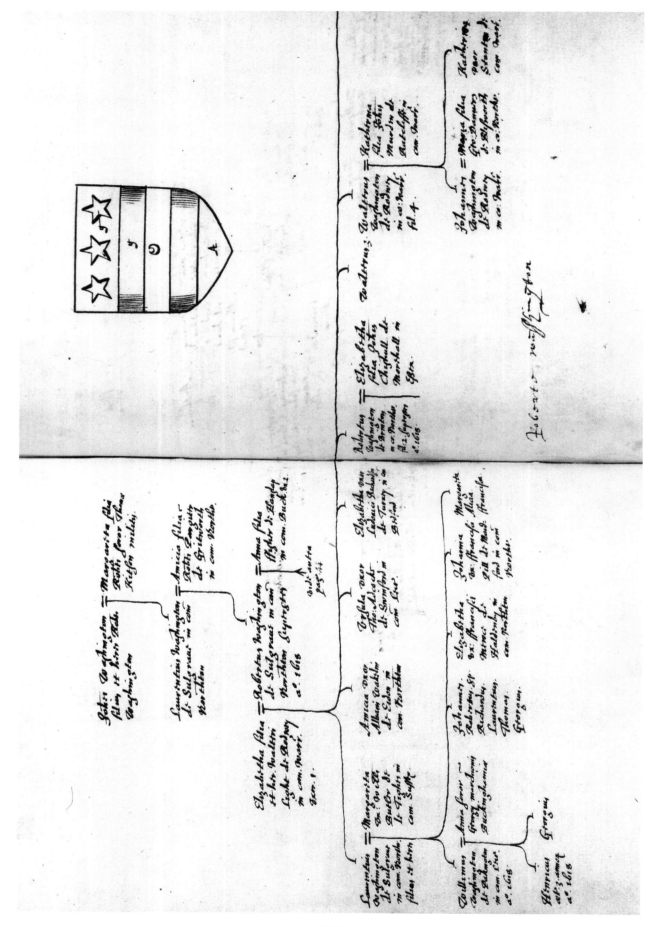

TRANSCRIPT

Pedigree in the Visitation of Northamptonshire, 1618-19

(College of Arms ref: C.14, ff. 87v-88r)

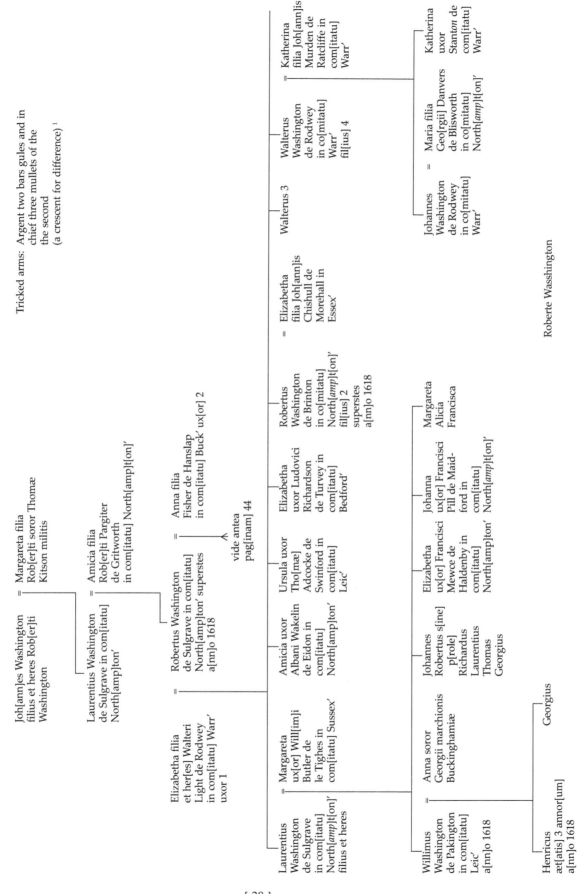

Tricked arms: Argent two bars gules and in chief three mullets of the second (a crescent for difference) [1]

Joh[ann]es Washington filius et heres Rob[er]ti Washington = Margareta filia Rob[er]ti soror Thomae Kitson militis

Laurentius Washington de Sulgrave in com[itatu] North[amp]ton' = Amicia filia Rob[er]ti Pargiter de Gritworth in com[itatu] North[amp]t[on]'

Robertus Washington de Sulgrave in com[itatu] North[amp]ton' superstes a[nn]o 1618 = Anna filia Fisher de Hanslap in com[itatu] Buck' ux[or] 2

vide antea pag[inam] 44

Elizabetha filia et her[es] Walteri Light de Rodwey in com[itatu] Warr' uxor 1

Laurentius Washington de Sulgrave in com[itatu] North[amp]t[on]' filius et heres = Margareta ux[or] Will[im]i Butler de le Tighes in com[itatu] Sussex'

Amicia uxor Albani Wakelin de Eidon in com[itatu] North[amp]ton'

Ursula uxor Tho[mae] Adcocke de Swinford in com[itatu] Leic'

Elizabetha uxor Ludovici Richardson de Turvey in com[itatu] Bedford'

Robertus Washington de Brinton in co[mitatu] North[amp]t[on]' fil[ius] 2 superstes a[nn]o 1618 = Elizabetha filia Joh[ann]is Chishull de Morehall in Essex'

Walterus 3

Walterus Washington de Rodwey in co[mitatu] Warr' fil[ius] 4 = Katherina filia Joh[ann]is Murden de Ratcliffe in com[itatu] Warr'

Willimus Washington de Pakington in com[itatu] Leic' a[nn]o 1618 = Anna soror Georgii marchionis Buckinghamiae

Johannes Robertus s[ine] p[role] Richardus Laurentius Thomas Georgius

Elizabetha ux[or] Francisci Mewce de Haldenby in com[itatu] North[amp]ton'

Johanna ux[or] Francisci Pill de Maidford in com[itatu] North[amp]t[on]'

Margareta Alicia Francisca

Johannes Washington de Rodwey in co[mitatu] Warr' = Maria filia Geo[rgii] Danvers de Blisworth in co[mitatu] North[amp]t[on]'

Katherina uxor Stanton de com[itatu] Warr'

Henricus aet[atis] 3 annor[um] a[nn]o 1618

Georgius

Roberte Wasshington

TRANSLATION

Pedigree in the Visitation of Northamptonshire, 1618-19

(College of Arms ref: C.14, ff. 87v-88r)

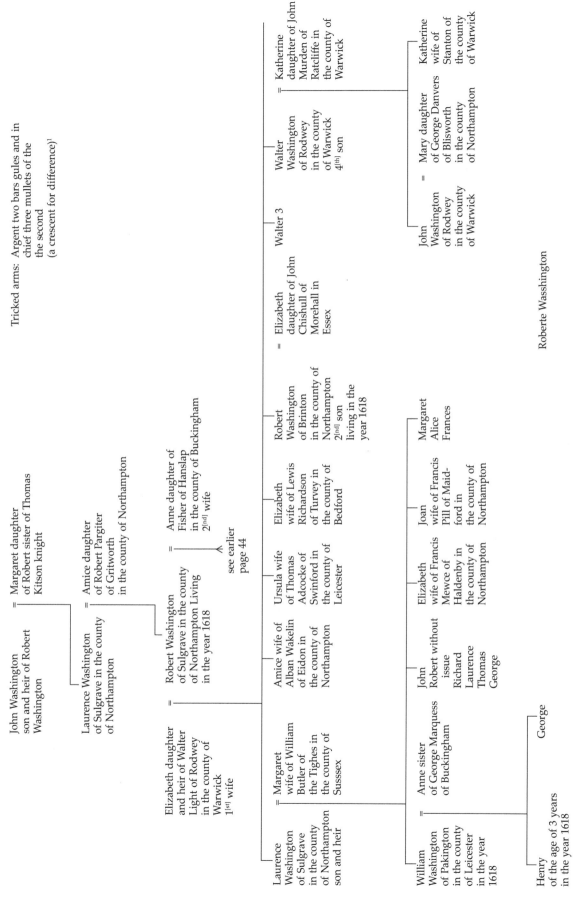

Tricked arms: Argent two bars gules and in chief three mullets of the second (a crescent for difference)[1]

John Washington son and heir of Robert Washington = Margaret daughter of Robert sister of Thomas Kitson knight

Laurence Washington of Sulgrave in the county of Northampton = Amice daughter of Robert Pargiter of Gritworth in the county of Northampton

Robert Washington of Sulgrave in the county of Northampton Living in the year 1618 = Anne daughter of Fisher of Hanslap in the county of Buckingham 2nd wife — see earlier page 44

Elizabeth daughter and heir of Walter Light of Rodwey in the county of Warwick 1st wife

Laurence Washington of Sulgrave in the county of Northampton son and heir = Margaret wife of William Butler of the Tighes in the county of Sussex

Amice wife of Alban Wakelin of Eidon in the county of Northampton

Ursula wife of Thomas Adcocke of Swinford in the county of Leicester

Elizabeth wife of Lewis Richardson of Turvey in the county of Bedford

Robert Washington of Brinton in the county of Northampton 2nd son living in the year 1618 = Elizabeth daughter of John Chishull of Morehall in Essex

Walter 3

Walter Washington of Rodwey in the county of Warwick 4th son = Katherine daughter of John Murden of Ratcliffe in the county of Warwick

William Washington of Pakington in the county of Leicester in the year 1618 = Anne sister of George Marquess of Buckingham

John
Robert without issue
Richard
Laurence
Thomas
George

Elizabeth wife of Francis Mewce of Haldenby in the county of Northampton

Joan wife of Francis Pill of Maidford in the county of Northampton

Margaret
Alice
Frances

Henry of the age of 3 years in the year 1618

George

John Washington of Rodwey in the county of Warwick = Mary daughter of George Danvers of Blisworth in the county of Northampton

Katherine wife of Stanton of the county of Warwick

Roberte Wasshington

COMMENTARY

Pedigree in the Visitation of Northamptonshire, 1618-1619
(College of Arms ref: C.14, ff. 87v-88r)

Document

The series of visitations (in which, county by county, arms and pedigrees of armigerous families were recorded) spans a period of some century and a half from 1530. This pedigree is reproduced by kind permission of the College of Arms from the Visitation of Northamptonshire, 1618-19. There is a small extension of the pedigree on f. 88v. The Washingtons of Sulgrave are said to be the ancestors of George Washington and there is a theory that the American Stars and Stripes may have been derived from this coat of arms. It is interesting to find at this period that the children in the last generation had in Robert Washington a living great-grandfather. The visitation is mentioned in *The Records and Collections of the College of Arms* (1952) by Anthony Wagner (then Richmond Herald, later Garter King of Arms) as an original, with signature, by Augustine Vincent, then Rouge Rose, whose hand he describes as 'admirable'. According to *A History of the College of Arms* by the Rev. Mark Noble (1805), Augustine Vincent was third son of William Vincent of Northamptonshire and, as a favourite of William Camden, then Garter, was sent by him as a deputy or marshal on some of his visitations. He is given as having been appointed Rouge Rose Pursuivant Extraordinary in February 1615/16.

Script

This neat hand, though small, is fairly regular. However, in some cases the letters *t* and *e* appear extremely similar (see *Walteri* in the third generation down). Similarly *a* and *o* are remarkably alike, so that place-names are sometimes slightly ambiguous.

Notes

To facilitate lay-out, the transcript in a few cases does not exactly reproduce the lines in the original. Extensions in brackets have followed aspects of the spelling of the writer in other instances e.g. in the use of the diphthong, and the form *Will[im]i* rather than the more usual *Will[elm]i*. Although it seems uncertain whether actual extension for a Latin ending is in all cases intended, the apostrophe usual for Latin endings of counties has been included in the transcript, and the final dot taken as a general abbreviation.

1. In the blazon: argent is silver; gules is red; mullets are stars, usually of five points. The crescent is a cadency mark indicating a second son.

(Plate and transcript on previous spread)

Mansfield ss: Cur Baron Dñi Barloy Ar et et Bauriettæ vxoris eius (colt arcat Dñus Dñus Barloy et Dñina Bauriatta Grandine Wilds Barloy) ibidem tent octavo dio Maij anno Dñi 1722. et anno regni Dñi nri Georgÿ nunc Regis Magn Britanniæ Octavo.

Ad hanc eandem Cur Johes Walker de Epperston ẙend et Maria vxor eius (que quondam Maria fuit vnica filia et heres Johis Seddon nuper de Baphwicke confectionez defunct) in proprijs personis suis Et hic in plena Cur (ipsa sola et separatim prius in absentia viri sui per senthu iudecand et confessa quo eohot vnimo fuit coact et) Sura in manibus Dñmni et Dñminæ Mano prædict Iunnia et singuka nightmay Maria Etcra Ecre̊ Euemonta et hore ditthamenta cum porlimo̊ infra Mano prædict que desccndebaut suo descendere debent prædict Maria vt filia vnica et heres prædict Johis Seddon nuper patris eius defunct Coluuququius statu fituip aliquid et Dcuiand iper prædict Johis Walker et Maria et eo̊ alteo̊ inuel et premiss prædict Ad opus et Vsum dict Johis Walker et Mariæ vxoris eius hore et Duraū vitis suis ac ac̊ Coruugququius statu fituip aliquid et Dcuiand iper prædict Johis Walker et Mariæ vxor maritaz et vit naturad eo̊ Duuthius ẙend et eo̊ hore de corpore dict Johis et ac̊ eius et Deceñminoo̊ Duuthius inter Tunc de opus et Vsum dict Johis Walker de Maria istuiů procreat vel procreand Et pro defochi faiis excitus Tunc ad opus et Vsum Rect de hore de dict Johis Walker impozpm Jluibus quid em Scti Walker et Mariæ Duus et Dua per senthu sud ibid concess inde spitur per virgam secud Cuo̊ Manuo̊ prædict hent et tenent profat Johis Walker et Mariæ vxor de eius pro et Duraū vitis suis naturad et vit naturad eo̊ Duuthius inter Romanoū Dul̊ locssorhir De Erb et Dua Manuo̊ prædict pro tempore existend per reddit Cunsududuuies et serit inde prius debit et de quruzenuisuot Et aut Dñū Dñū de fitis pro hiumoi statu et ingzu sic inde hore Duus seiñdos Et sic Denifs siutinde Soluculss.

per me Clay Ep̃i Seneschalt Manorÿ suprədict.

3 D
11

Copy of Manor Roll of Mansfield

Mansfield	1 Cur[ia] Baron[is] Ed[wa]r[d]i Harley Ar[migeri] et Henriettæ uxoris eius (co[mmun]iter vocat[orum]² Ed[wa]r[d]us D[omi]nus Harley et
2.	Domina Henrietta Cavendishe Holles Harley) ibidem tent[a] octavo die Maii anno D[omi]ni 1722
3.	et anno regni D[omi]ni n[ost]ri Georgii nunc Regis Magn[e] Britannie &c octavo
4.	**Ad hanc eandem Cur[iam]** Joh[ann]es Walker de Epperston gen[erosus] et Maria uxor eius (Quæ quedam
5.	Maria fuit unica filia et heres Joh[ann]is Seddon nuper de Paplewicke confectioner defunct[i]) in propriis personis
6.	suis Et hic in plena Cur[ia] (ip[s]a sola et seperatim prius in absentia viri sui per sen[esca]ll[u]m Cur[ie] exam[inata] et confessa quod
7.	ad hoc minime fuit coact[a] &c) Sur[sum]r[eddiderunt] in manus Domini et Dominæ Maner[ii] predict[i] Omnia et singula Messuag[ia]
8.	Cottagia Terr[as] Tenementa et heredittamenta³ cum pertinen[tiis] infra Maner[ium] predict[um] quæ descendebant sive
9.	descendere debent predict[æ] Mariæ ut filia unica & heres predict[i] Joh[ann]is Seddon nuper patris eius defunct[i]
10.	Totumq[ue] ius statu[m] titulu[m] clam[eum] et demand[am] ip[s]or[um] prefat[orum] Joh[ann]is Walker et Mariæ et eor[um] alter[ius] in et ad premiss[a]
11.	predict[a] **Ad opus et usum** dict[orum] Joh[ann]is Walker et Mariæ uxor[is] eius pro et duran[tibus] vitis suis
12.	natural[ibus] et vit[a] natural[i] eor[um] diutius viven[tis] Et immediate post decessum dict[orum] Joh[ann]is Walker et Mariæ uxor[is]
13.	eius et decessum eor[um] diutius viven[tis] **Tunc ad opus et usum** Hered[um] de corpore dicti Joh[ann]is
14.	Walker super corpus dict[æ] Mariæ l[eg]ittime⁴ procreat[orum] vel procreand[orum] Et pro defectu talis Exitus Tunc ad opus
15.	& usum Rect[orum] Heredu[m] dicti Joh[ann]is Walker imperp[etuu]m Quibus quidem Joh[ann]i Walker et Mariæ D[omi]nus et
16.	D[omi]na per sen[esca]ll[u]m suu[m] ib[ide]m concess[erunt] inde sei[si]n[am] per virgam⁵ s[e]c[un]d[u]m Cons[uetudinem] Maner[ii] predict[i] h[ab]end[um]⁶ et tenend[um]⁶ prefat[is] Joh[ann]i
17.	Walker et Mariæ uxor[i] eius pro et duran[te] vitis suis natural[ibus] et vit[a] natural[i] eor[um] diutius viven[tis] Remaner[e] ut
18.	prefertur De D[omi]no et D[omi]na Maner[ii] predict[i] pro tempore existen[ti] per reddit[um] Consuitudines⁷ et servic[ia] inde prius
19.	debit[a] et de iure consuet[a] Et dant D[omi]no & D[omi]ne de Fine pro hu[ius]mo[d]i statu et ingr[ess]u sic inde h[ab]end[is]⁸ duos solidos Et sic
20.	admissi sunt inde Tenentes
21.	per me J Clay Dep[utatum] Sen[es]call[i] Manerii supredict[i]

[39]

TRANSLATION

Copy of Manor Roll of Mansfield

Mansfield Court baron of Edward Harley esquire and Henrietta his wife (commonly called Edward Lord Harley and Lady Henrietta Cavendishe Holles Harley) held there on the eighth day of May in the year of the Lord 1722 and in the eighth year of the reign of our lord George now king of Great Britain &c.

To this same court John Walker of Epperston gentleman and Mary his wife (which certain Mary was the only daughter and heir of John Seddon late of Paplewicke confectioner deceased) [came] in person And here in full court (she being first examined alone and separately by the steward of the court in the absence of her husband and having acknowledged that she was in no way coerced &c to this) surrendered into the hands of the lord and lady of the aforesaid manor all and singular the messuages cottages lands tenements and hereditaments with appurtenances within the aforesaid manor which descended or ought to descend to the aforesaid Mary as only daughter & heir of the aforesaid John Seddon late her father deceased and all the right estate title claim and demand of the same aforesaid John Walker and Mary and either of them in and to the aforesaid premises **To the use and behoof** of the said John Walker and Mary his wife for and during their natural lives and the natural life of the longer living of them And immediately after the decease of the said John Walker and Mary his wife and the decease of the longer living of them **Then to the use and behoof** of the heirs of the body of the said John Walker upon the body of the said Mary lawfully begotten or to be begotten And for default of such issue then to the use and behoof of the right heirs of the said John Walker for ever To which indeed John Walker and Mary the lord and lady through their steward there granted seisin thereof by the rod according to the custom of the aforesaid manor to have and to hold to the aforesaid John Walker and Mary his wife for and during their natural lives and the natural life of the longer living of them To remain as is aforesaid from the lord and lady of the aforesaid manor for the time being for the rent customs and services first owed in respect thereof and of right accustomed And they give to the lord and lady for fine for such estate and entry thus to be had two shillings And thus they were admitted tenants thereof

By me J Clay deputy of the steward of the aforesaid manor

COMMENTARY

Copy of Manor Roll of Mansfield

Document

For a brief note on manor rolls, see plate 8. This kind of document (a copy of an entry on the court roll) would have been given to the tenant or tenants as proof of their holding, hence the term 'copyholder'. Taking a wife aside in this kind of circumstance, to ensure that pressure had not been brought to bear, was a usual occurrence. By searching for the surrenders and admissions recorded in court rolls, it can often be possible to deduce a number of generations of families holding the same messuage (usually taken to be a piece of land with a dwelling house on it). The land generally descended by primogeniture, but in some manors (e.g. Lambeth in Surrey and Edmonton in Middlesex) the custom of borough English obtained, whereby the youngest son was admitted. Where documents such as this survive they may well be, as this one is, in private ownership.

Script

The abbreviation marks are a little curious in that in some cases (e.g. *communiter* in l. 1) the abbreviation is placed over the second rather than the first part of the word; the abbreviation after a final *t* is like a colon, sometimes augmented to resemble the sign indicating *es*; and, in the case of *senescallum* (l. 6), it might be expected that the letter *m* rather than *u* would have been omitted. For what in classical Latin would be *ae*, the diphthong *æ* is used in most cases instead of the more usual *e* of medieval Latin. The transcript takes the differing forms into account in the extensions.

Notes

1. A paragraph mark appears here, similar to that on plate 17, resembling a double *s*.
2. The plural is used as it refers to Edward and Henrietta; the grammar is slightly curious and the ending of this word ambiguous.
3. This is an unusual spelling for the normal *hereditamenta*.
4. An extra *t* also appears in the word more usually spelt *legitime.*
5. By the rod: this was a formality whereby a rod was handed over to the new tenant by the steward, a ceremony still observed when *The Manor and Manorial Records* by Nathaniel Hone was published in 1906.
6. Thus sometimes extended, but such extensions can sometimes agree with the previous word to which they relate, in this case *seisinam.*
7. Another variation of spelling, *consuetudines* being usual.
8. The plural is used here to agree with *statu* and *ingressu.*

(Plate and transcript on previous spread)

[40]

TRANSCRIPT

Entry on Close Roll

(TNA:PRO ref: C 54/924)

In margin: De Rec[ognitione] int[er] Gerardu[m]' Croker et Annam Croker

1. Gerardus Croker de Staple Barton in Com[itatu] Oxon' Armig[er] coram D[omi]na Regina in Cancellar[ia] sua p[er]sonal[ite]r

2. constitut[a] recognovit se debere Anne Croker filie Joh[ann]is Croker de Todnam in Com[itatu] Glouc' gen[er]os[i]

3. quingentas libras bone & legalis monete Angl[ie] Solvend[as] eidem Anne Hered[ibus] Executorib[us] Administrat[oribus]

4. & Assign[atis] suis in festo Natalis d[omi]ni p[ro]x[imo] futur[o] post dat[um] p[re]sentiu[m] Et nisi fec[er]it vult & concedit p[ro] se Hered[ibus]

5. Executorib[us] & Administratorib[us] suis p[er] p[re]sentes Q[uo]d tunc p[re]d[i]c[t]a pecunie sum[m]a levet[ur] & recup[er]et[ur] de om[n]ib[us]

6. & singulis man[er]iis mesuagiis t[er]ris ten[ementis] bonis catallis possessionib[us] & hereditament[iis] suis quibuscumq[ue] ac

7. Hered[um] Executor[um] & Administrator[um] suor[um] ubicumq[ue] fu[er]int invent[a] ad p[ro]priu[m] opus & usum d[i]c[t]e Anne Hered[um]

8. Executor[um] & Administrator[um] suor[um] Teste d[i]c[t]a d[omi]na Regina Elizabeth[a]² dei gr[aci]a Angl[ie] Franc[ie] & Hib[er]n[ie] Regina

9. fidei defensor[e] &c apud Westm' decimo t[er]cio die Novembr[is] Anno regni sui decimo quinto³

10. The Condic[i]on of this Recognysaunce is suche That if thabovebounde Gerarde Croker his heires

11. Executors Administrators or assignes or any of them doe well and truly contente and paye or

12. cause to be contented and paied unto the abovenamed Anne Croker hir Executors Admynyst[r]ators

13. or assignes the full som[m]e of twoo hundred fourty and twoo pound[es] tenne shillyng[es] of good and

14. laufull money of England on the first daye of November next comyng after the date hereof at

15. or within the porche of the Guyldehall within the Citye of London betwene the houres of

16. one and foure of the clock in the afternone of the same daye without fraude covyn⁴ or ⁵

17. further delaye That then this p[re]sent Recognysaunce to be utt[er]ly voyde and of none effect Or ell[es]

18. to stande in full strength and v[er]tue

TRANSLATION

of Latin part

In margin: Concerning the recognizance between Gerard Croker and Anne Croker

Gerard Croker of Staple Barton in the county of Oxford esquire before the Lady Queen being personally in her chancery acknowledged that he owed to Anne Croker the daughter of John Croker of Todnam in the county of Gloucester gentleman five hundred pounds of good & lawful money of England to be paid to the same Anne her heirs executors administrators & assigns on the feast of the birth of [Our] Lord next coming after the date of [these] presents And if he shall not have done [so] she wills & grants for herself her heirs executors & administrators by [these] presents that then the aforesaid sum of money be raised & recovered from all & singular his manors messuages lands tenements goods chattels possessions & hereditaments whatsoever and [those] of his heirs executors & administrators wheresoever they shall have been found to the proper use & behoof of the said Anne her heirs executors & administrators The Lady Queen Elizabeth by the grace of God Queen of England France & Ireland defender of the faith &c. being witness at Westminster on the thirteenth day of November in the fifteenth year of her reign.

COMMENTARY

Entry on Close Roll

(TNA:PRO ref: C 54/924)

Document

See note on close rolls for plate 26.

Script

This is a type of script found in many formal documents – beautifully regular, but subject to the problem of unravelling minims, particularly in the first part which is in Latin and therefore more prone to a profusion of them. It will therefore be easier if the second part, in English, is deciphered first. In this hand the letters *h*, *l* and *w*, whether capital or small, are identical. In the English part a few formal abbreviations of no apparent significance appear (e.g. over the words 'full' and 'strength' in the last line).

Notes

1. A paragraph mark, resembling two minims (though evolving, it seems, from an original C) occurs here, confusing the end of the word.
2. The abbreviation mark above Elizabeth is extremely faint.
3. 1573.
4. Covyn: for covin, a legal or archaic term for collusion.
5. A line filler occurs here.

(Plate, transcript and translation on previous spread)

COMMENTARY

Entries in the Hallmote Court of Widnes
(TNA:PRO ref: DL 30/134/2069, rot 5r)

Document

For a note on manorial documents see plate 8. This part of the hallmote court roll predates the period of the Commonwealth from which the entries on plate 8 were taken and is therefore in Latin. It consists of part of the record of the hallmote court of Widnes held on 25 April 1648 and the entries are typical of those found in many manor rolls, recounting various types of misdemeanour and fines imposed. Often the amount of the fine is written over the name in question.

Script

The writing here appears much like that on plate 42, a slightly later part of the court.

Notes

1. Although this word appears to have an abbreviation, it would seem to be nominative, as in the entry above, and therefore does not need one.
2. This word is more usually spelt *cotagium*.
3. Thus apparently, though the abbreviation seems curious.
4. This word is more usually spelt *impanellati*.
5. *fuere* is an alternative form of the more frequently used *fuerunt*.

(Plate, transcript and translation on following spread)

TRANSCRIPT

Entries in the Hallmote Court of Widnes

(TNA:PRO ref: DL 30/134/2069, rot 5r)

1. **Et quod** Thomas Singleton et Thomas Robinson Insultu[m] fecer[unt] alter in alter[um] sine
2. sanguine Ideo uterq[ue] eor[um] in m[isericordia] xij^d In toto — ij^s
3. **Et quod** Ric[ard]us Parr de Rainhill et Joh[ann]es Whitfeild de Halewood affraia[m] fecer[unt]
4. alter[1] in alter[um] cu[m] sanguine Ideo uterq[ue] eor[um] in m[isericordia] iij^s iiij^d In toto — vj^s viij^d
5. **Et quod** Robertus Singleton Thomas Swinton Joh[ann]es Wood[es] et Ric[ard]us Marsh
6. Ludebant apud aleas (anglice plaide att dyce) p[ro] pecun[ia] in domo Joh[ann]is Naylor Ideo quil[i]b[e]t
7. eor[um] in m[isericordia] xij^d In toto — iiij^s
8. **Et quod** Joh[ann]es Willie et Matheus Savory de Warrington Ludebant pictis chartis
9. (anglice plaide att Card[es]) p[ro] Cervisia et pecun[ia] in domo Henrici Appleton Ideo uterq[ue] — iij^s
10. eor[um] in m[isericordia] xviij^d in toto
11. **Et quod** Will[el]mus Taylor de Farnworth permisit Jana[m] Taylor filia[m] eius pariri
12. cu[m] spurio (anglice to bee delivered of a bastard) in domo suo Ideo ipse in m[isericordia] — iiij^s iiij^d
13. **Et quod** Henricus Bold gen[erosus] edificavit Cottag[ium][2] infr[a] maner[ium] contra Statut[um] in — iiij^s iiij^d
14. eo Casu p[ro]vis[um][3] Ideo ipse in m[isericordia]
15. **Et quod** Ellena Chaddocke permisit Jana[m] Chaddocke filia[m] eius pariri cu[m] spurio — iiij^s iiij^d
16. (anglice to bee delivered of a bastard) in Domo suo Ideo ipsa in m[isericordia]
17. **Et quod** Thomas Wood[es] et Joh[ann]es Denton de Widnes impannellat[i][4] fuere[5] ad deserviend[um] — xx^s
18. ut Iurat[ores] p[ro] d[omi]na R[egi]na et exact[i] non vener[unt] in Cur[iam] Ideo uterq[ue] eor[um] in m[isericordia] x^s In toto

TRANSLATION

1. **And that** Thomas Singleton and Thomas Robinson made an assault one upon another without blood Therefore each of them [is] in mercy 12d. In all — 2s.
3. **And that** Richard Parr of Rainhill and John Whitfeild of Halewood made an affray one upon another with blood. Therefore each of them [is] in mercy 3s. 4d. In all — 6s. 8d.
5. **And that** Robert Singleton Thomas Swinton John Woodes and Richard Marsh were playing at dice (in English played at dice) for money in the house of John Naylor Therefore each of them [is] in mercy 12d. In all — 4s.
8. **And that** John Willie and Matthew Savory of Warrington were playing at cards (in English played at cards) for ale and money in the house of Henry Appleton Therefore each of them [is] in mercy 18d. In all — 3s.
11. **And that** William Taylor of Farnworth allowed Jane Taylor his daughter to be delivered of a bastard (in English to be delivered of a bastard) in his house Therefore he [is] in mercy — 3s. 4d.
13. **And that** Henry Bold gentleman built a cottage within the manor against the statute in that case provided Therefore he [is] in mercy — 3s. 4d.
15. **And that** Ellen Chaddocke allowed Jane Chaddocke her daughter to be delivered of a bastard (in English to be delivered of a bastard) in her house Therefore she [is] in mercy — 3s. 4d.
17. **And that** Thomas Woodes and John Denton of Widnes were empanelled to serve as jurors for the Lady Queen and being required did not come into court Therefore each of them [is] in mercy 10s. In all — 20s.

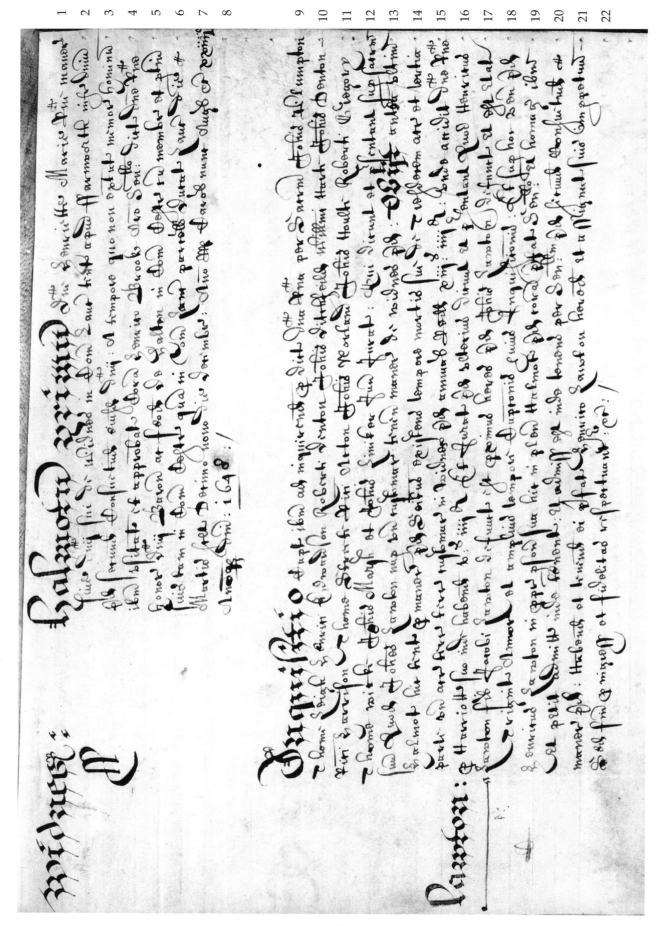

Heading and Admission in the Hallmote Court Roll of Widnes

(TNA:PRO ref: DL 30/135/2070, rot 3r)

In margin: **Widnes**[1]

1. **Halmotu[m] primu[m]** D[omi]ne Henriette Marie R[egi]ne[2] maner[ii]
2. sive d[omi]nii sui de Widnes in Com[itatu] Lanc' tent[um] apud Farnworth infr[a] d[omi]niu[m]
3. p[re]d[ictum] secund[um] Consuetud[inem] eiusd[em] d[omi]nii A tempore quo non ext[s]tat memor[ia] hominu[m]
4. ib[ide]m usitat[am] et approbat[am] Cora[m] Henrico Brooke Ar[miger]o Sen[esca]llo dict[e] d[omi]ne R[egi]ne
5. honor[is] D[omi]nii Baron[is] ac feod[i] de Halton in Com[itatu] Cestr' cu[m] membr[is] et p[er]tin[entiis]
6. suis tam in Com[itatu] Cestr' qua[m] in Com[itatu] Lanc' parcell[e] Ducat[us] Lanc' die
7. Martis sc[i]l[l]ice]t Decimo nono die Decembr[is] An[n]o R[egni] R[egis] Carol[i] nunc Angl[ie] &c xxiiij°
8. An[n]oq[ue] d[omi]ni 1648

In margin: **Lawton**

9. **Inquisitio** Capt[a] ib[ide]m ad inquirend[um] p[ro] dict[a] d[omi]na R[egi]na per Sacr[amentu]m Joh[ann]is Plumpton
10. Thome Leigh Henrici Edwardson[3] Roberti Denton Joh[ann]is Ditchfeild Will[el]mi Harte Joh[ann]is Denton
11. Ric[ard]i Harrison Thome Streete Ric[ard]i Acton Joh[ann]is Norland Joh[ann]is Houlte Roberti Gregory
12. Thome Wicke Joh[ann]is Marsh et Joh[ann]is Liniker Iun[ioris] Iurat[orum] Qui dicunt et p[re]sentant sup[er] sacr[amentu]m
13. suu[m] Quod Joh[ann]es Lawton nup[er] un[us] customar[iorum] tenen[tium] maner[ii] de Widnes p[re]d[ict'][4] **Obiit** antea[5] ultim[um]
14. Halmot[um] hic tent[um] p[ro] maner[io] p[re]d[icto] Sei[si]tus existens tempore mortis sue de Tresdecem acr[is] et tertia
15. parte un[ius] acr[e] terr[e] terr[e] customar[ie] in Widnes p[re]d[ict'] annual[is] Redd[itus] xiij[s] iiij[d] unde accidit d[omi]ne R[egi]ne
16. p[ro] Harriott[o] suo inde habend[o] v[s] iiij[d] Et Iurat[ores] p[re]d[icti] ulterius dicunt et p[re]sentant Quod Henricus
17. Lawton fil[ius] Jacobi Lawton defunct[i] est p[ro]ximus heres p[re]d[icti] Joh[ann]is Lawton defunct[i] et est etat[is]
18. Trigint[a] Annor[um] et amplius tempore Capc[i]onis[6] huius Inquisic[i]onis Et sup[er] hoc ven[it][7] p[re]d[ictus]
19. Henricus Lawton in p[ro]pr[ia] p[er]son[a] sua hic in plen[um] Halmot[um] p[re]d[ictum] cora[m] p[re]fat[o]
    Sen[esca]llo et homag[io] ib[ide]m
20. et petit admitt[i] inde tenent[em][8] et admiss[us][9] est inde tenens per Sen[esca]ll[u]m p[re]d[ictum] secund[um]
    Consuetud[inem]
21. maner[ii] p[re]d[icti] Habend[um] et tenend[um] ei p[re]fat[o] Henrico Lawton hered[ibus] et assignat[is] suis imp[er]petuu[m]
22. Sed fin[is] p[ro] ingress[u] et fidelitas respectuant[u]r &c

TRANSLATION

Heading and Admission in the Hallmote Court Roll of Widnes
(TNA:PRO ref: DL 30/135/2070, rot 3r)

Widnes

The first hallmote of the Lady Queen Henrietta Maria of her manor or lordship of Widnes in the county of Lancaster held at Farnworth within the aforesaid lordship according to the custom of the same lordship habitual and established in that place from a time from which the memory of man does not survive before Henry Brooke Esquire steward of the said Lady Queen of the honour of the lordship of the barony and fee of Halton in the county of Chester with its members and appurtenances both in the county of Chester and in the county of Lancaster parcel of the Duchy of Lancaster on Tuesday that is to say on the nineteenth day of December in the 24th year of the Reign of Charles now king of England &c. and in the year of the Lord 1648.

Lawton

Inquisition taken in the same place to enquire on behalf of the said Lady Queen by the oath of John Plumpton Thomas Leigh Henry Edwardson Robert Denton John Ditchfeild William Harte John Denton Richard Harrison Thomas Streete Richard Acton John Norland John Houlte Robert Gregory Thomas Wicke John Marsh and John Liniker junior jurors who say and present upon their oath that John Lawton late one of the customary tenants of the manor of Widnes aforesaid **died** before the last hallmote held here for the aforesaid manor being seized at the time of his death of thirteen acres and a third part of one acre of land, customary land in Widnes aforesaid of annual rent of 13s. 4d. wherefrom there accrues to the Lady Queen for her heriot to be had in respect thereof 5s. 4d. And the aforesaid jurors further say and present that Henry Lawton the son of James Lawton deceased is the next heir of the aforesaid John Lawton deceased and is of the age of thirty years and more at the time of the taking of this inquisition. And upon this the aforesaid Henry Lawton comes[7] here in person into the full aforesaid halmote before the aforesaid steward and homage in the same place and seeks to be admitted tenant thereof and he is[9] admitted tenant thereof by the aforesaid steward according to the custom of the aforesaid manor to have and to hold to him the aforesaid Henry Lawton his heirs and assigns in perpetuity but the fine for entry and the fealty are respited &c.

COMMENTARY

Hallmote Court Roll of Widnes

(TNA:PRO ref: DL/135/2070, rot 3r)

Document

The method of dating in the heading of this further extract from the hallmote court roll of Widnes is not untypical. The entry which follows exemplifies the immensely useful nature of manor rolls for family historians.

Script

This hand is reasonably clear. In some cases there is the usual ambiguity with minims, but in many instances there is good distinction between the letters which produce such problems. It is to be noted that the writer uses more than one form of some letters e.g. *D* and *H*, and *a*, *e* and *r*. *W* and *w*, as so often, are almost identical in form, but in this case a second type of capital letter is to be found.

Notes

1. Below this appears a paragraph mark which resembles a double *s* for which see the note for plate 17.
2. Queen consort of Charles I.
3. Presumably so; the letter *r* is far from clear, but there are others similar.
4. An ending has not been given here as there is no indication of what gender might apply to Widnes.
5. The word *antea*, normally an adverb, has been used here in place of the more usual preposition *ante*.
6. The second letter is written as a *u* which, uncrossed at the top, is the same in form as the *a* which was undoubtedly intended, and has been so taken in the transcript.
7. This verb is the same in perfect and present tense, but is translated as the present to fit with the tense of *petit*.
8. Here a nominative case might have been expected.
9. Following note 7, it seems that *admissus est* should be translated word by word, rather than as a perfect tense.

(Plate and transcript on previous spread)

Manor de Walton
Inferior

1
2
3
4
5
6
7
8
9
10
11
12
13
14
15
16
17
18
19
20
21
22
23
24

TRANSCRIPT

Copy of Manor Roll of Nether Wallop, Hampshire

(Hampshire Record Office ref: 11M49/332/bdl. 1)

In margin: Maner[ium] de Wallop Inferior[i]   1

1. Cur[ia] Baron[is] Nobilissimi Caroli Ducis de Bolton ib[ide]m tent[a] Vicessimo Octavo
2. die Aprilis Anno R[eg]ni D[omi]ni n[ost]ri Georgii Dei Gratia nunc Magn[e] Brittannie &c
3. R[egi]s Decimo Annoq[ue] D[omi]ni 1724 Coram Jacobo Crosse ar[miger]o Sen[es]c[all]o ib[ide]m.

4. Ad hanc Cur[iam] D[omi]nus Man[er]ii pr[e]d[icti] p[er] Sen[es]c[all][u]m suu[m] pr[e]d[ictum] concessit Will[elm]o Cowdry Ferrifabr[o]
5. Un[um] Messuag[ium] et Toft[um] Messuag[ii] et duas Virgat[as] t[er]re cum P[er]tin[entiis] infra hoc Maner[ium] nup[er]
6. in poss[ess]ione Josephi Shipton pro vita sua p[er] Cop[iam] Rot[u]lor[um] Cur[ie] huius Man[er]ii geren[tem]
7. Dat[am] Decimo Sexto die Aprilis 1708 Remanere inde Jacobo Shipton filio
8. suo Que omnia et Singula premissa dictus Josephus Shipton sursumredd[id]it
9. in manus D[omi]ni p[er] acceptac[i]on[em] Sen[es]c[all]i sui pr[e]d[icti] ad Cur[iam] tent[am] primo die Iulii
10. 1721 Et Idem Will[elm]us Cowdry h[ab]et Seizin[am] inde p[er] virgam H[ab]end[um] et tenend[um]
11. Messuag[ium] et Toft[um] Messuagii et Duas virgat[as] t[er]re cum P[er]tin[entiis] pr[e]d[ictis] dict[o] Will[elm]o
12. Cowdry nunc etatis Trigint[a] annor[um] et Ric[ard]o Cowdry nunc etatis triu[m] annor[um]
13. et Fortune Cowdry nunc etatis Quinq[ue] annor[um] filiis suis pro et durante
14. termino vitar[um] eor[um] et vite cuiuslibet eor[um] diutius viven[tis] successive ad
15. Vol[unta]tem D[omi]ni s[e]c[un]d[u]m consuetud[inem] Man[er]ii pr[e]d[icti] per Reddit[um] p[er] Ann[um] Un[ius] Libr[e] novem
16. Solidor[um] et Quatuor Denar[iorum] ac Herriot[um] cum acciderit ac p[er] o[mn]ia alia opera onera
17. sectas consuetud[ines] et Servitia inde prius debit[a] et de iure consuet[a] Et pro t[a]li
18. statu sic in pr[e]missis h[ab]end[o] Idem Will[elm]us Cowdry Dat D[omi]no pro Fine Centum et
19. Vigint[i] Libras pr[e]manib[us] solut[as] Et sic admissus est inde Tenens et fecit D[omi]no
20. fidelit[atem] sua[m] fidelitas pr[e]fact[orum]² Ric[ard]i et Fortune Cowdry respectua[n]t[ur]³ Quousq[ue] &c

21. May 13th 1747 Examined with the
22. Court Roll By me
23.   Mor. Keene⁴ }
24.   Steward.   }

In margin against lines 16-18:   Rent 1ˡ 9ˢ 4ᵈ
                                 Herr[io]t
                                 Fine 120ˡⁱ

[43]

TRANSLATION

Copy of Manor Roll of Nether Wallop

(Hampshire Record Office ref: 11M49/33/bdl.1)

In margin: Manor of Nether Wallop

The court baron of the most noble Charles Duke of Bolton held there on the twenty eighth day of April in the tenth year of the reign of Our Lord George by the grace of God now King of Great Britain &c. and in the year of the Lord 1724 before James Crosse esquire steward there.

At this court the lord of the aforesaid manor by his aforesaid steward granted to William Cowdry ironsmith one messuage and a toft of a messuage and two virgates of land with appurtenances within this manor late in the possession of Joseph Shipton for his life by copy of the rolls of the court of this manor bearing date the sixteenth day of April 1708 to remain in respect thereof to James Shipton his son All and singular which premises the said Joseph Shipton surrendered into the hands of the lord through the acceptance of his aforesaid steward at the court held on the first day of July 1721 And the same William Cowdry has seisin thereof by the rod to have and to hold the messuage and toft of the messuage and two virgates of land with the aforesaid appurtenances to the said William Cowdry now of the age of thirty years and to Richard Cowdry now of the age of three years and to Fortune Cowdry now of the age of five years his children for and during the term of their lives and of the life of each of them successively living the longer at the will of the lord according to the custom of the aforesaid manor for rent of one pound nine shillings and four pence a year and a heriot when it falls due and by all other works burdens suits customs and services first owed in respect thereof and of right accustomed And for such estate so to be had in the premises the same William Cowdry gives to the lord for fine a hundred and twenty pounds paid in advance[5] And thus he was admitted tenant thereof and made his fealty to the lord. The fealty of the aforesaid Richard and Fortune Cowdry is respited until &c.

COMMENTARY

Copy of Manor Roll of Nether Wallop

(Hampshire Record Office ref: 11M49/332/bdl. 1)

Document

For a brief note on manor rolls see plate 8, and for copies, plate 39. This copy of the record of admission would have been given to the incoming tenant as proof of his tenancy. Copied from an entry made in 1724, written in Latin, it was examined against it after Latin had been dropped for such documents.

Script

The writing here is mainly very clear. However there is a tendency for the final *o* to be written with a flourish so that it resembles an *s*. In some cases the scribe appears to have forgotten to include a mark of abbreviation.

Notes

1. Between the marginal heading and the text is the paragraph mark resembling a double long *s*.
2. Apparently for *prefatorum*.
3. The abbreviation sign such as that at the end of this word normally signifies, in different contexts, an ending *-us*, *-ue* or *-et*, but here apparently is intended for *-ur* ; that over the letter *a* indicates an omitted *n*, though does not seem relevant since *fidelitas* is singular, but perhaps the plural is used because there are two who are yet to make fealty.
4. Thus probably, but signatures are notoriously difficult to transcribe with certainty, being idiosyncratic and without text for comparison. The two diagonal lines are probably an individual embellishment.

(Plate and transcript on previous spread)

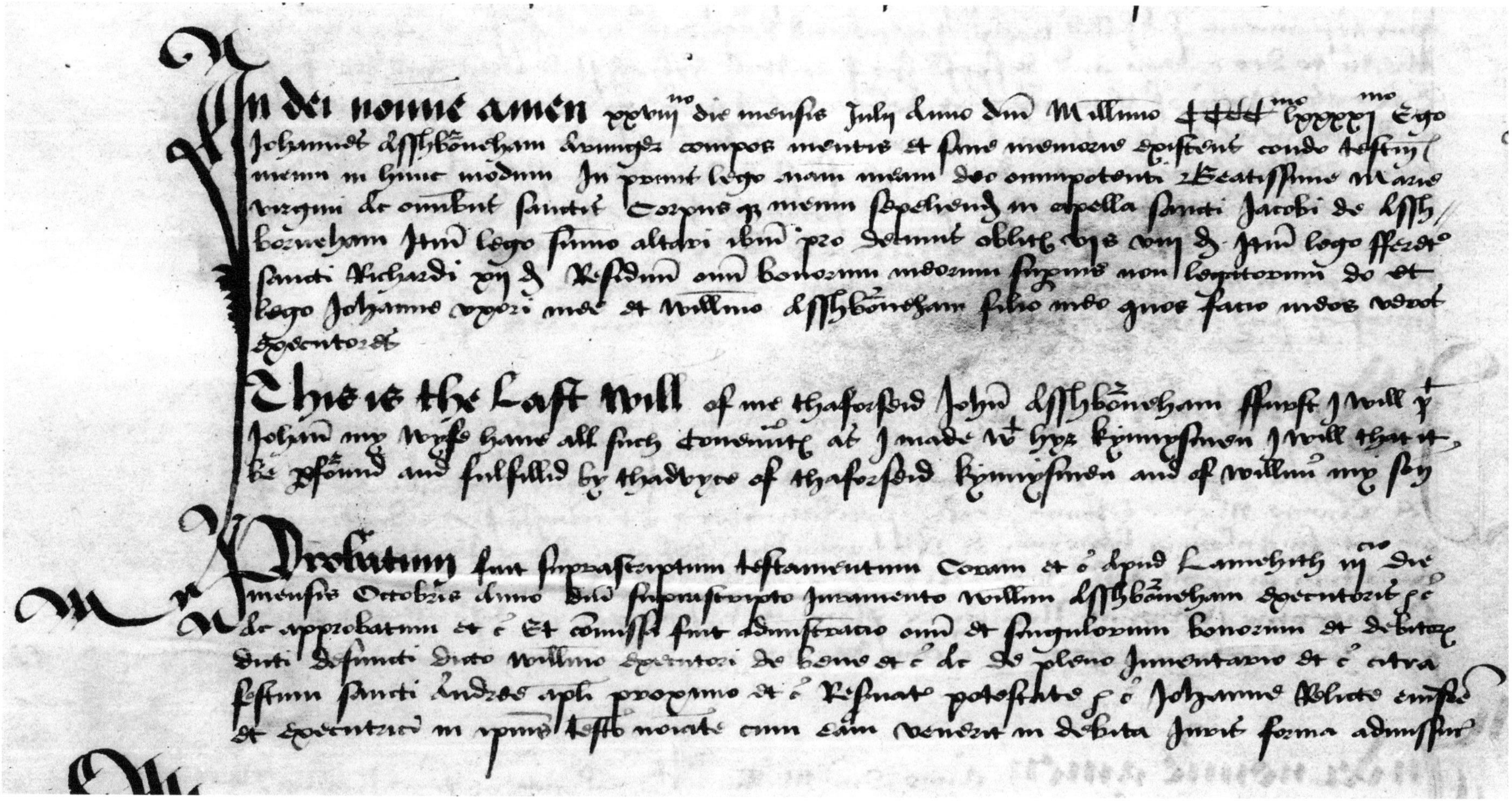

In dei nomine amen

1
2
3
4
5
6
7
8

This is the Last Will

9
10
11

12
13
14
15
16
17

1. **In dei nomi[n]e amen** xxviij[vo] [1] die mensis Iulii Anno d[omi]ni Mill[es]imo CCCC[mo] [2] lxxxxj[mo] [2] Ego
2. Johannes Asshbo[u]rneham Armiger compos mentis et sane memorie existens condo test[amentu]m
3. meum in hunc modum In primis lego a[n]i[m]am meam deo omnipotenti Beatissime Marie
4. virgini Ac om[n]ibus sanctis Corpus q[ue] [3] meum sepeliend[um] in capella sancti Jacobi de Assh
5. borneham It[e]m lego sum[m]o altari ib[ide]m pro decimis oblit[is] vjs viijd It[e]m lego Feret[r]o
6. sancti Richardi xijd Residuu[m] o[mn]i[u]m bonorum meorum su[per]ius non legatorum do et
7. lego Johanne uxori mee et Will[el]mo Asshbo[u]rneham filio meo quos facio meos veros
8. executores

9. **This is the Last Will** of me thaforseid John Asshbo[u]rneham Furst I will [tha]t
10. Johan my wyfe have all such Covena[u]nt[es] as I made w[i]t[h] hyr kynnysmen I will that it
11. be p[er]fo[u]rmid and fulfillid by thadvyce of thaforseid kynnysmen and of Willi[a]m my son

12. **Probatum** fuit suprascriptum testamentum Coram et c[etera] Apud Lamehith iij[cio] [4] die
13. mensis Octobris Anno d[omi]ni suprascripto Iuramento Will[el]mi Asshbo[u]rneham executoris & c
14. Ac approbatum et c[etera] Et co[m]missa fuit admi[ni]stracio o[mn]i[u]m et singulorum bonorum et debitor[um]
15. dicti defuncti dicto Will[el]mo executori de bene et c[etera] Ac de pleno Inventario et c[etera] citra
16. festum sancti Andree ap[osto]li proximo et c[etera] Res[er]vat[a] potestate & c[etera] Johanne Relicte eiusde[m]
17. et executrici in ip[s]ius test[ament]o no[m]i[n]ate cum eam [5] venerit in debita Iuris forma admissur[a] [6]

In the name of God Amen on the 28th day of the month of July in the one thousand four hundred and ninety first year of the Lord I John Asshbourneham esquire being of sound mind and good memory make my will in this manner First I bequeath my soul to Almighty God to the most blessed Virgin Mary and to all the saints and my body to be buried in the chapel of Saint James of Asshborneham Likewise I bequeath to the high altar there for forgotten tithes 6s. 8d. [7] Likewise I bequeath to the shrine of Saint Richard 12d. The residue of all my goods not above bequeathed I give and bequeath to Joan my wife and William Asshbo[u]rneham my son whom I make my true executors.

The abovewritten will was proved before etc. at Lambeth on the 3rd day of the month of October in the abovewritten year of the Lord by the oath of William Asshbourneham the executor &c. and approved etc. And administration was granted of all and singular the goods and debts of the said deceased to the said William the executor for well etc. And for a full inventory etc. before [8] the feast of Saint Andrew the Apostle [9] next etc. power being reserved &c. to Joan the relict of the same and the executrix named in the will of the same when she comes to accept it in due form of law.

COMMENTARY

Will of John Asshbourneham
(TNA:PRO ref: PROB 11/9/1)

Document

For a note on wills see commentary on plate 6. The expression 'will and testament' is often used in general terms, but in some early cases the will and testament were given separate identity. The distinction normally made is that the will relates to lands and tenements; the testament to goods and chattels. In this case the testament is in Latin, the will in English.

Script

This hand is typical of will registrations of the Prerogative Court of Canterbury at this period. The scribe has two forms of medial letter *r* (see *Armiger* and *memorie* in l. 2). The first of these is particularly deceptive. There is the recurrent problem with minims, compounded here by the economical use of a dot for the *i*. Note in the English the use of thorn and the elision of the word 'the' with the following word with an initial vowel.

Notes

1. The superscript *vo* indicates the final letters of the ordinal number *octavo*.
2. Similarly, *mo* here denotes ordinal number endings.
3. Note how the suffix *-que* is divorced from the previous word.
4. *cio* also denotes an ordinal number ending, in this case for *tercio*.
5. The word *eam* would seem to refer back to *administracio*.
6. *Admissura* is the fairly rare future participle, suggesting intention.
7. Forgotten tithes were often mentioned in wills.
8. *Citra* is an interesting word in that, meaning 'this side of' (relating to time), it can in fact indicate 'before' or 'after' according to context.
9. The feast of St Andrew fell on 30th November.

(Plate, transcript and translation on previous spread)

COMMENTARY

Final Concord
(TNA:PRO ref: CP 25(2)/237, Easter 39 Eliz I)

Document

For note on final concords see commentary on plate 10. This is the document drawn up for Shakespeare's purchase of New Place in Stratford-upon-Avon. Despite the great number of ways in which Shakespeare can be spelt, and the frequent variations of the spelling of names which can occur within a document, the spelling here is as we know it, and consistent. Further references to documents relating to Shakespeare can be found in *Shakespeare in the Public Records* by David Thomas (1985).

Script

The plaintiff here is exceptional but the writing not so, being typical of the kind of court hand in which many final concords are written. The letters *h*, *u* and *w* are identical whether small or capital. On the other hand there are two distinct forms of the medial letter *r* (see *Concordia* in l. 1 and Anderson in l. 3). The initial *s* is surprisingly large, though different from *S*; the *c* is often nearly closed up (and apparently entirely so when juxtaposed to another letter). Most of the surnames have an abbreviation mark not strictly suggesting any particular ending. This type of hand, found as the vehicle for so many legal documents, appears formidable to the unaccustomed eye but, as can be seen, is extremely regular. Once the unusual form of some of the letters has been mastered (by means of the examples of letters and transcript) the main problem lies in the minims. Most hands, including modern ones, display some degree of this difficulty, but it is enhanced in Latin texts (and especially in court hand) due to the wealth of words, particularly endings, which include combinations of *i*, *m*, *n*, *u*, and *v*.

Notes

1. This word is plural, relating to the places mentioned.
2. The year is 1597; Easter day fell on 27th March in that year.

(Plate, transcript and translation on following spread)

TRANSCRIPT

Final Concord

(TNA:PRO ref: CP 25(2)/237, Easter 39 Eliz I)

1. Hec est finalis Concordia f[a]c[t]a in Cur[ia] d[omi]ne Regine apud Westm' A die Pasche in quinq[ue]
2. septimanas Anno regnor[um]¹ Elizabeth[e] dei gr[aci]a Angl[ie] Franc[ie] & Hib[er]nie Regine fidei
3. defens[oris] &c A conq[uest]u tricesimo Nono² coram Ed[uard]o Anderson Thoma Walmysley
4. Francisco Beaumont & Thoma Owen Iustic[iariis] & aliis d[omi]ne Regine fidelib[us] tunc
5. ibi p[re]sentib[us] Int[er] Will[elmu]m Shakespeare quer[entem] et Will[elmu]m Underhill gen[er]osum defor[ciantem]
6. de uno Mesuagio duob[us] horreis & duob[us] gardinis cum p[er]tin[enciis] in Stratford' sup[er]
7. Avon' unde Pl[ac]it[u]m convenc[i]o[n]is sum[monitum] fuit int[er] eos in eadem Cur[ia] Scil[ice]t q[uo]d
8. p[re]d[i]c[t]us Will[elmu]s <Underhill> recogn[ovit] p[re]d[i]c[t]a ten[ementa] cum p[er]tin[enciis] esse ius ip[s]ius Will[elm]i Shakespeare
9. ut ill[a] que idem Will[elmu]s h[ab]et de dono p[re]d[i]c[t]i Will[elm]i Underhill et ill[a] remisit &
10. quiet[um]clam[avit] de se & hered[ibus] suis p[re]d[i]c[t]o Will[elm]o Shakespeare & hered[ibus] suis
11. Imp[er]p[etuu]m et p[re]t[er]ea idem Will[elmu]s Underhill concessit p[ro] se & hered[ibus] suis q[uo]d ip[s]i
12. warant[izabunt] p[re]d[i]c[t]o Will[elm]o Shakespeare & hered[ibus] suis p[re]d[i]c[t]a ten[ementa] cu*m* p[er]tin[enciis]
13. Imp[er]p[etuu]m et p[ro] hac recogn[icione] remissione quiet[a]clam[acione] warant[ia] fine & Concordia
14. idem Will[elmu]s Shakespeare dedit p[re]d[i]c[t]o Will[elm]o Underhill Sexaginta libras
15. sterlingor[um]
16.

Warr'   ex[aminatur]

TRANSLATION This is the final agreement made in the court of the Lady Queen at Westminster in five weeks of Easter day in the thirty ninth year of the reign(s) of Elizabeth by the grace of God Queen of England France & Ireland defender of the faith etc from the conquest before Edward Anderson Thomas Walmysley Francis Beaumont & Thomas Owen justices and other faithful men of the Lady Queen then there present between William Shakespeare plaintiff and William Underhill gentleman defendant concerning one messuage two barns & two gardens with appurtenances in Stratford upon Avon whereof a plea of covenant was summoned between them in the same court That is to say that the aforesaid William Underhill has acknowledged the aforesaid tenements with appurtenances to be the right of the same William Shakespeare as those which the same William has of the gift of the aforesaid William Underhill and he has remised & quitclaimed them from himself & his heirs to the aforesaid William Shakespeare & his heirs for ever and moreover the same William Underhill has granted for himself & his heirs that they themselves will warrant to the aforesaid William Shakespeare & his heirs the aforesaid tenements with appurtenances for ever and for this acknowledgement remise quitclaim warrant fine & agreement the same William Shakespeare has given to the aforesaid William Underhill sixty pounds sterling

Warwickshire it is examined

TRANSCRIPT

Deed

(Surrey History Centre ref: 371/8/223)

1. Sciant p[re]sentes & futuri q[uo]d ego Ricardus Stapelere Bouchier[1] & Civis London' dedi concessi & hac p[re]senti carta mea
2. confirmavi Ric[ard]o Stevene Civi London' & Eve uxori sue totum mesuagium meum cum omnib[us] domib[us] sup[er]edificatis cu[m]
3. gardino adiacente situatis in Burgo de Reigate que quond[a]m fuerunt Philippi Broun que quid[e]m nup[er] adquisivi de
4. Johanne Fether & Andrea Gattyn Habend[um] & tenend[um] omnia p[re]dicta mesuagium & gardinu[m] cum omnib[us] domib[us] sup[er]edificat[is]
5. cum omnib[us] suis p[er]tinenciis p[re]fatis Ric[ard]o Stevene & Eve uxori sue heredib[us] & assignatis suis de capitali d[omi]no feodi illius p[er]
6. redditus & servicia inde debita & consueta imp[er]petuu[m] Et ego vero p[re]dictus Ric[ard]us Stapelere & heredes mei omnia p[re]fata me
7. suagiu[m] & gardinu[m] cum omnib[us] domib[us] sup[er]edificatis & omnib[us] aliis suis p[er]tinenc[iis] p[re]fatis Ricardo Stevene & Eve heredib[us] &
8. assignatis suis contra omnes gentes warrantizabimus & imp[er]petuum defendemus In cuius rei testimoniu[m] huic p[re]senti carte
9. mee sigillum meum apposui Hiis testib[us] Joh[an]ne Fether Walt[er]o Wrig'[2] Henrico Flaynesford Joh[an]ne Skynn[er]e Rogero
10. Chaunce Joh[an]ne Hammeshurne[3] Ric[ard]o Turnour & Joh[an]ne Kny[g]t[4] tunc ballivo de Reigate cum multis aliis Dat[a][5] apud
11. Reigate p[re]dictam sextodecimo die Maii Anno regni Regis Henrici quarti post conquestum Anglie Nono[6]

[46]

TRANSLATION

Let all present & future men know that I Richard Stapelere butcher & citizen of London have given granted & by this my present deed confirmed to Richard Stevene citizen of London & Eve his wife my whole messuage with all houses built thereon with the garden adjacent situated in the borough of Reigate which were sometime Philip Broun's which indeed I lately bought of John Fether & Andrew Gattyn to have and to hold all the aforesaid messuage & garden with all the houses built thereon with all their appurtenances to the aforesaid Richard Stevene & Eve his wife their heirs & assigns from the lord in chief of that fee by rents & services owed & accustomed in respect thereof for ever And I truly the aforesaid Richard Stapelere & my heirs shall warrant & for ever defend all the aforesaid messuage & garden with all the houses built thereupon & all other their appurtenances to the aforesaid Richard Stevene & Eve their heirs & assigns against all people In witness whereof I have affixed my seal to this my present deed These being witnesses John Fether Walter Wrig' Henry Flaynesford John Skynnere Roger Chaunce John Hammeshurne Richard Turnour & John Knygt then bailiff of Reigate with many others Given at Reigate aforesaid on the sixteenth day of May in the ninth year of the reign of King Henry the fourth after the conquest of England.

COMMENTARY

Document

Deeds of title were formal legal documents (sometimes indented) relating to ownership or occupation of real estate. They might thus embrace the transfer of lands (corporeal hereditaments) or intangible rights such as tithes, advowsons or annuities (incorporeal hereditaments). This document is part of the archive of Reigate Borough Council.

Script

As so often, it appears that the letters *h* and *w*, whether small or capital, are extremely similar, if not in some cases identical. The mark over the letter *i*, doing duty as a dot, often looks similar to some abbreviation marks. The dotting of the *i* is, however, arbitrary.

Notes

1. Bouchier: this has the form of the Anglo-Norman French for butcher but is perhaps a variant of the obsolete English word 'boucher' with that meaning.
2. This is an unorthodox abbreviation and appears, by comparison with other documents in the series, to complete a name such as Wright.
3. Allowing for the letter *i* in this hand being in many cases without its dot, there could be other possibilities for these six minims e.g. *-unn-*.
4. Note the yogh.
5. *Data*: feminine to agree with *carta*.
6. 1408.

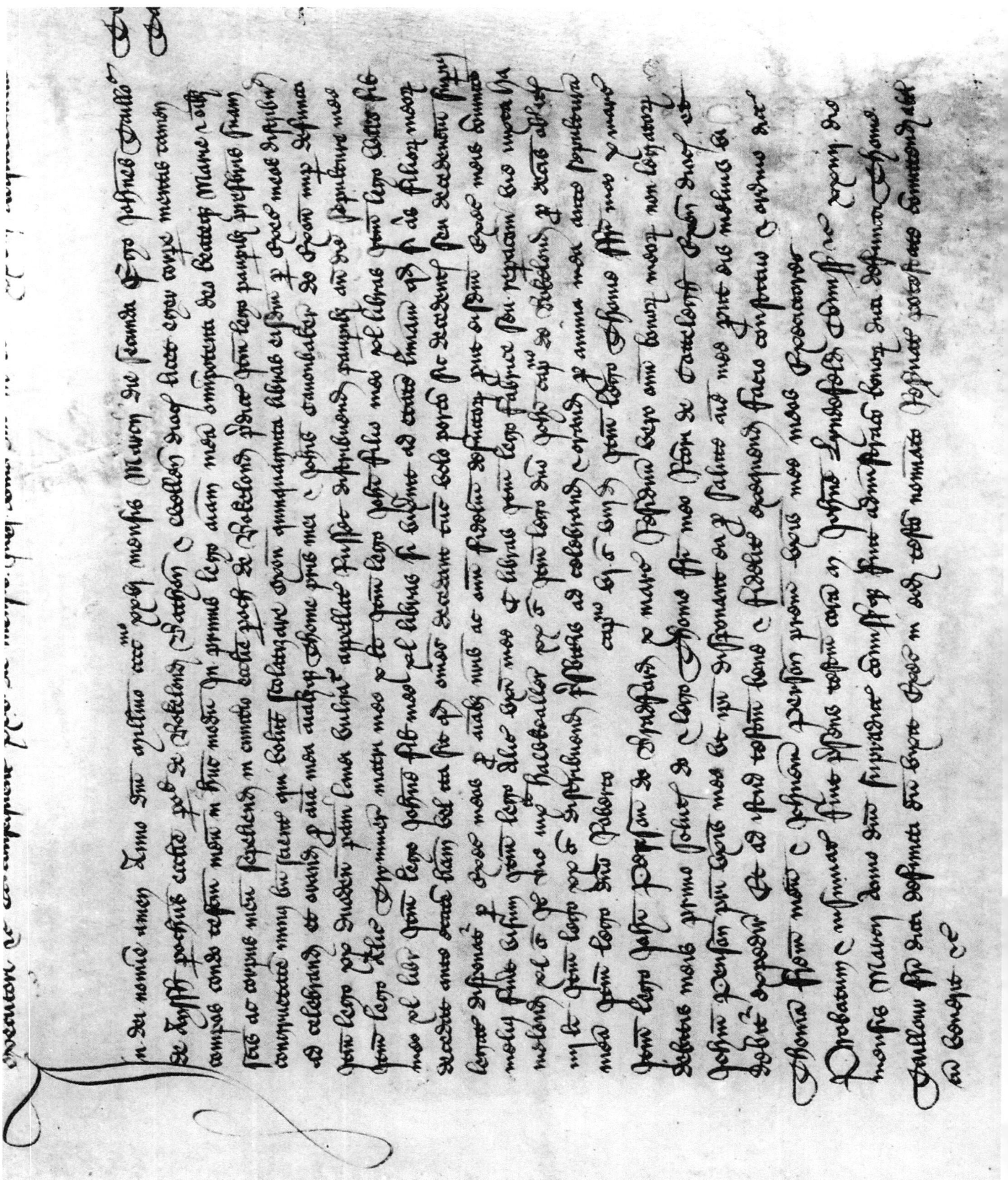

The Will of John Taillour

(TNA:PRO ref: PROB 11/3/55)

1. In dei nomi[n]e amen Anno d[omi]ni mill[esi]mo cccc[mo][1] xxvj mensis Marcii die secunda[2] Ego Joh[a]n[n]es Taillo[u]r

2. de Ayssh' p[ar]och[ian]us eccl[es]ie p[ar]och[ial][is] de Bokelond' Bathon[iensis] & Wellen[sis] dioc[esis] licet eger corp[or]e mentis tamen

3. compos condo test[amentu]m meu[m] in[3] hu[n]c modu[m] In primis lego a[n]i[m]am mea[m] om[n]ipotenti deo beateq[ue] Marie & o[mn]ib[us]

4. s[an]c[t]is ac corpus meu[m] sepeliend[um] in cimit[er]io eccl[es]ie p[ar]och[ialis] de Bokelond' p[re]dict'[4] It[e]m lego paup[er]ib[us] presb[ite]ris suam

5. congruetate[m] min[us] b[e]n[e] scient[ibus] qui volu[n]t scolatizare Oxon'[5] quinquaginta libras eisd[e]m p[er] Exec[utores] meos distribu[en]d[as]

6. ad celebrand[um] et orand[um] p[ro] a[n]i[m]a mea a[n]i[m]ab[us]q[ue] Thome p[at]ris mei & Joh[ann]is Canonbaker de Exon' nup[er] defuncti

7. It[e]m lego xx duoden[as][6] pan[n]i lanei vulga[ri]t[er] appellat[i] Russet distribuend[as] paup[er]ib[us] an[te] die[m] sepulture mee

8. It[e]m lego Alic[ie] Trymmer matri mee x li[bras] It[e]m lego Joh[ann]i filio meo xl libras It[e]m lego Will[elm]o fil[io]

9. meo xl libr[as] It[e]m lego Joh[a]n[n]e fil[ie] mee xl libras si vix[er]int ad etate[m] l[egit]imam q[uo]d si a[l]iqu[is] filior[um] meor[um]

10. decedat ante etate[m] l[egit]i[m]am vel ita sit q[uo]d om[n]es decedant tu[n]c volo porc[i]o sic decedent[is] seu decedentiu[m] sup[er]ji[us]

11. legat[a] disponat[u]r p[er] Exec[utores] meos p[ro] a[n]i[m]ab[us] n[ost]ris ac o[mn]i[u]m fideliu[m] defu[n]ctor[um] p[ro]ut eisd[e]m Exec[utoribus] meis co[n]iuncti[m][7]

12. meli[us] fu[er]it visum It[e]m lego Alic[ie] ux[or]i mee C libras It[e]m lego fabrice seu rep[ar]ac[i]oni vie iuxta Ha[8]

13. melond' xl s[olidos] It[em] vie iux[t]a Hawkealler' xx s[olidos] It[e]m lego d[omi]no Joh[ann]i cap[ella]no de Bokelond' p[ro] dec[im]is oblit[is]

14. iiij li[bras] It[e]m lego xx s[olidos] distribuend[os] p[re]sbit[er]is ad celebrand[um] & orand[um] p[ro] anima mea ante sepultura[m]

15. mea[m] It[e]m lego d[omi]no Roberto   cap[ella]no vj s[olidos] viij d[enarios] It[e]m lego Thome Fr[atr]i meo x marc[as]

16. It[e]m lego Joh[ann]i Person'[9] de Bradford'[10] x marc[as] Residuu[m] vero o[mn]i[u]m bonor[um] meor[um] non legator[um]

17. debitis meis primo solut[is][11] do & lego Thome fr[atr]i meo R[e]c[t]ori de Cottelegh[10] Exon[iensis] dioc[esis] et

18. Joh[a]n[n]i Penson p[at]ri ux[or]is mee ut ip[s]i disponant ea p[ro] salute a[n]i[m]e mee p[ro]ut eis melius vi[8]

19. debit[u]r expedir[e] Et ad istud test[amentu]m bene & fidelit[er] exequend[um] facio constituo & ordino dict[os]

20. Thoma[m] fr[atr]em meu[m] & Joh[a]n[n]em Person p[at]rem ux[or]is mee meos Executores

21. Probatum & insinuat[um] fuit p[re]sens test[amentu]m cora[m] M[agistro] Joh[a]n[n]e Lyndefeld Co[m]miss[ario][12] &c xxiiij die

22. mensis Marcii Anno d[omi]ni supradict[o] co[m]miss[a]q[ue] fuit admi[n]istrac[i]o bonor[um] dicti defuncti Thome

23. Taillour fr[atr]i dicti defuncti du[m] vixit Exec[utori] in eod[em] test[ament]o nomi[n]ato Res[er]vat[a] potestate co[m]mittend[i] alt[er]i

24. cu[m] venerit &c

[47]

TRANSLATION

The Will of John Taillour

(TNA:PRO ref: PROB/11/3/55)

In the name of God Amen in the fourteen hundred and twenty sixth year of the Lord on the second day of the month of March I John Taillour of Ayssh a parishioner of the parish church of Bokelond of the diocese of Bath & Wells despite [being] ill in body nonetheless sound of mind compose my will in this manner Firstly I bequeath my soul to Almighty God and to the Blessed Mary & to all the saints and my body to be buried in the churchyard of the parish church of Bokelond aforesaid Also I bequeath to the poor priests less well knowing their [grammatical] correctness who wish to study at Oxford fifty pounds to be distributed to the same by my executors to celebrate[13] and to pray for my soul and the souls of Thomas my father & of John Canonbaker of Exeter lately deceased[14] Also I bequeath 20 dozen[15] [pieces] of woollen cloth commonly called russet to be distributed to the poor before the day of my burial Also I bequeath to Alice Trymmer my mother 10 pounds Also I bequeath to John my son 40 pounds Also I bequeath to William my son 40 pounds Also I bequeath to Joan my daughter 40 pounds if they live to legal age that if any of my sons[16] should die before legal age or it so be that they all die then I will that the portion above bequeathed of that one or those so dying[17] should be disposed by my executors for our souls and [those] of all the faithful departed as it shall seem best[18] jointly to my same executors Also I bequeath to Alice my wife 100 pounds Also I bequeath for the fabric or repair of the way next to Hamelond 40 shillings Also for the way next to Hawkealler 20 shillings Also I bequeath to Sir[19] John chaplain of Bokelond for forgotten tithes 4 pounds Also I bequeath 20 shillings to be distributed to priests to celebrate & to pray for my soul before my burial Also I bequeath to Sir Robert chaplain 6 shillings 8 pence Also I bequeath to Thomas my brother 10 marks Also I bequeath to John Person of Bradford 10 marks The residue however of all my goods not bequeathed my debts being first paid I give & bequeath to Thomas my brother rector of Cottelegh of the diocese of Exeter and to John Penson the father of my wife that they may dispose them for the well-being of my soul as shall best seem to them to be right And for well and truly performing this will I make constitute & ordain the said[20] Thomas my brother & John Person the father of my wife my executors.

The present will was proved & registered before Master John Lyndefeld commissary &c. on the 24th day of the month of March[21] in the abovesaid year of the Lord and administration of the goods of the said deceased was granted to Thomas Taillour the brother of the said deceased while he lived the executor named in the same will, power being reserved for granting to the other when he comes &c.

COMMENTARY

Document

See general note on wills for plate 6. Wills were proved in the Prerogative Court of Canterbury from 1383. This example, proved in 1427, shows many of the early features of the time and has the advantage of indicating three generations of a family.

Script

Here the letter *t* is very low and in some cases almost identical with the letter *c*. Note for instance the very slight difference between the words *sit* and *sic* in l. 10. In l. 4, similarly, the word *s[an]c[t]is*, with the second letter joined by ligature to the letter *s*, is the likely reading, although s[anc]tis is as suitable from the form of the letters. In some cases *o* and *a* are very much alike. The scribe is not consistent with forms of capital letters, having two types of *A* and of *M*. There are two types of abbreviation for the ending -ur.

Notes

1. The year: the superscript ending of *cccc^mo* is an indication, as seen previously and often found, of an ordinal number in the ablative case as in *vij^mo*, *x^mo*, for *septimo*, *decimo*. This or other suitable ordinal ending tends to occur on the end of each part of the number, and one might here have expected *xxvj^to* to follow.
2. The word *dies* (day) can be masculine or feminine, generally the former, here the latter as indicated by *secunda*.
3. Note the use here of the preposition *in* with the accusative, where classical Latin would expect the ablative, or omit the preposition.
4. This word has not been fully extended since it is unknown whether Bokelond was considered to be masculine or feminine.
5. *Oxon'* is here taken as locative case (*Oxonie*).
6. *duedena* or *duodenarios* could be alternatives here.
7. The end of this word is not clear in the manuscript, but the beginning indicates the full word *coniunctim*.
8. Note that this word is continued on the following line.
9. The third letter appears to be written over an *n*, rather than the reverse, but both Penson and Person appear subsequently.
10. Despite appearance, these place-names seem likely to include examples of this scribe's rendering of the letter *o*, joining it so that it resembles an *a* (see *o[mn]i[u]m* in l. 16).
11. *debitis ... solutis*: an example of the ablative absolute.
12. Although a general abbreviation which indicates an omitted *m* is normally taken to signify a second *m*, here and subsequently in this document it is clear that the first *m* has been omitted.
13. E.g. mass (here and subsequently).
14. The word 'deceased' strictly refers only to John Canonbaker.
15. Apparently a word for e.g. pieces is understood; however, it is interesting to note that, with regard to kersey (a woollen cloth) at least in the following century, a Devonshire kersey of a particular size was known as a dozen (*O.E.D.*).
16. This is the literal translation but perhaps *filiorum* might here be taken to mean 'children' since the masculine can be used for a combination of masculine and feminine.
17. Literally, dying (singular) or dying (plural).
18. Literally, here and subsequently, 'better', but *melius* is commonly translated as 'best' in this type of context.
19. Sir (*dominus*), here and subsequently: often used as a courtesy title for clergy.
20. The Latin *dictos*, more succinct than in English, relates to both executors.
21. Thus (see p. 11) the date given was in 1426 but, falling (as does that of the will) during the period 1 January – 24 March, was in the historical year 1427. The will was proved on the last day of 1426 as then computed.

N.B. Note here the distinction between the cases of *Johannes* and *Johanna*. See (l. 8) for *Johanni*, the dative of *Johannes*; and (l. 9) *Johanne*, dative of *Johanna*. In another context *Johanne* could be the ablative of *Johannes*.

(Plate and transcript on previous spread)

Final Concord (1648)

1. Hec est finalis Concordia f[a]c[t]a in Cur[ia] D[omi]ni Regis apud Westm' in Crastino s[an]c[t]i Martini Anno regnor[um] Caroli Dei
gr[aci]a Angl[ie] Scocie

2. Franc[ie] & Hib[er]nie Regis fidei defens[oris] &c A Conqu[estu] vicesimo quarto¹ Coram Petro Phesant & Ric[ard]o Cresheld Iustic[iariis]
& aliis D[omi]ni Regis

3. fidelib[us] tunc ibi p[re]sentib[us] Int[er] Rob[er]tum Fretchwell quer[entem] et Alanu[m] Snowe seniorem gen[er]osum & Elizabeth[am]²
ux[or]em eius Joh[ann]em Snowe

4. gen[er]osum Ric[ardu]m Snowe Iuniorem Samuelem Snowe Alanu[m] Snowe Saram Taylor viduam Franciscum Hanson & Mariam
ux[or]em eius & Will[elmu]m

5. Bankes & Elizabeth[am] ux[or]em eius deforc[iantes] de uno mesuagio & uno gardino cum p[er]tin[enciis] in parochia s[an]c[t]i Andree
Holborne unde Pl[ac]it[u]m Convenc[i]o[n]is

6. sum[monitum] fuit int[er] eos in eadem Cur[ia] Scil[ice]t q[uo]d p[re]d[i]c[t]i Alanus & Elizabeth[a] Joh[ann]es Ric[ard]us Alanus Samuel
Sara Franciscus & Maria & Will[elmu]s &

7. Elizabeth[a] recogn[overunt] p[re]d[i]c[t]a ten[ementa] cum p[er]tin[enciis] esse ius ip[s]ius Rob[er]ti ut ill[a] que idem Rob[er]tus h[ab]et
de dono p[re]d[i]c[t]or[um] Alani & Elizabeth[e] Joh[ann]is

8. Ric[ard]i Alani Samuelis Sare Francisci & Marie & Will[elm]i & Elizabeth[e] Et ill[a] remiser[unt] & quietclam[averunt] de ip[s]is Alano &
Elizabeth[a] Joh[ann]e Ric[ard]o

9. Alano Samuele Sara Francisco & Maria & Will[elm]o & Elizabeth[a] & hered[ibus] suis p[re]d[i]c[t]o Rob[er]to & hered[ibus] suis
imp[er]p[etuu]m Et p[re]f[at]ea idem Alanus

10. Snowe senior & Elizabeth[a] uxor eius concesser[unt] p[ro] se & hered[ibus] ip[s]ius Elizabeth[e] q[uo]d ip[s]i warant[izabunt] p[re]d[i]c[t]o
Rob[er]to & hered[ibus] suis p[re]d[i]c[t]a

11. ten[ementa] cum p[er]tin[enciis] cont[r]a p[re]d[i]c[t]os Alanu[m] & Elizabeth[am] & hered[es] ip[s]ius Elizabeth[e] imp[er]p[etuu]m Et
ult[er]ius idem Joh[ann]es concessit p[ro] se & hered[ibus]

12. suis q[uo]d ip[s]i warant[izabunt] p[re]d[i]c[t]o Rob[er]to & hered[ibus] suis p[re]d[i]c[t]a ten[ementa] cum p[er]tin[enciis] cont[r]a
p[re]d[i]c[tu]m Joh[ann]em & hered[es] suos imp[er]p[etuu]m Et insup[er] idem Ric[ard]us

13. concessit p[ro] se & hered[ibus] suis q[uo]d ip[s]i warant[izabunt] p[re]d[i]c[t]o Rob[er]to & hered[ibus] suis p[re]d[i]c[t]a ten[ementa] cum
p[er]tin[enciis] cont[r]a p[re]d[i]c[tu]m Ric[ardu]m & hered[es] suos imp[er]p[etuu]m

14. Et eciam idem Alanus <Snowe> Iun[ior] concessit p[ro] se & hered[ibus] suis q[uo]d ip[s]i warant[izabunt] p[re]d[i]c[t]o Rob[er]to &
hered[ibus] suis p[re]d[i]c[t]a ten[ementa] cum p[er]tin[enciis] cont[r]a ³

15. p[re]d[i]c[tu]m Alanu[m] & hered[es] suos imp[er]p[etuu]m Et eciam idem Samuel concessit p[ro] se & hered[ibus] suis q[uo]d ip[s]i
warant[izabunt] p[re]d[i]c[t]o Rob[er]to & hered[ibus]

16. suis p[re]d[i]c[t]a ten[ementa] cum p[er]tin[enciis] cont[r]a p[re]d[i]c[tu]m Samuelem & hered[es] suos imp[er]p[etuu]m Et eciam eadem
Sara concessit p[ro] se & hered[ibus] suis

17. q[uo]d ip[s]i warant[izabunt] p[re]d[i]c[t]o Rob[er]to & hered[ibus] suis p[re]d[i]c[t]a ten[ementa] cum p[er]tin[enciis] cont[r]a
p[re]d[i]c[t]am Saram & hered[es] suos imp[er]p[etuu]m Et eciam idem

18. Franciscus & Maria concesser[unt] p[ro] se & hered[ibus] ip[s]ius Marie q[uo]d ip[s]i warant[izabunt] p[re]d[i]c[t]o Rob[er]to & hered[ibus]
suis p[re]d[i]c[t]a ten[ementa] cum p[er]tin[enciis] cont[r]a

19. p[re]d[i]c[t]os Franciscum & Mariam & hered[es] ip[s]ius Marie imp[er]p[etuu]m Et eciam iidem Will[elmu]s & Elizabeth[a] uxor eius
concesser[unt] p[ro] se &

20. hered[ibus] ip[s]ius Elizabeth[e] q[uo]d ip[s]i warant[izabunt] p[re]d[i]c[t]o Rob[er]to & hered[ibus] suis p[re]d[i]c[t]a ten[ementa] cum
p[er]tin[enciis] cont[r]a p[re]d[i]c[t]os Will[elmu]m & Elizabeth[am] & hered[es]

21. ip[s]ius Elizabeth[e] imp[er]p[etuu]m Et p[ro] hac recogn[icione] remissione quietclam[acione] warant[ia] fine & Concordia idem
Rob[er]tus dedit p[re]d[i]c[t]is Alano &

22. Elizabeth[e] Joh[ann]i Ric[ard]o Alano Samueli Sare Francisco & Marie & Will[elm]o & Elizabeth[e] Centum libras sterlingor[um]

TRANSLATION

Final Concord (1648)

This is the final concord made in the court of the Lord King at Westminster on the morrow of Saint Martin the twenty fourth year of the reign(s) of Charles by the grace of God King of England Scotland France & Ireland defender of the faith &c from the conquest before Peter Phesant & Richard Cresheld justices & other faithful men of the Lord King then there present Between Robert Fretchwell querent and Alan Snowe senior gentleman & Elizabeth his wife John Snowe gentleman Richard Snowe Alan Snowe junior Samuel Snowe Sarah Taylor widow Francis Hanson & Mary his wife & William Bankes & Elizabeth his wife deforciants concerning one messuage & one garden with appurtenances in the parish of Saint Andrew Holborne whereof a plea of covenant was summoned between them in the same court That is to say that the aforesaid Alan & Elizabeth John Richard Alan Samuel Sara Francis & Mary & William & Elizabeth acknowledged the aforesaid tenements with appurtenances to be the right of the same Robert as those which the same Robert has of the gift of the aforesaid Alan & Elizabeth John Richard Alan Samuel Sarah Francis & Mary & William & Elizabeth And they remised & quitclaimed them from the same Alan & Elizabeth John Richard Alan Samuel Sarah Francis & Mary & William & Elizabeth & their heirs to the aforesaid Robert & his heirs for ever And furthermore the same Alan Snowe senior and Elizabeth his wife have granted for themselves & the heirs of the same Elizabeth that they will warrant to the aforesaid Robert and his heirs the aforesaid tenements with appurtenances against the aforesaid Alan & Elizabeth & the heirs of the same Elizabeth for ever And further the same John has granted for himself & his heirs that they will warrant to the aforesaid Robert & his heirs the aforesaid tenements with appurtenances against the aforesaid John & his heirs for ever And moreover the same Richard has granted for himself & his heirs that they will warrant to the aforesaid Robert & his heirs the aforesaid tenements with appurtenances against the aforesaid Richard & his heirs for ever And also the same Alan Snowe junior has granted for himself & his heirs that they will warrant to the aforesaid Robert & his heirs the aforesaid tenements with appurtenances against the aforesaid Alan & his heirs for ever And also the same Samuel has granted for himself & his heirs that they will warrant to the aforesaid Robert & his heirs the aforesaid tenements with appurtenances against the aforesaid Samuel & his heirs for ever And also the same Sarah has granted for herself & her heirs that they will warrant to the aforesaid Robert & his heirs the aforesaid tenements with appurtenances against the aforesaid Sarah & her heirs for ever And also the same Francis & Mary have granted for themselves & the heirs of the same Mary that they will warrant to the aforesaid Robert & his heirs the aforesaid tenements with appurtenances against the aforesaid Francis & Mary & the heirs of the same Mary for ever And also the same William & Elizabeth his wife have granted for themselves & the heirs of the same Elizabeth that they will warrant to the aforesaid Robert & his heirs the aforesaid tenements with appurtenances against the aforesaid William & Elizabeth & the heirs of the same Elizabeth for ever And for this acknowledgement remise quitclaim warrant fine & concord the same Robert has given to the aforesaid Alan & Elizabeth John Richard Alan Samuel Sarah Francis & Mary & William & Elizabeth a hundred pounds sterling.

COMMENTARY

Final Concord (1648)

Document

For notes on the final concord, see commentary for plate 10 where the original tripartite documents are mentioned. The feet were retained by the court and now form the vast series at The National Archives. According to C.A.F. Meekings in his introduction to the Surrey Record Society's volume XIX, *Surrey Fines, 1509-1558,* 'the upper portions were delivered to the parties, the right-hand copy to the deforciants and the left-hand copy to the plaintiffs'. One can tell from the indentations therefore that this copy (which is in private ownership) was the part given to the plaintiff, or querent, Robert Fretchwell, who was buying the land. The right side of this document would have adjoined part of the top of the foot which is, of course, in The National Archives. It is unusual for so many parties to feature in a final concord, and it seems likely that not only those deforciants who had the surname Snowe were related.

Script

This kind of court hand, though daunting at first (but similar to the Tudor document, plate 45) and, as so often in Latin documents, full of abbreviations, is nonetheless also very regular. The examples of letters in the book and an observant eye should be of help in unravelling the writing. Those abbreviations consisting of a horizontal line above the word are in some cases extremely thin. The curious custom of crossing *ll* (as in Fretchwell) is particularly noticeable here, thus on first impact suggesting *tt*, although further scrutiny will show that the tops and height of the letters *l* and *t* differ. Elsewhere the crossing of *ll* indicates different endings of *ille*. However, perhaps the main difficulty, as with many other hands, is in dealing with the minims, particularly as the letter *i* is bereft of its dot. At the ends of some words the scribe indulges in some rather grandiose flourishes (having no particular significance, but not untypical).

Notes

1. There are several dates for St Martin. The date here seems likely to have been 5 July 1648. Curiously the document is endorsed (perhaps in a later hand) Michaelmas 24 Car. 1st 1649, which seems contradictory, since Michaelmas 24 Car 1st was in 1648, and Michaelmas 1649 was after the execution.
2. The horizontal line over this name to indicate the Latin ending is consistently very faint.
3. Here there is a rather elaborate line filler.

(Plate and transcript on previous spread)

TRANSCRIPT

Chancery Proceeding
(TNA:PRO ref: C 1/10/189)

1. A t[re]srev[er]ent pier en dieu Levesq[ue] de
2. Bathe Chaunceller Denglet[er]re[1]
3. Supplie humblement William Mayowe fitz & heir [2] Joh[a]n Mayowe q[ue] come le dit Joh[a]n enfeffa Joh[a]n Gerveys[3] Joh[a]n Balon William Tystede & aut[re]s ja mortz en c[er]teins t[er]res & ten[emen]tz
4. en la ville de Sutton Rople en le Countee de Sutht'[4] a lentent de refeffer le dit Joh[a]n Mayowe ou ses heirs q[u]aunt ils p[ar] le dit Joh[a]n Mayowe ou ses heirs s[er]roit requiz[5] puis la
5. mort de quell[e] Joh[a]n Mayowe le dit William sovent foitz ad requiz les ditz Joh[a]n Gerveys Joh[a]n Balon & William Tystede de luy enfeffer en les ditz t[er]res & ten[emen]tz & ils le
6. refusent pur que please a v[ost]re t[re]sgraciouse s[eigneur]ie[6] de considerer les p[re]misses & auxi q[ue] le dit William nad mye ascun remedie a la co[mun]e ley saunz v[ost]re g[r]aciouse eide & socour en celle
7. partie Et sur ceo denvoier p[ur][6] les ditz Joh[a]n Gerveys Joh[a]n Balon & William Tystede de comparer deva[u]nt vous soubz c[er]tein peine a c[er]tein jo[ur][6] p[ar] vous alimiter[7] pur
8. dieu & en oevre de charite

Thomas Overton &

pleg[ii] de p[ro]s[equendo]

Will[elmu]s Bele

TRANSLATION

To the Very Reverend Father in God the Bishop of
Bath Chancellor of England

William Mayowe son & heir of John Mayowe humbly beseeches that whereas the said John enfeoffed John Gerveys[3] John Balon William Tystede & others now deceased in certain lands & tenements in the town of Sutton Rople in the county of Southampton with the intent of re-enfeoffing the said John Mayowe or his heirs when they should be requested by the said John Mayowe or his heirs since the death of which John Mayowe the said William was oft-times requested the said John Gerveys John Balon & William Tystede to enfeoff him in the said lands & tenements and they refuse [to do] it wherefore may it please your very gracious lordship to consider the premise & also that the said William has not any remedy at the common law without your gracious aid & succour in that matter And thereupon to send for the said John Gerveys John Balon & William Tystede to appear before you under a certain pain on a certain day by you to be appointed for God & in work of charity

Thomas Overton &

William Bele

sureties for the prosecution

COMMENTARY

Document

Many of the quite early chancery proceedings (which date from temp. Richard II) were written in Anglo-Norman French. The early documents are far smaller than the later cases which are often very extensive. Most are fairly legible but in general are in less good condition than this example, so excellent for its age.

Script

This careful and beautifully written script is very clear. The *W* appears identical in form but marginally larger than *w*.

Notes

1. As noted in in the commentary for plate 23 this kind of address is often the only means of dating by internal evidence. See the *Handbook of British Chronology* by E.B. Fryde and others for a list of chancellors to give approximate dates for such documents. In this list John Stafford appears to be the only name before the 1460s shown as Bishop of Bath (and Wells). He is given as being appointed to the chancellorship in 1432, but as becoming Archbishop of Canterbury in 1443. Another Bishop of Bath and Wells, however, was Chancellor during parts of the period 1467-1473.
2. Notice the absence of the word *de*, a common occurrence in Anglo-Norman French.
3. The two minims of this name here and subsequently could be read as *n*.
4. The county of Southampton, as is often the form for Hampshire.
5. The verb here should be plural (*serroient requiz*) rather than singular.
6. The abbreviation here is not strictly a superscript *r* as is more usual, but a separate sign. It is not always easy to determine the difference between the two.
7. *a* has been joined with *limiter*.

[49]

TRANSCRIPTION

Writ of Diem Clausit Extremum

(TNA:PRO ref: C 139/81/38, no 3)

1. Henricus dei gr[ati]a Rex Angl[ie] & Franc[ie] & D[omi]n[u]s Hib[er]n[ie] Escaetori suo in Com[itatu]
   Suff' sal[ult[e]m[1] Quia Thomas Andrewe fil[ius] & heres Elizabeth[e] que fuit ux[or] Will[elm]i Andrewe
   defuncte que de

2. d[omi]no H[enrico] nup[er] Rege Angl[ie] Avo n[ost]ro tenuit in capite nup[er] dum infra etatem &
   in custodia d[omi]ni H[enrici] nup[er] Regis Angl[ie] p[at]ris n[ost]ri fuit diem clausit extremu[m] ut
   accepim[us] tibi p[re]cipim[us] q[uo]d

3. p[er] sacr[amentu]m p[ro]bor[um] & leg[alium] ho[m]i[n]u]m de balliva tua p[er] quos rei v[er]itas melius
   sciri pot[er]it diligent[er] inquiras que t[er]re & [2] ten[ementa] p[er] mortem p[re]d[i]c[t]e Elizabeth[e] &
   r[ati]one minoris etatis

4. p[re]d[i]c[t]i Thome ad manus p[re]d[i]c[t]i Avi n[ost]ri devenerunt & in manu n[ost]ra adhuc existunt &
   de quo vel de quib[us] teneant[ur] & p[er] quod s[er]viciu[m] & quantum valeant p[er] annu[m] in

5. om[n]ib[us] exitib[us] & quo die idem Thomas obiit & quis p[ro]pinquior heres eius sit & cuius etatis Et
   inquisic[i]o[n]em inde distincte & ap[er]te f[a]c[t]am nob[is] in Cancellar[iam] n[ost]ram sub

6. sigillo tuo & sigillis eor[um] p[er] quos f[a]c[t]a fu[er]it sine dil[ati]one mittas[3] & hoc br[ev]e T[este] me
   ip[s]o apud Westm' quinto die Decembr[is] Anno r[egni] n[ostri] quintodecimo[4]

                                                                                          Wymbyssh

TRANSLATION

Henry by the grace of God King of England & France & lord of Ireland to his escheator in the county of Suffolk [sends] greeting. Because Thomas Andrewe son & heir of Elizabeth, who was the wife of William Andrewe, deceased[5] who[5] held in chief of the Lord Henry late king of England our grandfather, lately while he [Thomas] was under age & in the wardship of the Lord Henry late king of England our father, has died as we have learned, we order you diligently to make enquiry by the oath of upright & law-worthy men of your jurisdiction through whom the truth of the matter may better be able to be known what lands & tenements, through the death of the aforesaid Elizabeth & by reason of the minor age of the aforesaid Thomas came into the hands of our aforesaid grandfather & are yet in our hand & from which man or which men they may be held & by what service & how much they may be worth a year in all profits & on which day the same Thomas died and who may be the next heir & of what age; and without delay to send to us at our chancery the inquisition distinctly and clearly made in respect thereof under your seal & the seals of those through whom it shall have been made & this writ I myself being witness at Westminster on the fifth day of December in the fifteenth year of our reign.

Wymbyssh

COMMENTARY

Document

The writ of *diem clausit extremum* (he/she closed [his/her] last day) was sent by the king to the local escheator (an official concerned with revenue which, for various reasons, might accrue to the king) in the expectation that, upon the death of one of his tenants in chief, particularly if leaving an heir under age, he would be entitled to some financial gain.

Script

This cramped script is typical of writs of the period. However, as these writs run very much to a formula (and, it must be admitted, seldom add more of interest than the date), they do not ordinarily, require or warrant much time to search. This writ, bound as is usual with the resultant inquisition, is fuller than most due to the slightly complex nature of the situation (see document 51).

Notes

1. This word is in the accusative case as the verb (as is usual in such cases) is omitted (see translation).
2. The mark here possibly covers an erasure.
3. The subjunctive (as *inquiras* above) is used after *precipimus*.
4. The document is temp. Henry VI. The year therefore is 1436.
5. These words refer, as can be seen from the Latin, to Elizabeth.

Inquisicio capta apud Cippenhm in com Dunelm duodecimo die ...

... ordator dni Regem in com pdca virtute brs ome ...

... Robt Godbald Rici Hadley Johis Celoys Willi Hoboch Johis

longys jurp Anis dicum dns Rogn ont pdr corconn et viginti ...

... de Sanndyssh in com pdco tenenpnt ad manus dni H gnappo ...

... Thome Andie in eodm brs naidl et Whne in manu pd ...

ipse p annum p omnib dincys de Celoys p annum in omnib ...

pdcus Thomas filius pdice Elizaboth obijt vicessimo die ...

omnia illa trie et tenementa in Sanndyssh pdict desendepnt ...

Andie fratris omsd Thome et ... idem Thomas obijt ...

et tenementa in Sanndyssh pdict gubnst ... Andie ...

et filiab Willi Andie fratris pdci Johis patris pdca ...

... dicunt ... justa ... dce ... et Johna sunt ...

fratris omsd Thome et ... eadm ... cus filiar ...

Johna alia filiar pdca Willi et etatis viginti et quatuor annor ...

pdce Elizaboth pdict minoris etatis omsdm Thome ad manus ...

in manu dni Regis nunc existunt. In cui p testom jurat ...

[51]

1 ...dam Anno regni Regis Henrici Regis post conquestum quintodecimo ...

2 ...m Regis ordinem spectatori deputat' ... Inquisic'o consuet' p' ... Henrico ...

3 ...o Willi potter Willi clyppe Joh'o Bacon Willi hoker Joh'o hoker e ...

4 ...the quindecim acq' prat' decem acq' pastur' e quindecim acq' bosc' in villa ...

5 ...m D'no Regis suo p' mortem Elizabeth in t'p' p'dc'o pacificat' jacuit minoris

6 D'no Regis suo existunt' quo tenent' de d'no Rege in capite p' d'ctum ...

7 ...ux' p'jus decem e septem solidos e nonam Donat' p' d'cm' ordin' q' ...

8 Anno regni Regis Henrici quint' post conquestum nonas ... p' cui' mortem ...

9 ...cto Andrewe ut consanguineos e h'edes emist'm' th'o no' ... de filio Joh'o

10 h'edes de corpore suo exeunt' ... de eadem ... victo descendend ...

11 e Joh'o exon' potui collyng de consanguineis e h'edes p'd' victo ...

12 ... de q' idem victus dicit' suo h'edes ... de corpore suo exeunt'

13 ...anguineos e p'pinquiores h'edes p'dict' thom' victo filio p'dict' Willi

14 ...d' Willi est etatis viginti e octo annor' e amplius ... q' eodem

15 amplius. Dicunt' eadem ip'm q' nulla alia con plur' the e tenement' p' mortem

16 ...dict' d'no ... quib'sp' nup' Regis angl' an' p'dict' D'no Regis suo Donaverunt' nec

17 ...e sigill' sua apposuerunt' Dat' loco die e Anno sup'dict'

TRANSCRIPT

Inquisition Post Mortem

(TNA:PRO ref: C 139/81/38, no 4)

1. Inquisic[i]o capta apud Gippewicum in Com[itatu] Suff' duodecimo die Februarii anno regni Regis Henrici sexti post conquestum quintodecimo[1] coram Joh[ann]e

2. Rypley escaetore d[omi]ni *Regis* in Com[itatu] p[re]d[i]c[t]o virtute br[ev]is eiusd[e]m d[omi]ni Regis eid[e]m escaetori directi & huic Inquis[icioni] consut[i] p[er] sacr[amentu]m Henrici Vany

3. Rog[er]i Godbald Ric[ard]i Hawker Joh[ann]is Waleys Will[elm]i Hoberd Joh[ann]is Page Will[elm]i Potter Will[elm]i Cryspe Joh[ann]is Bacon Will[elm]i Hoker Joh[ann]is Hoker & Rob[er]ti

4. Longys Iur[atorum] Qui dicunt sup[er] sacr[amentu]m suu[m] q[uo]d *Cen*tum & triginta acre t[er]re quindecim acre prati decem acre pasture & quindecim acre bosci in villa

5. de Caundyssh' in Com[itatu] p[re]d[i]c[t]o devenerunt ad manus d[omi]ni H[enrici] quarti avi d[omi]ni Regis nu[n]c p[er] mortem Elizabeth[e] in br[ev]i p[re]d[i]c[t]o specificat[e] rac[i]o[n]e minoris

6. etatis Thome Andrew in eod[e]m br[ev]i no[m]i[n]ati et adhuc in manu p[re]d[i]c[t]i d[omi]ni Regis nu[n]c existunt que tenent[ur][2] de d[omi]no Rege in capite p[er] s[er]viciu[m] uni[us]

7. *r*ose p[er] annum p[ro] om[n]ib[us] s[er]viciis et valent p[er] annu[m] in om[n]ib[us] exitib[us] ult[r]a rep[ri]s[as] decem & septem solidos & novem denarios Dicunt eciam q[uo]d

8. p[re]d[i]c[t]us Thomas filius p[re]dict[e] Elizabeth[e] obiit vicesimo die Octobr[is] anno regni Regis Henrici quinti post conquestum nono[3] post cui[us] mortem

9. om[n]ia illa t[er]re & tenementa in Caundyssh' p[re]dict'[4] descenderunt Nich[ola]o Andrew ut consang[u]ineo & hered[i] eiusd[e]m Th*ome* videl[ice]t ut filio Joh[ann]is

10. Andrew fratris eiusd[e]m Thome eo q[uo]d idem Thomas obiit sine hered[e] de corpore suo exeunt[i] Et de eod[e]m Nich[ola]o descenderunt ead[e]m t[er]re

11. & tenementa in Caundyssh' p[re]dict'[4] quibusdam[5] Margarete Andrew & Joh[ann]e uxori Rob[er]ti Codlyng ut consanguineis & hered[ibus] p[re]d[i]c[t]i Nich[ola]i videl[ice]t

12. ut filiab[us] Will[elm]i Andrew fratris p[re]d[i]c[t]i Joh[ann]is patris p[re]d[i]c[t]i Nich[ola]i eo q[uo]d id[e]m Nich[ola]us obiit sine hered[e] de corpore suo exeunt[i]

13. Et sic dicunt iid[e]m Iuratores q[uo]d dict[e] Margareta & Joh[an]na sunt consang[u]inee & p[ro]pinquiores hered[es] p[re]ldict[i] Thome videl[ice]t filie p[re]d[i]c[t]i Will[elm]i

14. fratris eiusd[e]m Thome Et q[uo]d ead[e]m Margareta una filiar[um] p[re]d[i]c[t]i Will[elm]i est etatis viginti & sex annor[um] & amplius Et q[uo]d ead[e]m

15. Joh[an]na alt[er]a filiar[um] p[re]d[i]c[t]i Will[elm]i est etatis viginti & quatuor annor[um] & amplius Dicunt eciam iid[e]m <Iurat[ores]> q[uo]d nulla alia seu plur[a] t[er]re & tenement[a] p[er] mortem

16. p[re]dict[e] Elizabeth[e] rac[i]o[n]e minoris etat[is] eiusd[e]m Thome ad manus p[re]dict[i] d[omi]ni H[enrici] quarti nup[er] Regis Angl[ie] avi p[re]dict[i] d[omi]ni Regis nu[n]c devenerunt nec

17. in manu d[omi]ni Regis nu[n]c existunt In cui[us] rei testi[m]o[niu]m Iurat[ores] p[re]dict[i] sigill[a] sua apposuerunt Dat[a] loco die & anno supradict[is]

[51]

TRANSLATION

Inquisition Post Mortem

(TNA:PRO ref: C 139/81/38, no 4)

Inquisition taken at Ipswich in the county of Suffolk on the twelfth day of February in the fifteenth year of the reign of King Henry the sixth after the conquest before John Rypley the eschaetor of the Lord King in the aforesaid county by virtue of a writ of the same Lord King directed to the same eschaetor & sewn to this inquisition by the oath of Henry Vany Roger Godbald Richard Hawker John Waleys William Hoberd John Page William Potter William Cryspe John Bacon William Hoker John Hoker & Robert Longys jurors who say on their oath that one hundred & thirty acres of land fifteen acres of meadow ten acres of pasture & fifteen acres of woodland in the township of Caundyssh in the aforesaid county came into the hands of the Lord Henry the fourth the grandfather of the present Lord King through the death of Elizabeth specified in the aforesaid writ by reason of the minor age of Thomas Andrew named in the same writ and are yet in the hand of the aforesaid present Lord King which are held of the Lord King in chief by service of one rose a year for all services and are worth in all profits beyond outgoings seventeen shillings & nine pence a year They say also that the aforesaid Thomas the son of the aforesaid Elizabeth died on the twentieth day of October in the ninth year of the reign of King Henry the fifth after the conquest after whose death all those lands & tenements in Caundyssh aforesaid descended to Nicholas Andrew as kinsman & heir of the same Thomas that is to say as the son of John Andrew the brother of the same Thomas because the same Thomas died without an heir issuing of his body And the same lands & tenements in Caundyssh aforesaid descended from the same Nicholas to a certain Margaret Andrew and Joan the wife of Robert Codlyng as kinswomen & heirs of the aforesaid Nicholas that is to say as daughters of William Andrew the brother of the aforesaid John father of the aforesaid Nicholas because the same Nicholas died without an heir issuing of his body And thus the same jurors say that the said Margaret & Joan are kinswomen & next heirs of the aforesaid Thomas that is to say daughters of the aforesaid William the brother of the same Thomas And that the same Margaret one of the daughters of the aforesaid William is twenty six years of age & more And that the same Joan the other of the daughters of the aforesaid William is twenty four years of age & more The same jurors say also that no other or further lands & tenements came through the death of the aforesaid Elizabeth by reason of the minor age of the same Thomas to the hands of the aforesaid Lord Henry the fourth late king of England grandfather of the aforesaid present Lord King nor are in the hand of the present Lord King In witness whereof the aforesaid jurors have affixed their seals Given in the place on the day & in the year abovesaid.

COMMENTARY

Inquisition Post Mortem

(TNA:PRO ref: C 139/81/38, no 4)

Document

These records (temp. Henry III-Charles II) provide excellent evidence for the pedigrees of families of some substance, particularly for the date of death of the subject of the inquisition, and the name and age of the heir and description of lands held. Inquests were held, following a writ of *diem clausit extremum*, to ascertain details of the heir of a deceased tenant thought to hold land of the king in chief. The object was to prevent the king from losing any advantage which could accrue to him, such as right of wardship of an heir under full age, reversion of holding for want of heir or fine on livery of the land to an adult heir etc. Where gavelkind obtained (as in Kent) more than one heir might be named. Till the reign of James I a copy of the chancery record was sent to the exchequer; also, from 1540, if the heir was a minor, to the Court of Wards and Liveries. These copies can be extremely useful if the chancery record is defective through fading, injudicious use of restorative fluids etc. Some of the later inquisitions relate to tenants not deceased but deemed no longer capable of running their affairs. There are other series, as in the records of the Duchy of Lancaster. This I.P.M. is rich in genealogical detail. Sometimes only a son and heir is mentioned, but at the other extreme, for example, there is mention of some 20 relations or relations-in-law (not counting others in excerpts of quoted wills) in the I.P.M. of an Essex knight who died without issue in 1560.

Script

The small and capital letters *h* and *s* are very similar and have been transcribed as seems appropriate. The *d* sometimes appears surprisingly large, though distinct in form, it seems, from the capital letter. The scribe gives a few of the surnames the appearance of being abbreviated.

Notes

1. 1436/7, the historical year 1437.
2. The abbreviation here is by a sign rather than a superscript letter.
3. The year is 1421. A mark of no apparent significance follows, perhaps to fill in after an erasure or after a gap had been filled.
4. This word is not extended as the supposed gender of Caundyssh is not known.
5. Here, as sometimes happens, there appears to be no omission despite the superscript letter.

(Plate, transcript and translation on previous spreads)

Select Bibliography

Although listed under the most likely categories, some of the books will also belong satisfactorily in other categories. Books mentioned in the text and relating to specific types of document or the finding of documents are not included in the bibliography.

Books useful to transcribers of documents for dates, unusual terms, place-names &c.

Bond, John J., *Handy-Book of Rules and Tables for Verifying Dates with the Christian Era, &c.* (1869)

Bristow, Joy, *The Local Historian's Glossary & Vade Mecum* , 2nd edn (1994)

Burness, Lawrence R., *A Scottish Genealogist's Glossary* (1991)

Chapman, Colin R., *How Heavy, How Much and How Long* (1995)

Cheney, C.R. (ed.), *A Handbook of Dates for Students of British History,* rev. edn (2000)

Cook, Chris, *Dictionary of Historical Terms,* (1983)

Cowie, L.W., *A Dictionary of British Social History* (1973)

Darby, H.C., and Versey, G.R., *Domesday Gazetteer* (1975)

Ekwall, Eilert, *The Concise Oxford Dictionary of English Place-Names,* 4th edn (1960)

Fisher, John H., Richardson, Malcolm and Fisher, Jane L., *An Anthology of Chancery English* (1984)

Forster, K., *A Pronouncing Dictionary of English Place-Names including standard local and archaic variants* (1981)

Fryde, E.B., Greenway, D.E., Porter, S., and Roy, I., *A Handbook of British Chronology,* 3rd edn (1986)

Halliwell, James Orchard, *A Handbook of Archaic and Provincial Words,* 2 vols, 7th edn (1872)

Harris, Maureen and Glen, *Concise Genealogical Dictionary* (1989)

Markwell, F.C. and Saul, Pauline, *The Family Historian's Enquire Within* (1988)

Milward, Rosemary, *Glossary of Household, Farming and Trade Terms from Probate Inventories,* 2nd edn (1982)

Moore, John S., *The Goods and Chattels of Our Forefathers* (1976)

Nicolas, Nicholas Harris, *Notitia Historica: Containing Tables, Calendars and Miscellaneous Information for the use of Historians, Antiquaries and the Legal Profession* (1824)

Public Record Office, Guide to the Contents of, vol. 1 (glossary, pp. 201-211) (1963)

Richardson, John, *The Local Historian's Encyclopedia,* 3rd edn (2003)

Smith, Frank, *A Genealogical Gazetteer of England* (1982)

Humphery-Smith, Cecil R. (ed.), *The Phillimore Atlas and Index of Parish Registers*, 3rd edn (2003)

Humphery-Smith, Cecil R., *A Genealogist's Bibliography* (glossary, pp. 95-113) (1985)

Vincent, Benjamin, *Haydn's Dictionary of Dates*, 14th edn (1873)

Way, Albertus (ed.), *Promptorum Parvulorum* (1843-65)

Webb, Clifford, *Dates and Calendars for the Genealogist* (1989)

Withycombe, E.G., *The Dictionary of English Christian Names,* 3rd edn (1977)

A law dictionary is also very useful e.g.:

Jacob, Giles, *New Law Dictionary* (1729)

Osborn's Concise Law Dictionary, 7th edn (1983)

Rushen, Percy C., *The Genealogists Legal Dictionary* (1909)

Wharton's Law Lexicon, 14th edn (1938), 5th impression (1957)

as also:

Gazetteers etc:

Bartholomew, John, *Gazetteer of the British Isles* (1963)

Lewis S. & Co., *Lewis's Topographical Dictionary of England*, 4 vols (1831) (also *of Wales and of Scotland*)

Mills, A.D., *A Dictionary of English Place Names* (1991)

The National Gazetteer of Great Britain (Virtue & Co.) 3 vols (1868)

and:

The Oxford English Dictionary

Books &c. which relate to Palaeography and include reproductions of documents with transcriptions

Barrett, John, and Iredale, David, *Discovering Old Handwriting* (1995)

Emmison, F.G., *How to Read Local Archives 1550-1700* (1967)

Gardner, Frank, and Smith, David E., *Genealogical Research in England and Wales*, vol. III (1964)

Grieve, Hilda E.P., *Some Examples of English Handwriting* (1949)

Grieve, Hilda E.P., *Examples of English Handwriting, 1150-1750* (reprint 1978)

Haydon, Edwin, and Harrop, John (eds.), *Widworthy Manorial Court Rolls 1453-1617* (1997)

Hector, L.C., *The Handwriting of English Documents*, 2nd edn (1966)

Jenkinson, Hilary, *The Later Court Hands in England, 1390-1620*, 2 vols. (1927)

Johnson, Charles, and Jenkinson, Hilary, *English Court Hand, A.D. 1066-1500*, 2 vols (1915)

Munby, Lionel, *Reading Tudor and Stuart Handwriting* (1988)

Newton, K.C., *Mediaeval Local Records: A Reading Aid* (1971)

Preston, Jean F. and Yeandle, Laetitia, *English Handwriting 1400-1650* (1999)

Stuart, Denis, *Manorial Records: An introduction to their transcription and translation* (1992)

Thompson, Sir Edward Maunde, *An Introduction to Greek and Latin Palaeography* (1912)

Also Borthwick Wallets:

Ryecraft, Ann, *Sixteenth and Seventeenth Century Handwriting* – series 1, 3rd edn (1972) and series 2, 3rd edn (1972)
  English Mediaeval Handwriting, 2nd edn (1973)
Sheils, W.J., *The Reformation in the North to 1558* (1976)
Smith, D.M., *Mediaeval Latin Documents, series 1: Diocesan Records*, 3rd edn (1979)

Also useful:

(for types of letter): Buck, W.S.B., *Examples of Handwriting* (1973)
(for commentary): Thoyts, E.E., *How to Read Old Documents* (1893, reprinted 2001)

Books offering particular help for the transcription or translation of documents in medieval Latin

Cappelli, Adriano, *Lexicon Abbreviaturarum (Dizionario di Abbreviature latine ed italiane)* (1929, reprint 1979)
Chassant, L.-Alphonse, *Dictionnaire des Abréviations Latines et Françaises (Usitées dans les ... Manuscrits ... du Moyen Age)* (1866)
Fisher, John L., revised Powell, Avril and Raymond, *A Medieval Farming Glossary of Latin and English Words*, 2nd edn (1997)
Gooder, Eileen A., *Latin for Local History*, 2nd edn (1978)
Gosden, David, *Starting to Read Medieval Latin Manuscript* (1993)
Kennedy, B.H., revised by Bartram, J.W., *The Shorter Latin Primer* (1931)
Latham, R.E., *Revised Medieval Latin Word-List from British and Irish Sources* (1965)
Latham, R.E., Howlett, D.R. and others, *Dictionary of Medieval Latin from British Sources* – A-O in eight fascicules (1975-2004). Further fascicules in course of publication.
Martin, Charles Trice, *The Record Interpreter*, 2nd edn (1910, reprint 1976)
Morris, Janet, *A Latin Glossary for Family and Local Historians* (1989)
Peltzer, Auguste, *Abréviations Latines Médiévales (Supplément au Dizionario Di Abbreviature latine ed italiane)* (1982)
Sims, Richard, *A Manual for the Genealogist, Topographer, Antiquary and Legal Professor* (the glossary, pp. 527-542) (1888)
Stuart, Denis, *Latin for Local and Family Historians* (1995)
Wright, Andrew, *Court-Hand Restored or, the Student's Assistant in Reading Old Deeds, Charters, Records, etc.*, 8th edn (1867)

A classical dictionary is also required e.g.:

Lewis, C.T. and Short, C., *A Latin Dictionary* (1879, impression of 1975)

or the smaller

Lewis, C.T., *An Elementary Latin Dictionary* (1891, impression of 1975)

Books in which specific Latin documents etc. of interest to genealogists and local historians are included

Those marked * do not include translation
Those marked ** do not include reproduction of document
Those marked *** include only translation

Accounts

**Gooder, Eileen, *Latin for Local History*, 2nd edn (1978)
**Page, Frances M., *Wellingborough Manorial Accounts A.D. 1258-1323* (1936)

Administration

**FitzHugh, Terrick V.H., *The Dictionary of Genealogy* (1985)
Scott, Miriam, *Prerogative Court of Canterbury Wills and Other Probate Records* (1997)

Bishops registers

**Gooder, Eileen, *Latin for Local History*, as above

Bond

**Stuart, Denis, *Latin for Local and Family Historians* (1995)

Chapter act book

**Gooder, Eileen, *Latin for Local History*, as above

Deeds, charters &c.

Alcock, N.W., *Old Title Deeds: A Guide for Local and Family Historians* (1986)
Cornwall, Julian, *Reading Old Title Deeds* (1993)
Dibben, A.A., *Title Deeds* (1968)
**Gooder, Eileen, *Latin for Local History*, as above
*Grieve, Hilda E.P., *Some Examples of English Handwriting* (1949)
Newton, K.C., *Medieval Local Records* (1971)
* **Rye, Walter, *Records and Record Searching: A Guide to the Genealogist and Topographer*, (1897)
**Stuart, Denis, *Latin for Local and Family Historians*, as above

Feet of fines

**Cornwall, Julian, *Reading Old Title Deeds* (1993)
**Gooder, Eileen, *Latin for Local History*, as above
*Hector, L.C., *The Handwriting of English Documents* (1966)
* ** Meekings, C.A.F., *Abstracts of Surrey Feet of Fines, 1509-1558* (intro.) (1968)
* **Rye, Walter, *Records and Record Searching*, as above (pp. 36-38)
**Stuart, Denis, *Latin for Local and Family Historians* as above

Inquisitions post mortem (with writ of diem clausit extremum)

**Gooder, Eileen, *Latin for Local History* as above
* **Rye Walter, *Records and Record Searching*, as above

Institution and induction

**Gooder, Eileen, *Latin for Local History,* as above

Manorial Documents

**Gooder, Eileen, *Latin for Local History,* as above
***Hone, Nathaniel J., *The Manor and Manorial Records* (1906)
Newton, K.C., *Medieval Local Records,* as above
**Stuart, Denis, *Manorial Records, An introduction to their transcription and translation* (1992)

Power of Attorney

**Gooder, Eileen, *Latin for Local History,* as above

Rental

Newton, K.C., *Medieval Local Records,* as above

Will (with probate act)

**Gooder, Eileen, *Latin for Local History,* as above

Books of forms of Latin documents

Hall, Hubert, *A Formula Book of English Historical Documents* (1909)
Madox, Thomas, *Formulare Anglicanum* (1702)

Extensive printed parallel texts showing transcripts of Latin with translations

The following books do not treat of palaeography (unless stated to do so) but are useful for acquiring a familiarity with typical Latin wording in particular documents, to facilitate transcription and translation.

Haydon, Edwin and Harrop, John, *Widworthy Manorial Court Rolls 1453-1617* (1997) (includes facsimiles)
London County Council, *Court Rolls of Tooting Beck* (1909)
London Borough of Sutton Libraries and Arts Services, *Courts of the Manors of Bandon and Beddington 1498-1552* (1983)
The Wimbledon Common Committee, *Extracts from the Court Rolls of The Manor of Wimbledon* (1866) (record type)

See also many parallel texts in the publications of the Selden Society and elsewhere listed in:

Mullins, E.L.C., *Texts and Calendars (An Analytical Guide to Serial Publications),* vol. I (1958); vol. II (1983)
Stevenson, David and Wendy B., *Scottish Texts and Calendars* (1987)

Anglo-Norman French

Baker, J.H., *Manual of Law French* (1979)

Einhorn, E., *Old French* (1974)

Kelham, R., *A Dictionary of the Norman or Old French Language* (1779, reprint 1978)

Rothwell, William, and others (eds.), *Anglo-Norman Dictionary* (in seven fascicules, 1977-1992, or one volume)

See also volumes of the Selden Society

Latin Vocabulary

The following vocabulary of classical and medieval Latin words is intended only as a guide to the words to be found in the Latin documents in this book. Medieval Latin particularly is notable for its varied definitions and spellings, and those given, with only a few amplifications, relate to these documents. Parts of speech are generally designated, but verbs and nouns are taken to be easily recognisable. Most place-names, being often abbreviated and of unknown ending, are not included. Genitive cases of regular 1st, 2nd and 4th declension nouns have been abbreviated, being shown as additions to the stem; otherwise the full form of cases has been given. Genders are normally included for adjectives but, when more appropriate, the genitive case is given. The letters *i* and *j* appear as shown in the transcripts (i.e. generally as *i*); also the letters *c* and *t*, which can in many cases be interchangeable. To help those whose remembrance of Latin grammar has faded, some irregular forms are included, and reference made to a word elsewhere in the list. The following abbreviations have been used:

abl.	ablative case	inf.	infinitive
adj.	adjective	lit.	literally
acc.	accusative case	m.	masculine
adv.	adverb	n.	neuter
comp.	comparative	nom.	nominative case
conj.	conjunction	p.	participle
dat.	dative case	perf.	perfect
dep.	deponent	pers.	person
etc.	*et cetera*	pl.	plural
f.	feminine	prep.	preposition
gen.	genitive case	pres.	present
gram.	grammatical	pron.	pronoun
Heb.	Hebrew	sing.	singular
i.e.	*id est*	subj.	subjunctive
imp.	imperfect	sup.	superlative
indecl.	indeclinable	usu.	usually

absentia, -e (f.)	absence
ac (conj.)	and
accipio, -ere, accepi, acceptum	understand, learn; receive
acceptacio, acceptacionis (f.)	acceptance
accido, -ere, accidi, -	accrue; fall due
acra, -e (f.)	acre
ad (prep. with acc.)	to, towards
adhuc (adv.)	yet, still, till now
adiaceo, -ere, -ui, -	lie adjacent to
administracio, administracionis (f.)	administration
administro, -are, -avi, -atum	administer

administrator, administratoris (m.)	administrator
administratrix, administratricis (f.)	administratrix
admitto, -ere, admisi, admissum	admit
adquiro, -ere, adquisivi, adquisitum	acquire; buy
Ægidius, -i	Giles (as *Egidius*)
affraia, -e (f.)	affray
Agneta, -e (f.)	Agnes
Alanus, -i (m.)	Alan
Albanus, -i (m.)	Alban
alea, -e (f.)	die (sing. of dice)
Alexander, Alexandri (m.)	Alexander
alias (adv.)	otherwise

Alicia, -e (f.)	Alice
aliquis, -quis, -quid (pron.)	anyone, anything, any
alius, -a, -ud (adj. and noun)	other; another
allinigenus, -i (m.); *allinigena, -e* (f.)	foreigner, alien
altare, altaris (n.)	altar
alter, altera, alterum (gen. *alterius*; dat. *alteri*) adj.	one or other (of two)
amen (Heb.)	Amen
Amicia, -e (f.)	Amice
amplius (indecl.)	more
Andreas (acc. *Andream*; gen. and dat. *Andree*; abl. *Andrea*) (m.)	Andrew
Anglia, -e (f.)	England
Anglice (adv.)	in English
anima, -e (f.)	soul
Anna, -e (f.)	Ann(e)
annualis, -e (adj.)	annual
annus, -i (m.)	year
Annys (f.)	Agnes
ante (prep. with acc.)	before
antea (adv.)	before
Antonius, -i (m.)	Anthony
aperte (adv.)	clearly, openly
apostolus, -i (m.)	apostle
appello, -are, -avi, -atum	name, call (by name)
appono, -ere, apposui, appositum	affix (seal)
approbo, -are, -avi, -atum	approve
Aprilis, Aprilis (m.)	April
apud (prep. with acc.)	at
armiger, armigeri (m.)	esquire
assignatus, -a (m., f.) (past p., as noun)	assign
avus, -i (m.)	grandfather
balliva, -e (f.)	bailiwick, (area of) jurisdiction
ballivus, -i (m.)	bailiff
baptizo, -are, -avi, -atum	baptise
Barnardus, -i (m.)	Barnard
baro, baronis (m.)	baron
Bathoniensis (gen. *Bathoniensis*)	of Bath (and Wells) – relating to diocese
beatus, -a, -um (adj.)	blessed
beatissimus, -a, -um (sup. adj.)	most blessed
bene (adv.)	well
bonus, -a, -um (adj.)	good
bona, -orum (n. pl.)	goods
boscus, -i (m.)	woodland
breve, brevis (n.); *brevis, brevis* (m.)	writ
Britannia, -e (f.)	Britain
burgus, -i (m.)	borough
cancellaria, -e (f.)	chancery
capcio, capcionis (f.)	taking (of inquisition etc.) (as *captio*)
capella, -e (f.)	chapel
capellanus, -i (m.)	chaplain
capitalis, -e (adj.)	capital; in chief
capio, -ere, cepi, captum	take
captio, captionis (f.)	taking (of inquisition etc.) (as *capcio*)
caput, capitis (n.)	head
in capite	in chief
Carolus, -i (m.)	Charles
carta, -e (f.)	deed
carta picta	playing card
casus, -us (m.)	case; set of circumstances
catallum, -i (n.)	chattel
celebro, -are, -avi, -atum	celebrate (mass)
centum (indecl.)	a hundred
cervisia, -e (f.)	ale
ceterus, -a, -um (adj.)	other
charta, -e (f.)	see *carta*
Christopherus, -i; Christoferus, -i sometimes spelt with first letters as Greek χ, *chi* (ch) and ρ, *rho* (r)	Christopher
cimiterium, -i (n.)	graveyard
citra (prep. with acc.)	this side of (of time – thus before or after)
civis, -is (m., f.)	citizen
clameum, -i (n.)	claim
claudo, -ere, clausi, clausum	close
Clemens, Clementis (m.)	Clement
coactus, -a, -um (past p.)	see *cogo*
cogo, -ere, coegi, coactum	force
comitatus, -us (m.)	county
commissarius, -i (m.)	commissary (delegate appointed by bishop)
commissio, commissionis (f.)	grant; commission (legal)
committo, -ere, commisi, commissum	grant; entrust (to)
communiter (adv.)	commonly, jointly
compos (gen. *compotis*)	sound, in full possession of faculties
concedo, -ere, concessi, concessum	grant
concordia, -e (f.)	agreement, concord
condo, -ere, condidi, conditum	compose (will etc.)
confessus	see *confiteor*
confirmo, -are, -avi, -atum	confirm
confiteor, -eri, confessus sum (dep.)	confess
congruetas, congruetatis (f.)	correctness (gram.)
coniunctim (adv.)	jointly
conquestus, -us (m.)	conquest, the Conquest
consanguineus, -a (adj. used as noun)	kinsman, kinswoman
constituo, -ere, -ui, -utum	appoint; constitute (will)
consuetudo, consuetudinis (f.)	custom
consuetus, -a, -um (adj.)	accustomed
consuo, -ere, consui, consutum	sew
contra (prep. with acc.)	against
convencio, convencionis (f.)	covenant
copia, -e (f.)	copy
coram (prep. with abl.)	in the presence of
corpus, -oris (n.)	body
cot(t)agium, -i (n.)	cottage
crastinum, -i (n.)	the morrow
credo, -ere, credidi, creditum	believe
credita, -orum (n. pl.)	credits
cuius (gen. m., f., and n. of *qui*)	see *qui*
cuiuslibet (gen. m., f., and n. of *quilibet*)	see *quilibet*
cum (prep. with abl.)	with
cum (conj.)	when, since; whereas
curia, -e (f.)	court
custodia, -e (f.)	custody, wardship
customarius, -a, -um (adj.)	customary
data, -e (f.); *datum, -i* (n.) (past p. of *do* as noun)	date
datus, -a, -um (past p. of *do*)	given; dated
de (prep. with abl.)	concerning; from; of
debeo, -ere, debui, debitum	ought; owe
debitum, -i (n.) (past. p. of *debeo* as noun)	debt
debitus, -a, -um (past p. of debeo)	due
decedo, -ere, decessi, decessum	die
decem (indecl.)	ten
December, Decembris (m.)	December

decessus, -i (m.); decessa, -e (f.)   the deceased
     (past p.of decedo used as noun)
decessus, -us (m.)   decease
decima, -e (f.) (i.e. for decima pars, tithe
     a tenth part)
decimus, -a, -um (adj.)   tenth
dedi   see do
defectus, -us (m.)   default
defendo, -ere, defendi, defensum   defend
defensor, -oris (m.)   defender; defendant
deforcians, deforciantis (m., f.)   deforciant, defendant
defunctus, -a (past p.)   deceased
deus, -i (m.)   God
demanda, -e (f.)   demand, claim
denarius, -i (m.)   penny
deputatus, -i (m.) (past p. as noun)   deputy
descendo, -ere, -scendi, -scensum   descend, descend (of
                                        property)
devenio, -ire, deveni, -   come (into the hands,
                                        possession)
dico, -ere, dixi, dictum   say
dies, diei (m. or f.)   day
     diem clausit extremum   he/she died (lit. closed
                                        [his/her] last day)
dilatio, dilationis (f.)   delay; adjournment
diligenter (adv.)   diligently
diocesis, diocesis (f.)   diocese
Dionisius, -i (m.)   Denis
dirigo, -ere, direxi, directum   direct
dispono, -ere, disposui, dispositum   dispose
distincte (adv.)   distinctly
distribuo, -ere, distribui, distributum distribute
diutius (comp. adv.)   longer (of time)
do, dare, dedi, datum   give
domina, -e (f.)   lady
dominium, -i (n.)   demesne; lordship
dominus, -i (m.)   lord; sir (sometimes
                                        used as courtesy title
                                        for clergy)
domus, -us (f.)   house
donum, -i (n.)   gift
Dorothea, Dorothee (f.)   Dorothy
dum (conj.)   while
duo, due, duo (acc. m. duos: dat.   two
     and abl., m. and n. duobus)
duodecimus, -a, -um   twelfth
duodena, -e (f.); duodenum, -i (n.) etc. dozen
duos   see duo
durante (abl. sing. m., f. and   during (from duro)
     n. pres. p.)
duro, -are, -avi, -atum   endure; last
dux, ducis (m.)   duke

eadem (nom. f. sing.; nom. and   see idem
     acc. n. pl. of idem)
eandem (acc. f. sing. of idem)   see idem
ecclesia, -e (f.)   church
eciam (adv., sometimes conj.)   also; even (as etiam)
edifico, -are, -avi, -atum   build
Eduardus, -i; Edwardus, -i (m.)   Edward
Egidius, -i (m.)   Giles (as Ægidius)
eger, egra, egrum (adj.)   ill
ego (acc. me; gen. mei; dat. mi[c]hi;   I, me etc.
     abl. me)
ei (dat. m., f. and n. sing.; and   see is
     nom. m. pl. of is)
eidem (dat. m., f. and n. sing.; and   see idem
     nom. m. pl. of idem)
eisdem (dat. and abl. m., f. and n.   see idem
     pl. of idem)

eius (gen. m., f. and n. sing.   see is
     of is)
eiusdem (gen. m., f. and n. sing.   see idem
     of idem)
Elizabetha, -e (f.)   Elizabeth
emano, -are, -avi, -atum   issue
eo quod   because
eodem (dat., abl. m. and n.   see idem
     sing. of idem)
eorum (gen. m. and n. pl. of is)   see is
eos (acc. m. pl. of is)   see is
erat (3rd pers. sing. imp. of sum)   see sum
escaetor, -oris (m.)   escheator (an officer
                                        concerned with the
                                        monarch's revenue)
esse (inf. of sum)   see sum
est (3rd pers. sing. pres. of sum)   see sum
et   and
etas, etatis (f.)   age
etiam (adv., sometimes conj.)   also; even (as eciam)
Eva, -e (f.)   Eve
exactus, -a, -um (past p.)   see exigere
examino, -are, -avi, -atum   examine
executor, executoris (m.)   executor
executrix, executricis (f.)   executrix
exeo, exire, exi(v)i, exitum   go out
exequor, exequi, executus sum (dep.)   fulfil; execute (will)
exeuns (gen. exeuntis) (pres. p.   issuing; going out
     of exeo)
exigo, -ere, exegi, exactum   require; compel
existo, -ere, exstiti, exstitum   be, exist
exitus, exitus (m.)   profits; issue; death
Exonia, -e   Exeter
Exoniensis, Exoniensis (adj.)   of Exeter – relating to
                                        diocese
expedio, -ire, expedivi, expeditum   be right, suitable
exsto, -are, -, -   exist, be extant
     a tempore quo non exstat   from a time from
     memoria   which the memory
                                        does not survive
extremus, -a, -um (adj.)   last

fabrica, -e (f.)   fabric, structure (of
                                        building)
facio, -ere, feci, factum   do; make
Februarius, -i (m.)   February
fecit, fecerunt   see facio
feodum, -i (n.)   fee (legal)
feretrum, -i (n.)   tomb, shrine
ferrifaber, ferrifabri (m.)   ironsmith
festum, -i (m.)   feast(-day); festival
fidelis, (gen. fidelis) (adj.)   trustworthy
fidelitas, fidelitatis (f.)   fealty; faithfulness
fideliter (adv.)   faithfully
fides, fidei (f.)   faith, trust
filia, -e (f.) (dat. and abl. pl. filiabus) daughter
filius, -i (m.)   son
finalis, -e (adj.)   final
finis, finis (m. or f.)   fine; boundary
forma, -e (f.)   form (i.e. of law)
Fortuna, -e (f.)   Fortune (as a name)
Francia, -e (f.)   France
Francisca, -e (f.)   Frances
Franciscus, -i (m.)   Francis
frater, fratris (m.)   brother
fui, fuit (etc.)   see sum
futurus, -a, -um (adj.)   future, coming

gardinum, -i (n.); gardinus, -i (m.)   garden, enclosed
                                        ground etc.

generosus, -i (m.)	gentleman
gens, gentis (f.) (in sing. or pl.)	people
Georgius, -i (m.)	George
Gerardus, -i (m.)	Gerard
gero, -ere, gessi, gestum	bear (date)
Gippewicum, -i	Ipswich
gracia, -e (f.)	grace (as gratia)
Gracia, -e; Gratia, -e (f.)	Grace
gratia, -e (f.)	grace (as gracia)
habeo, -ere, habui, habitum	have, hold
halmotum, -i (n.)	hallmote, hall-moot (manorial court)
hac (abl. f. sing. of *hic*)	see *hic*
hanc (acc. f. sing. of *hic*)	see *hic*
harriotum, -i (as *herriotum* and similar variants)	heriot (form of feudal death duty)
hec (nom. f. sing.; and nom. and acc. n. pl of *hic*)	see *hic*
Helena, -e (f.)	Helen
Henricus, -i (m.)	Henry
Henrietta, -e (f.)	Henrietta
heredit(t)amentum -i (n.)	hereditament
heres, heredis (m., f.)	heir
herriotum, -i (n.)	see *harriotum*
Hibernia, -e (f.)	Ireland
hic, hec, hoc (adj. and pron.)	this
hic (adv.)	here
hiis; his (dat. and abl. m., f. and n. pl. of *hic*)	see *hic*
hoc (nom. and acc. n. sing.; and abl. sing. m. and n. of *hic*)	see *hic*
homagium, -i (n.)	homage (manorial jury)
homo, hominis (m.)	man
honor, honoris (m.)	honour (estate; possessions held under one lord)
horreum, -i (n.)	barn; granary
huic (dat. m., f. and n. sing. of *hic*)	see *hic*
huius (gen. m., f. and n. sing of *hic*)	see *hic*
huiusmodi (indecl.)	of such kind
Humfredus, -i (m.)	Humphrey
hunc (acc. m. sing. of *hic*)	see *hic*
Ianuarius, -i (m.)	January
ibi (adv.)	there
ibidem (adv.)	in the same place
idem, eadem, idem (pron., used as adj.)	the same
ideo (adv.)	therefore
iidem (as *eidem* - nom. m. pl. of *idem*)	see *idem*
illa (nom. f. sing.; nom.and acc. n. pl. of *ille*)	see *ille*
ille, illa, illud (adj. and pron.)	that; he, she, it
illius (gen. m., f. and n. sing. of *ille*)	see *ille*
immediate (adv.)	immediately
impan(n)ello, -are, -avi, -atum	impanel
imperpetuum (adv.)	for ever
in (prep. with acc.)	into; onto; at
in (prep. with abl.)	in; on
in primis	firstly
inde (adv.)	thereof, in respect thereof; then
infans (m., f.)	infant
inferior, inferius (gen. *inferioris*) (adj.)	nether, lower
infra (prep. with acc.)	within
infra etatem	under age
ingressus, ingressus (m.)	entry
inquiro, -ere, inquisivi, inquisitum	make enquiry
inquisicio, inquisicionis (f.)	enquiry, inquisition
insinuo, -are, -avi, -atum	register, enter
insultus, -us (m.)	assault
insuper (adv.)	moreover, furthermore
inter (prep. with acc.)	between
intellego, -ere, intellexi, intellectum	understand
invenio, -ire, -veni, -ventum	find, discover
ipse, ipsa, ipsum (gen. *ipsius*)(adj. and pron.)	this, that (often translated as: the same); he, she or it (emphatic); he himself, she herself etc.
is, ea, id (pron.)	he, she, it
iste, ista, istud (adj. and pron.)	this, that; he, she, it
ita (adv.)	thus
item (adv.)	likewise; also
iunior (gen. *junioris*)	younger
Iunius, -i (m.)	June
iura	see *ius*
iuramentum, -i (n.)	oath
iurator, iuratoris (m.)	juror
iuro, -are, -avi, -atum	swear, make an oath
ius, iuris (n.)	right; law
iusticiarius, -i (m.)	judge; (a) justice
iuxta (prep. with acc.)	next to
Jacobus, -i (m.)	James
Jana, -e (f.)	Jane
Januarius, -i (m.)	January
Jocosa, -e (f.)	Joyce
Johanna, -e (f.)	Joan
Johannes, Johannis (m.)	John
Josephus, -i (m.)	Joseph
Katherina, -e (f.)	Katherine
Lamehitha, -e (and variants)	Lambeth
laneus, -a, -um (adj.)	woollen
Laurentius, -i (m.)	Laurence
legalis, -e (adj.)	law-worthy, lawful
legitimus, -a, -um (adj.)	lawful, legitimate
legit(t)ime (adv.)	lawfully, legitimately
lego, -are, -avi, -atum	bequeath
lego -ere, legi, lectum	read
levo, -are, -avi, -atum	raise
libra, -e (f.)	pound (weight or money)
licet (impersonal verb) (used as conj.)	it is allowed despite, although
locus, -i (m.)	place
Ludovicus, -i (m.)	Lewis
magister, magistri (m.)	master
magnus, -a, -um (adj.)	great
Maius, -i (m.)	May
manerium, -i (n.)	manor
manus, -us (f.)	hand
marca, -e (f.)	mark (usually 13s. 4d. i.e. two-thirds of £1)
marchio, marchionis (m.)	marquis (marquess)
Marg(a)reta, -e (f.)	Margaret
Maria, -e (f.)	Mary
maritus, -i (m.)	husband
Martinus, -i (m.)	Martin
Martius, -i (m.)	March
mater, matris (f.)	mother
matrimonium, -i (n.)	marriage
me	see *ego*
melius (comp. adv.)	better (sometimes translatable as: best)

membrum, -i (n.)	member, part (of manor etc.)
memoria, -e (f.)	memory
mens, mentis (f.)	mind
mensis, mensis (m.)	month
mes(s)uagium, -i (n.)	messuage (usu. land with dwelling-house etc.)
meus, mea, meum (adj.)	my
mi(c)hi	see *ego*
millesimus, -a, -um (adj.)	thousandth
Milo, Milonis (m.)	Miles
minime (adv.)	least
minor (gen.*minoris*) (comp. adj.)	minor
minus (comp. adv.)	less
misericordia, -e (f.)	mercy (usu. with reference to a fine)
mitto, -ere, misi, missum	send
modus, -i (m.)	manner
moneta, -e (f.)	money
mors, mortis (f.)	death
multi, -e, -a (pl.)	many
natalis (gen. *natalis*) (adj. used as noun)	birthday
Nathaniel, Nathanielis (m.)	Nathaniel
naturalis, -e (adj.)	natural
nec (conj.)	nor
Nicholaus, -i (m.)	Nicholas
nisi (conj.)	unless, except, if … not
nobilissimus, -a, -um (sup. adj.)	most noble
nobis (dat., abl. of *nos*)	see *nos*
nomen, nominis (n.)	name
nomino, -are, -avi, -atum	name
non (adv.)	not
nonus, -a, -um (adj.)	ninth
nos (nom. and acc.; abl. *nobis*)	we, us
noster, nostra, nostrum (adj.)	our
novem (indecl.)	nine
November, Novembris (m.)	November
nullus, -a, -um (adj.)	not any, no, none
nunc (adv.)	now
nuper (adv.)	lately
obeo, obire, obi(v)i, obitum	die
oblitus, -a, -um (past p.)	see *obliviscor*
obliviscor, oblivisci, oblitus sum (dep.)	forget
octavus, -a, -um (adj.)	eighth
October, Octobris (m.)	October
omnipotens (gen. *omnipotentis*) (adj.)	almighty
omnis, omne (adj.)	all
onus, oneris (n.)	burden
opus, operis (n.)	work
ad opus et usum	to the use and behoof
oro, -are, -avi, -atum	pray, beseech
ordino, -are, -avi, -atum	arrange; appoint (to office)
Oxonia, -e; Oxonium, -i	Oxford
pagina, -e (f.)	page
pannus, -i (m.)	cloth
pannus laneus (m.)	(piece of) woollen cloth
parcella, -e (f.)	part, parcel
pario, -ire, peperi, partum	give birth
parochia, -e (f.)	parish
parochialis, parochiale (adj.)	parochial
parochianus, -i (m.)	parishioner
Pascha, -e (f.)	Easter Sunday
pastura, -e (f.)	pasture; right of pasturage

pater, patris (m.)	father
pauper, pauperis (m.) (adj. as noun)	pauper
pecunia, -e (f.)	money
per (prep. with acc.)	through; by
permitto, -ere, permisi, permissum	allow
personaliter (adv.)	personally
persona, -e (m.)	parson; or (m., f.) person
pertinencia, -e; pertinentia, -e (f.)	appurtenance
peto, -ere, peti(v)i, petitum	seek; ask
Petrus, -i (m.)	Peter
Philippus, -i (m.)	Philip
pictus, -a, -um (past p.)	see *pingo; carta*
pingo, pingere, pinxi, pictum	paint
placitum, -i (n.)	plea
plegius, -i (m.)	(one who acts as) pledge
plenus, -a, -um (adj.)	full
plura	(nom. and acc. n. pl. of *plus*) see *plus*
plus (gen. *pluris*)	more
porcio, porcionis (f.)	share, portion
possessio, possessionis (f.)	possession
possum, posse, potui, -	can, am able
post (prep. with acc.)	after
potestas, potestatis (f.)	power
pratum, -i (n.)	meadow
precipio, -cipere, precepi, preceptum	order, command
predictus, -a, -um (past p.)	aforesaid
prefatus, -a, -um (past p.)	aforesaid
prefero, preferre, pretuli, prelatum	mention previously
premanibus	in advance; cash down
premissa (n. pl.)	premises; things previously mentioned
presbiter, presbiteri (m.)	priest
presens (gen. *presentis*) (adj.)	present
presentes (gen. *presentium*, f. pl.)	[these] presents (referring to deed etc.)
presento, -are, -avi, -atum	present, make presentment
preterea (adv.)	moreover, furthermore
primus, -a, -um (adj.)	first
prius (adv.)	first, previously
pro (prep. with abl.)	for, on behalf of
probo, -are, -avi, -atum	prove (a will)
probus, -a, -um (adj.)	good, honest, upright
procreo, -are, -avi, -atum	beget
proles, prolis (f.)	offspring
propinquior (gen. *propinquioris*) (comp. adj.)	nearer; often translated as: next (heir)
proprius, -a, -um (adj.)	own; proper
in propria persona sua	in person
in propriis personis suis	
prosecutio, prosecutionis (f.)	prosecution
prosequor, prosequi, prosecutus sum (dep.)	prosecute; bring or proceed with suit
prout (conj.)	as
proviso quod	provided that
proximus, -a, -um (adj.)	next
puer, pueri (m.)	boy
quam (acc. f. sing. of *qui*)	see *qui* (see also *tam*)
quantum (adv.)	how much
quartus, -a, -um (adj.)	fourth
quat(t)uor (indecl.)	four
que (nom. f. sing.; nom. f. pl.; nom. and acc. n. pl. of *qui*)	see *qui*
-que (suffix conj.)	and (translated as if before the word to

quedam (nom. f. sing.; nom. f. pl.; nom and acc. n. pl. of *quidam*) — which it is affixed) see *quidam*

querens, querentis (m., f.) — querent, plaintiff

qui, que, quod (pron.) — who, which

quia (conj.) — because

quibus (dat. and abl. m., f. and n. pl. of *qui*) — see *qui*

quicumque, quecumque, quodcumque (pron.) (cases as for *qui + cumque*) — whosoever whatsoever,

quidam, quedam, quoddam (pron.) (cases as for *qui + dam*) — a certain, certain

quidem (adv.) — indeed, in fact

quiet(um)clamacio, quietclamacionis (f.) quitclaim

quiet(um)clamo, -are, -avi, -atum — quitclaim

quilibet, quelibet, quodlibet (pron.) (cases as for *qui + libet*) — anyone, anything, each

quindecim (indecl.) — fifteen

quingenti, -e, -a (adj.) — five hundred

quinquaginta (indecl.) — fifty

quinque (indecl.) — five

quintus, -a, -um (adj.) — fifth

quintusdecimus, quintadecima, quintumdecimum; also *quintus decimus* etc. (adj.) — fifteenth

quis/qui, quis/que, quid/quod (pron.) — who?, what?

quis/qui, qua/que, quid/quod (pron.) — anyone, anything

quo (abl. m. and n. sing. of *qui*) — see *qui*

quod (nom. and acc. n. sing. of *qui*) — see *qui*

quod (conj.) — that; because

quondam (adv.) — once, at some time

quos (acc. m. pl. of *qui*) — see *qui*

quousque (adv.) — until

racio, racionis; ratio, rationis (f.) — reason

recognicio, recognicionis; recognitio, recognitionis (f.) — recognizance; acknowledgement

recognosco, -ere, recognovi, recognitum — acknowledge

rector, rectoris (m.) — rector

rectus, -a, -um (adj.) — right (heir)

recupero, -are, -avi, -atum — recover (land etc.)

redditus, -us (m.) — rent

regina, -e (f.) — queen

regnum, -i (n.) — reign; kingdom

relicta, -e (f.) — relict

remaneo, -ere, remansi, - — remain

remissio, remissionis (f.) — remission; written grant

remitto, -ere, remisi, remissum — remise

reparacio, reparacionis (f.) — repair

reprisa, -e (f.) — outgoings; deduction from profit

res, rei (f.) — thing; matter

reservo, -are, -avi, -atum — reserve

residuum, -i (n.) — remainder

respectuo, -are, -avi, -atum — adjourn; respite

rex, regis (m.) — king

Ric(h)ardus, -i (m.) — Richard

Robertus, -i (m.) — Robert

Rogerus, -i (m.) — Roger

rosa, -e (f.) — rose

rotulus, -i (m.) — roll

russetum, -i (n.) — russet (cloth)

sacramentum, -i (n.) — oath

salus, salutis (f.) — well-being, salvation; greeting

Samuel, Samuelis (m.) — Samuel

sanctus, -a, -um (adj.) — holy

sanctus, -a (m., f.) — saint

sanus, -a, -um (adj.) — sound, reasonable

sanguis, sanguinis (m.) — blood

Sara, -e (f.) — Sarah

scilicet (adv.) — that is to say, namely

scio, scire, scivi, scitum — know

Scocia, -e — Scotland (as *Scotia*)

scolatizo, -are, -avi, -atum — study

Scotia, -e — Scotland (as *Scocia*)

se (acc., abl. – no nom.) (pron.) — himself, herself, itself, themselves

secta, -e (f.) — suit (of court)

secundus, -a, -um (adj.) — second

secundum (prep. with acc.) — according to

seisina, -e (f.) — seisin, possession (as *seizina*)

seisitus, -a (past p.) — seized, possessed (of land)

seizina, -e (f.) — seisin, possession (as *seisina*)

senescallus, -i (m.) — steward

senior (gen. *senioris*) (comp. adj.) — elder

sepelio, -ire, sepelivi, sepultum — bury

separatim; seperatim (adv.) — separately

septem (indecl.) — seven

September, Septembris (m.) — September

septimana, -e (f.) — week

sepultura, -e (f.) — burial; tomb, burial-place

sepultus, -a, -um (past p.) — see *sepelio*

servicium, -i; servitium, -i (n.) — service

seu (conj.) — or

seu ... seu — whether ... or

sex (indecl.) — six

sexaginta (indecl.) — sixty

sextus, -a, -um (adj.) — sixth

sextusdecimus, sextadecima, sextumdecimum (adj.) — sixteenth

si (conj.) — if

Sibilla, -e (f.) — Sybil

sic (adv.) — so, thus

sigillum, -i (n.) — seal

sine (prep. with abl.) — without

singuli, -e, -a (pl.) — singular, every single one

sit (3rd. pers. sing. pres. subj. of *sum*) — see *sum*

situatus, -a, -um (adj.) — situated

sive (conj.) — or

solemnizo, -are, -avi, -atum — solemnise (matrimony)

solidus, -i (m.) — shilling

solus, -a, -um (adj.) — alone

soluta, -e (f.) — spinster

solutus, -a, -um (past p.) — see *solvo*

solvo, -ere, solvi, solutum — pay

soror, sororis (f.) — sister

specifico, -are, -avi, -atum — specify

spuriosus, -a (adj.) — illegitimate

spurius, -a (adj.) — illegitimate

status, -us (m.) — estate, title, interest (in property)

statutum, -i (n.) — statute, regulation

Stephanus, -i (m.) — Stephen

sterlingus, -a, -um (adj.) — sterling

sub (prep. with abl.) — under

successive (adv.) — successively

sum, esse, fui, - — am etc. (verb to be)

summa, -e (f.) — sum

summoneo, -ere, summonui, summonitum	summon	*unicus, -a, -um* (adj.)	only (child etc.)
summus, -a, -um (adj. and adv.)	highest (but translated before *altare* as: high)	*unius*	see *unus*
sunt (3rd pers. pl. pres. of *sum*)	see *sum*	*unus, -a, -um* (gen. *unius*)	one
super (prep. with acc.; and adv.)	on	*Ursula, -e* (f.)	Ursula
supera (adv.)	above	*usitatus, -a, -um* (past p. as adj.)	habitual
superedifico, -are, -avi, -atum	build upon	*usus, -us* (m.)	use
superius (adv.)	above	*ut* (adv. and conj.)	as; in order that, so that
superstes (gen. *superstitis*) (adj.)	surviving, living		
supra (adv., and prep. with acc.)	above	*uterque, utraque, utrumque* (pron.)	each
supradictus, -a, -um (past p.)	abovesaid	*uxor, uxoris* (f.)	wife
suprascriptus, -a, -um (past p.)	abovewritten		
sursumreddo, -ere, sursumreddidi, sursumredditum	surrender (land)	*valeo, -ere, valui, valitum*	be worth
		vel (conj.)	or
suus, sua, suum (adj.)	his, her, its, their	*venio, -ire, veni, ventum*	come
		veritas, veritatis (f.)	truth
talis, tale (adj.)	such, of such a kind	*vero* (adv.)	indeed, in fact
tam (adv.)	so much	*verus, -a, -um* (adj.)	true
tam ... quam	both ... and	*via, -e* (f.)	road, way
tempus, -oris (n.)	time	*vices(s)imus, -a, -um* (adj.)	twentieth
tenementum, -i (n.)	tenement, holding	*videlicet* (adv.)	that is to say, namely
teneo, -ere, tenui, tentum	hold (land etc.)	*video, -ere, vidi, visum*	see
tercius, -a, -um (adj.)	third (as *tertius*)	*videor* (passive of *video*)	seem
terra, -e (f.)	land	*vidua, -e* (f.)	widow
tertius, -a, -um (adj.)	third (as *tercius*)	*viginti* (indecl.)	twenty
testamentum, -i (n.)	testament, will	*villa, -e* (f.)	township, town
testimonium, -i (n.)	testimony, witness	*vir, viri* (m.)	man
in cuius rei testimonium	in witness whereof	*virga, -e* (f.)	rod
testis, testis (m., f.)	witness	*virgata, -e* (f.)	virgate (variable area of land, usu. about 30 acres)
Thomas (acc. *Thomam*; gen., dat. *Thome*; abl. *Thoma*)	Thomas		
tibi	see *tu*	*virgo, virginis* (f.)	maiden, virgin
titulus, -i (m.)	title, claim	*virtus, virtutis* (f.)	virtue, force (of meaning etc); courage
tofta, -e (f.); *toftum -i* (n.)	toft (house, or land on which house stood)		
		visus, -a, -um (past p.)	see *video*
totus, -a, -um (adj.)	whole, all	*vita, -e* (f.)	life
tre(s)decim (indecl.)	thirteen	*vivo, -ere, vixi, -*	live
tres, tres, tria (gen. *trium*; abl. *tribus*)	three	*vixi*	see *vivo*
		voco, -are, -avi, -atum	call
tricesimus, -a, -um (adj.)	thirtieth	*volo, velle, volui, -*	will, wish
triginta (indecl.)	thirty	*voluntas, voluntatis* (f.)	will, wish
trium	see *tres*	*vulgariter* (adv.)	commonly
tu (acc. *te*; dat. *tibi*)	you	*vult* (3rd pers. sing. pres. of *volo*)	see *volo*
tunc (adv.)	then		
tuus, tua, tuum (adj.)	your (sing.)	*Walterus, -i* (m.)	Walter
		warantia, -e (f.)	warrant, guarantee
ubicumque (adv.)	wheresoever	*war(r)antizo, -are, -avi, -atum*	warrant
ulterius (adv.)	furthermore	*Wellensis, -is*	of Wells – relating to diocese
ultimus, -a, -um (adj.)	last		
ultra (prep. with acc.)	exceeding, beyond	*Westmonasterium, -i*	Westminster
unde (adv.)	whence; whereof	*Wilfridus, -i,* (m.)	Wilfred
		Willelmus, -i; Willimus, -i (m.)	William

Anglo-Norman French Vocabulary

The words below are intended only as a basic guide for the translation of the example from chancery proceedings (plate 49). Anglo-Norman French offers a great diversity of spellings and only those appearing in this document are listed below. It should be taken into account that a few words in the document appear with an initial *a*, *d* (for *de*), *l* (for *le, la*) or *n* (for *ne*) attached, and in some cases therefore reference to the vocabulary should be made omitting these letters. The addition of the letter *s* or *z* may indicate a plural.

a	to
ad	has
ascun	any
autre	other
auxi	also
Bathe	Bath
celle (f.)	that
ceo	it; this, that (see *sur*)
certein	certain
charite	charity
chauncellor	chancellor
come	whereas; as
comune (adj.)	common
comparer	to appear
considerer	to consider, take into consideration
countee	county
de	of; to (with infinitive)
envoier	to send
devaunt	before
dieu	God
dit	said
eide	aid
en	in
enfeffer	to enfoeff
Engleterre	England
entent	intent
et	and
evesque	bishop
fitz	son
foitz	time(s) (see *sovent*)
graciouse	gracious
heir	heir
humblement	humbly, meekly
ils	they
ja	now
Johan	John
jour	day
la (f.)	the
le (m.)	the
le	it
les (pl.)	the
limiter	appoint, specify

ley	law
luy	him
mort (noun)	death
mort (adj.)	dead
mye	see *ne*
ne ... mye	not any
oevre	work
ou	or
par	by
partie	behalf; matter
peine	pain, penalty
pier	father
please	may it please
premisses (pl.)	premise; aforesaid things
puis	then
pur	for
pur que	wherefore
quaunt	when
que	that (see also *pur que*)
quelle	which
refeffer	to re-enfeoff
refuser	to refuse
remedie	remedy
requiz	requested (see *serroit*)
saunz	without
seigneurie	lordship
serroit requiz	(he) should be requested
ses	his
socour	succour
soubz	under
sovent	often
sovent foitz	oft-times
supplier	supplicate, beseech
sur	on
sur ceo	thereupon
tenement	tenement
terre	land
tresgraciouse	very gracious
tresreverent	very reverend
ville	town, township
vostre	your
vous	you

Index

The following list includes aspects of palaeography, transcriptions, translations and means of identifying confusibilia, but does not refer to documents or their content. Mention of letters and abbreviations relating to specific plates is to be found separately in the commentaries. A **bold** number refers to a document – its plate, transcript, translation or commentary – identified in square brackets at the base of a page.

* see also under Latin

Magnifying glass, 8, 9
Minims, 8, 29, **6**, **40**, **42**, **45**, **48**
Money, 2, 15, **15**, **16**
Months:
    method of indicating, 10, **3**
    Quakers' reckoning, **2**

Numbers, **3**, **11** *

Paragraph mark, **17**, **32**, **39**, **40**, **42**
Place-names, 3, 7, 8, 16, 23 *
Punctuation, 3

Record type, 1
Regnal years, 12, 14
Roman numbers, 15, 29

Secretary hand, 7, 23, **13**, **14**, **17**, **20**, **35**
Signatures, **9**, **11**, **20**, **43**
Spelling, 3, 5, 9, 18
Standard wording, 6, 10, 12
Subjunctive mood, 13
Superscript letters and symbols, 2, 18-22, 24
Surnames, 3, 7, 8, 23 *
Suspension, 18

Thorn, 3, 10, 38, **1**, **2**, **22**

Ultra-violet lamp, 9

Yogh, 3, 10, 39, **35**, **46**